HART CRANE

The Life of an American Poet

HART CRANE

THE LIFE OF AN AMERICAN POET

BY PHILIP HORTON

NEW YORK: THE VIKING PRESS

Acknowledgments

For her unfailing sympathy and insight, the author is especially grateful to Miss Lorna Dietz; and to Mrs. Grace Hart Crane for her generous co-operation in making material available.

Special thanks are due to Malcolm Cowley, Samuel Loveman, Allen Tate, Slater Brown, and all the friends of Crane for contributing reminiscences and correspondence.

The author is also indebted to the Ohio State University Library for the Munson letters; and to Liveright Publishing Corporation for permission to quote from Crane's *Collected Poems*.

⚘CONTENTS⚘

vii

VI.

VII.

VIII.

IX.

X

"Now while thy petals spend the suns about us, hold—
(O Thou whose radiance doth inherit me)
Atlantis,—hold thy floating singer late!"

XI.

"Hasten, while they are true,—sleep, death, desire,
Close round one instant in one floating flower."

XII.

CONCLUSION

"And so it was I entered the broken world
To trace the visionary company of love, its voice
An instant in the wind (I know not whither hurled)
But not for long to hold each desperate choice."

APPENDIX

I.

General Aims and Theories

*"Each seemed a child, like me, on a loose perch,
Holding to childhood like some termless play."*

On SUMMER afternoons in the year 1905 the citizens of Warren, Ohio, passing in front of the shaded porch of Mrs. Sutcliff's home, often saw the old lady holding forth to a little boy at her feet. Sometimes they smiled at the sight of her lace cap bobbing with emphasis, for they could well imagine the stories she was telling which held the boy fixed in rapt attention: stories of the opening of the Western Reserve, of wars with the Indians, their customs and way of life, encounters with marauding bears in the forests, her own log cabin and the long years of struggle to settle the land and build the villages. As one of Warren's oldest inhabitants, her memory spanned the greater part of the preceding century and furnished as stirring a record of adventure as any boy's book of historical legend. At least, Harold Crane, the little visitor from across the street, found it so. By comparison the games of his playmates seemed commonplace and colorless and worn from daily repetition. Sitting on Mrs. Sutcliff's porch, his round solid face puckered with intense excitement, his dark eyes wide with a sense of peril or wonder, he was transported to a life more spacious, more thrilling, and infinitely more real than any to be found in the backyards of Warren. It was less cruel, too; the hostilities and barriers he felt between himself and the other children had no part in the primitive landscapes of these stories, where he could move with the free will of imagination. And his familiarity with that world was encouraged by Mrs. Sutcliff's occasional descriptions and anecdotes of his own forbears.

The Cranes were among the first settlers in the Western Reserve. In 1801 Simeon Crane and his family of Saybrook, Connecticut, had joined the great migration, travelling by ox-team for forty days over the Alleghenies into the new territory to purchase land near the shores of Lake Erie. During the decades that followed the family gradually entrenched itself, first as farmers, and later as merchants, the proprietors of Crane Brothers, the leading store of Garretsville, a village some thirty miles south of Cleveland. It was here, towards the end of the century, that Clarence A. Crane grew up, the only son of Arthur Crane, one of the town's most prosperous citizens, a director of the First National Bank, senior member of the family firm, and owner of a thriving maple syrup cannery. A restless, strong-willed young man, passionately ambitious, Clarence had little use for scholastic discipline, and after a two-year course at Allegheny College returned to Garretsville to undertake more profitable pursuits. While still living at home, however, casting about for a suitable career of his own, he met Grace Edna Hart, a lovely young woman from Chicago who was visiting friends in town. Characteristically, he decided that he must have her at all costs, and at once. By the time her visit had come to an end he had proposed to her several times over; receiving no definite reply, he carried his suit to the station platform; and finally, at the last moment, leaped aboard the train and pursued her with protestations all the way to Cleveland. Throughout the following weeks the strenuous courtship continued with an immoderate display of emotion that scarcely augured well for married happiness. There were impetuous visits to Chicago, stormy scenes, letters, pleas, and threats until, in the end, Clarence Crane had his way. After a large wedding in Chicago in the early summer of 1898, he returned to Garretsville with his bride.

From their parents' point of view the match was a splendid one, for the two families had been friends for many years. The Harts, like the Cranes, came of old New England stock, and traced their direct descent back to Deacon Stephen Hart, one of the pillars of the Reverend Thomas Hooker's Hartford Church. Furthermore, they, too, had prospered in the new country. Clinton Hart, the father of the bride, as county treasurer and a successful clothing merchant had been a prominent citizen of Warren, Ohio, for many years; and having amassed a comfortable fortune, increased it considerably by removing to Chicago to become a partner in the Sykes Steel Roofing Company. The elder Crane, in fact, was so pleased by the wisdom of his son's choice of a wife that upon the return of the young couple to Garretsville, he built them a comfortable home next to his own. And here they lived for the first few years of their married life; none too happily, however, for the young wife soon found her husband's intemperate moods and desires increasingly difficult to understand.

It was in this house on July 21, 1899, when the last summer of the nineteenth century lay hot over the Mahoning Valley, that their first and only child was born, a boy, who was christened Harold Hart Crane. Both father and grandfather rejoiced as they looked at him; for since the father was himself an only son, it would necessarily be little Harold who would ultimately receive the bulk of the accumulated worldly goods of two generations, and be responsible in furthering the family fortunes. And why should he not? He was clearly a healthy sturdy child. What more was needful that he should be worthy and capable of this trust, except that he be trained for it? There was no dissenting voice, least of all from Harold, who gave big-eyed and tacit approval, and by his very presence involuntarily promised to fulfill their plans.

As he grew older, he developed a passionate love of color and began to show a stubborn devotion to the creating of fine, if somewhat eccentric, artistic effects. In his third year this aptitude received a sudden stimulus when he discovered in his mother's closet a large bandbox stuffed with the leavings of the dressmaker and milliner—scraps of brilliant cloth, ribbons, feathers, patches and buttons of all shapes and sizes. Thereafter, he was content to spend hours contriving striking decorations for such cast-off hats as he could acquire, until one day, swept away by creative enthusiasm, he appropriated the bonnet of a visitor for alterations and so sealed his own doom. His Aunt Bess, who had long been concerned over so effeminate a diversion in a male child, seized upon the incident as an excuse to separate him from his bandbox once and for all. The two days of brazen-lunged clamor which followed should have been sufficient to convince her that, whatever his weaknesses might be, effeminacy would not be one of them. Years later, however, the boy compensated for this early frustration and indulged his love of color and dash to his heart's desire, appearing variously as a French sailor in Mexico City; as a sergeant major on a transatlantic liner in a sailor hat, dress breeches, and a scarlet coat lined with brandy bottles; and not least dramatically as an African chief in a Connecticut farmhouse, complete with lampblack paint and original weapons—albeit over winter underwear.

Before the boy's legs were long enough to permit independent sorties into the village, Mr. Crane removed the family to Warren, not far distant, but a much larger and more prosperous town than Garretsville, where a young man might find opportunities worthy of his ambitions. There he undertook to open a cannery for maple syrup, and in this he was substantially aided by his father-in-law, who built him a factory. It was a wise investment, for the business flourished so rapidly that within a few years Mr. Crane was able to sell it for a solid sum to the Corn Products Company of Chicago and to accept at the same time a fat salary as the manager of a new plant recently established by the firm in the vicinity of Warren. But though such success brought much gaiety in its wake and new luxuries—a handsome carriage for Mrs. Crane and a new-fangled vociferous motor car for her husband—there was no more harmony between them than there had been in their first home.

Harold, in the meantime, had grown into a sturdy boy of six or seven, and was properly enrolled in the grade school. In a group picture taken at that time his figure stands out from those of the other children with a kind of incisive three-dimensional solidity, which derived possibly from the conjunction of his chunkiness of body with a dark rebelliousness of expression in his round face and big eyes. His short convict-like haircut, moreover, added not a little to the effect of forcefulness. There was also a specific quality of brooding in his eyes, too concentrated to be sullen, too watchful and full of wonder to be felt as morbid. Gradually his parents were becoming aware that there was a great sensitivity in the child. Despite his obvious physical health, sudden attacks of acute nausea and fever seized him from time to time, inexplicable not only to them but to the doctors as well. More often than not, only the boy himself knew the correct diagnosis, and after the dark way of children, concealed it for fear of ridicule. But occasionally the causes of his mysterious seizures were clear enough. There was the day, for instance, when his mother dressed him in his best bib-and-tucker and dispatched him with a card of birthday greetings for their next-door neighbor, Mrs. Hall. Unfortunately, Harold misunderstood the instructions. Farther across the town, but much closer to his heart, lived the Misses Hall, two maiden sisters of whom he was very fond, and whose old-fashioned house, filled with the polished ornate furniture that he had classified as "curly leg," had always held a powerful fascination for him. Thither he bent his steps, and being admitted by one of the sisters, chanted a cheerful "Happy Birthday, Miss Mary." Later, returning home, highly inflated with the success of his mission and still ignorant of his mistake, he told his mother about how very nice Miss Mary had been to him. But when she explained with no little amusement the error he had made, his pride shrivelled away before a blast of mortification. The rest of the day he was very quiet; and that night, when he had been put to bed after his supper, he became very ill with a nausea for which no remedy could be found.

A similar incident took place about the same time in the dining room of a large hotel on Mackinac Island where the family were staying for a few weeks. Mrs. Crane, thinking Harold old enough to learn the etiquette of adult society, had taken the opportunity of dining in public to teach him his table manners. One evening she had just been instructing him in the gesture of rising from one's place to greet anyone stopping to speak, when some acquaintances paused at the table to say good evening. Properly observing the requirements of form, Mr. Crane rose from his seat; but Harold, wide-eyed and watchful, remained as he was, forgetful of everything but the interests of the moment. When their friends had passed on, his mother chided him good-humoredly on his lapse of manners and asked him what, indeed, would people think of him now. The boy said nothing, and his defection was forgotten; by all except himself. Late that night his parents were awakened by his illness, which was so severe that a doctor was summoned, who reported that the child was running a high fever. For some time the nature of this sickness, which kept him in bed for two days, remained a mystery. Nor did Harold himself offer any clue, until several days after they had left the hotel, when he made some remark to his mother which threw a sudden and oblique illumination on the incident at the dinner table that evening.

Since such sturdy children were not commonly supposed to be over-sensitive, Mr. and Mrs. Crane continued to be somewhat disturbed and puzzled by Harold's recurrent "fits," as they were called. Quite naturally, they could not see that their son had inherited from both of them a peculiarly high-strung nervous organism, which, though protected in themselves by the complex devices of maturity, was left cruelly exposed in him. But this alone hardly accounted for his attacks and the striking fact that they invariably followed upon real or imagined humiliations, and furthermore, that the fear of being humiliated was a daily torment throughout his life. This obsession, in later years, it is true, was aggravated by more concrete circumstances, which multiplied and closed in on him with what seemed to be appalling malice. Still, it did not spread its pattern of tortuous shadow over his life without having first struck roots, however threadlike, in earlier soil.

Certainly a child who suffered such real anguish from the fear of ridicule must have been completely lacking in a sense of self-confidence and security. To hang so desperately on the regard of comparative strangers; to be consumed by fear and shame at the slightest suspicion of failure: what could this mean except that without their approval the very ground would crumble beneath him? But a child's most solid ground is usually founded sturdily in his family. It is with one foot confidently planted there that he gingerly tests with his other foot the unknown plots of experience around him, so that if they sink, he need not drown, but safely retreat to his island. But what if this central and most certain ground were unbased and threatened to founder? What if he were constantly aware of violent quarrels and a widening gap of estrangement between his parents, and of himself as a precarious pawn, pushed now this way, now that, liable at any moment to be lost or forgotten in the shuffle? Then there might well be an urgent need for the approval and devotion of others, which in time would yield a sense of independent security and confidence. For such a child, a blunder or a rebuff might well give anguish, might well be a world lost.

This was more or less the background of the years in Warren. As Harold was turning seven, the unhappy tension between his parents, which had existed since the beginning of their married life, became increasingly acute. There were frequent scenes, recriminations, tears. Sociable and lively by disposition, Mrs. Crane resented her husband's jealous possessiveness which prohibited many of the pleasures she had been accustomed to. Gifted with a fine voice, she had enjoyed taking part in private musicales and concerts before her marriage; but the first time she appeared in Warren in a benefit performance, Mr. Crane stormed out of the hall and afterwards insisted she give up her singing. Underlying such incidents as this, however, was a basic conflict—the struggle between two positive, highly strung temperaments, focused in what seems to have been an unfortunate sexual incompatibility and resulting in nerve-wracking alternations of attraction and repulsion.

The role to be played by Harold was clearly indicated by the circumstances. He naturally sided with his mother, for there had been little chance for any solid affection to grow up between him and his father. Like many ambitious business men eager to found a family fortune, Mr. Crane was not so much interested in his child as in his son; and he was content to wait until the metamorphosis had taken place, and the boy was of an age to share in his business, before devoting much time or attention to him. Consequently, in Harold's eyes he became a rather unique phenomenon which belonged to him but in which he had no share; which, moving for the most part in another world, was mostly surely his father, as his mother was his mother, yet somehow very different. It was hardly strange that he stood a little in fear of him. In later years, when Mr. Crane was eager to enlist his son's support and affection, he felt this fear, and, ironically, was hurt by it. The correspondence that passed between them during those years, full of pathetic attempts to effect a reconciliation and a natural relationship, showed much of such unconscious irony. In a letter of 1923 Mr. Crane wrote to his son: "Your letter doesn't ring true of affection—rather it emphasizes the fear that I have always held, that you feel yourself humbled if you suggest a warm affection for your father—a sort of condition where you feel that I should come to you rather than you come to me."

But more than simple neglect fostered this early estrangement between father and son. As the breach between his parents widened, creating more hysterical tensions, there was added to the boy's childish forebodings the constant distress of his mother, whose nervous temperament often broke down under the strain and precipitated on him the full impact of her accumulated bitterness and resentment. His loyalty and devotion, already withdrawn from his father, doubled their allegiance to her; and sharing her suffering with the whole-hearted passion of a child, he came to accept without question the fact of his father's guilt. She was the one remaining bulwark in the crumbling devastation of his home, and clinging to her for security, he made common cause with her in all things. Her humiliations were his; he passed through the vicissitudes of scenes and reconciliations with her; and with exaggerated imagination saw his father through her eyes, now as a cruel tyrant, now as a faithless husband. Often during the nights when he knew his father had not come home, he came to his mother's room where she lay awake and stood beside her bed in the dark, speechless with emotions he was too young to know how to phrase. The identification was complete; throughout the crisis Harold and his mother stood as one.

Years later when he was old enough to understand what he had felt and heard, he spoke his mind only too clearly. In one letter he complained of the "avalanche of bitterness and wailing that has flooded me ever since I was seven years old"; and again that "family affairs and fusses have been my destruction since I was eight years old when my mother and father began to quarrel." Even when he was a grown man he could not forget the painful days and nights in Warren. "The slightest disturbance now," he confessed, "tends to recall with consummate force all the past and its horrid memories on pretext of the slightest derangement of equilibrium." And a casual misunderstanding with his mother in his twentieth year brought forth the bitter observation that "I don't want to fling accusations etc. at anybody, but I think it's time you realized that for the last eight years my youth has been a rather bloody battleground for yours and father's sex life and troubles."

But his childhood was not entirely compounded from unhappiness. There were also the homely natural incidents common to every child:

> . . . the whip stripped from the lilac tree
> One day in spring my father took to me . . .

or on luckier days the discovery of a new excitement:

> The cinder pile at the end of the backyard
> Where we stoned the family of young
> Garter snakes under . . . And the monoplanes
> We launched—with paper wings and twisted
> Rubber bands . . .

For the most part, however, his pleasures were solitary. As much as he longed for the companionship of his playmates and however heartily he was welcomed to their games, he felt curiously alienated from them, partly from fear, partly from the sense of a great difference between himself and them. Sometimes he confessed his loneliness to his mother, but more often, keeping it to himself, he wandered off into the country beyond the town to find more solid consolation. When spring came to the Mahoning Valley and an iridescent green blurred like fog through the gathered groves of oaks and maples and flushed slowly up across the hills from the quickening creeks, the boy followed in its tracks. He "left the village for dogwood," and paddling the streams back into the hills, left his "sleek boat nibbling margin grass."

> I took the portage climb, then chose
> A further valley-shed; I could not stop.
> Feet nozzled wat'ry webs of upper flows;
> One white veil gusted from the very top.

Here in the upper reaches of the hills he steeped himself in the sensations of nature and stored away a rich fund of impressions which later in a Connecticut farmhouse and a plantation in the Caribbean Sea would yield up a magnificent harvest. There were also corners in the town where his watchful curiosity found more complex mysteries: the impressive noises of industry, odds and ends of cast-off machinery and people, which aroused a vivid sympathy in him. Above all, there was the place where—

>   Behind
> My father's cannery works I used to see
> Rail-squatters ranged in nomad raillery,
> The ancient men—wifeless or runaway
> Hobo-trekkers that forever search
> An empire wilderness of freight and rails.
> Each seemed a child, like me, on a loose perch,
> Holding to childhood like some termless play.

His own childhood, however, and the years in Warren came to an abrupt end in his ninth year when the tension between his parents finally snapped, scattering the little family to the winds. In the midst of the final recriminations and threats of divorce Mrs. Crane collapsed and was hurried away to a sanatarium in the East. Harold was carried off to his new home in Cleveland by his grandmother; and Mr. Crane, whose business activities had been transferred to Chicago, temporarily made his home there.

Harold's new home was by far the largest he had ever known. Bought by Mr. Hart upon his retirement from active business, number 1709 East 115th Street stood in one of the most pleasant residential sections of the city near the park, a symbol of the solid success of its owner. Its white wooden façade of three stories was flanked on either side by circular peaked towers in the elaborate taste of the period, and across the front extended a generous shaded porch. Harold was given his quarters on the third floor, happily including the round tower room with its four windows. Here in his "ivory tower," as it inevitably came to be known, he maintained an invincible privacy, collecting his books, victrola records, and prints of the modern painters without interference. He pored over the first little magazines there, wrote his first lines of poetry, drank his first jugs of red wine, and flushed with a new sense of power, entertained his first friends hilariously by kicking up his heels in the Russian "Gasotski." For the Hart home became the only home he would ever know. There the family gradually came together again under one roof: first his mother, considerably refreshed after several months in the East; and later, his father, once more caught in the irresistible swing of affection for his wife, and as impetuous as he had been before his marriage. For the next few years there was a semblance, at least, of comparative harmony. Although the household was a large one—besides the Harts, the Crane family and the servants there was always a maiden aunt or so—few occasions for quarrels arose. Mr. Crane, having resigned his former position, was busy day and night organizing and launching the Crane Chocolate Company, and a short time later, the Crane Company, a retail organization, which opened the first of the stores that soon became a popular Cleveland institution. In this latter enterprise he was aided by his wife, who supervised the details of management, finding in such activities a satisfactory release for the restless impulses of her temperament. As for Harold, he was as happy as a boy could well be who was suffering the growing pains of adolescence and the mysterious gestation of poetic genius. He still passed most of his time alone, for he had no friends in Cleveland; but his new home suited him nonetheless. He had his own rooms, where he could read and brood at will; he had a piano that he practised on with vigorous, undisciplined pleasure; and he fairly worshipped his grandmother, the little old lady who presided over the house, whom, as he grew older, he delighted to catch up in his arms, rushing her from one room to another in a burst of high spirits.

In 1913 after his grandfather's death, when his parents decided to make the Hart house their permanent home, he enrolled, somewhat belatedly, as a student at East High School. During his brief and sporadic attendance there, however, he found little to enlist his sympathy or attention. His scholastic record, though passing, was quite ordinary with the exception of his grades in English, in which he took honors. Even in this chosen field it was not any precocity or brilliant piece of writing that drew his teacher's attention and by which she recalled him in later years, but "his shining brown eyes as he argued with eager interest about everything that came up for discussion." She remembered above all that "he wanted so much to find out about things." Otherwise, he was quiet and unobtrusive; companionable with the other students, but rarely taking them into his confidence.

Among all the students of his acquaintance there was only one whom he chose as his confidant and with whom he had a continuous friendship throughout his life. In William Wright, a boy somewhat younger than himself, who was also beginning to write his first poems, he found a companion with whom he could share the enthusiasms nearest his heart. On afternoons after school hours they often retired to Harold's tower room to compare their efforts or passages from their favorite poets and discuss the state of poetry in the world. They also had a less pleasant bond of community in their enforced attendance every Saturday afternoon at the same dancing class, which, however disagreeable, served to mark in Wright's mind a memorable day. It was one evening in the early winter of 1915 when the two were on their way home from the class that Harold announced to his friend his first literary achievement—the publication of one of his poems in *Bruno's Bohemia*. The magazine, it is true, was an obscure one. Published in a Greenwich Village garret by the Greenwich Village character whose name it bore, the little paper contained in its cheap pulp pages a curious agglomeration of gleanings from the English literature of the 1890's together with the bizarre poetic whimsies of the contemporary Villagers. In the delicate and subtle evil of the Beardsley drawings, which served as cover decorations, as well as in the not dissimilar faces and festoons of many of its contributors, could be traced its lineage to a preceding generation. Still, it was a New York magazine, and to Harold's mind, a seal of approval had been set upon his work. His mind focused intensely on these omens, and swinging his black silk bag containing his dancing pumps, he said calmly and seriously to his friend, "I believe I have found my life's work." Wright said nothing. His own mind, crowded with the two-inch headlines of war news, famines, and empires crumbling, could not concede any great importance to this occasion. In truth, he was not a little shocked at so much single-mindedness in the older boy. Years later in 1923 he found in him the same fixity of purpose and devotion when, one evening after a long separation, they were walking along lower Fifth Avenue and Crane, though harassed by a long period of unemployment, said with the same seriousness, "I believe I have it in me to become the greatest singer of our generation." Indeed, throughout the following years, despite family complications, unemployment, friendships, betrayals, drunkenness and debauchery—through all the excessive turmoil of his life—his devotion to poetry was his one constant lodestar.

That Saturday afternoon was the last the two friends spent together for some time. A few days later Harold dropped out of school to accompany his mother on a trip to the Isle of Pines, south of Cuba, where they were to spend the winter with his grandmother on the Hart plantation. Excepting a few weeks' visit to Boston and Rye Beach the year before, it was his first extensive glimpse of the vast reaches of the country. And vast it must have seemed to him as day after day the various earth roared past beneath the southbound train: the black loam, the rolling hills of Ohio and Maryland giving place to the red clays of Virginia and the silent pine wastes of North Carolina; the mountain ranges, now near, now far, succeeding each other down the continent—the Alleghenies, the Blue Ridge, the Great Smokies; and at last the thickening

heat and brilliant tropical colors of Florida fringing the intense and level blue of the sea. Then the ship and his first
ocean voyage; and at the end, the plantation with its broad
white house set low in a glossy orange grove, shading its
porch towards the misshapen blue mountains inland. Like the
first voyage of another great American poet, who sailed
through the tropical seas during his early impressionable
years, this trip and the several months' stay on the island sank
plummet-wise into the depths of his being, where it lived and
grew secretly, later to put forth in his poetry curious and
moving images of tropical seascapes. In the work of both
Melville and Crane there is a profound sea spell: eloquent
evocations of the subterranean peace, of the mysterious and
primeval life-forces, and the paradisaical beauty of the tropical ocean—a nostalgia, one suspects, for another world than
the one from which they felt so deeply estranged. But Crane,
though he had not yet read Melville, needed no literary guide
to sharpen his sensibilities for this new setting. Free to wander at will about the plantation, he spent his days swimming,
sunning himself, exploring the beaches, the groves and the
brush, constantly soaking up the sensuous profusion of the
island. There was the royal palm, "unshackled, casual of its
azured height," the eucalyptus of the "wrinkled shadows,"
poincianas and poinsettias with fiery blossoms, mango trees
and curious species of cactus: all the brilliant botanical wealth
of the tropics. With his passion for colors and the intense curiosity he had for the structure of leaf and petal, the days must
have passed swiftly enough. But in his delight in the beauties
of the island he was not insensible to the presence of death all
around him—in the "tarantula rattling at the lily's foot," in the
relentless cannibalism of its animal life, in the sinister silences
and the polished desiccated drift along the shores.

Perhaps it was his too sensitive awareness of this sinister
quality of the island that caused the one strange incident of

his visit there. One night his mother and grandmother, awakened by noises outside the house and investigating the disturbance from their windows, discovered a small herd of indistinct cattle cropping the lawn in the grey moonlight. Harold was quickly roused from bed and sent to drive them away. Throwing on some clothes, he went out into the night, followed by the house dog, and soon raised a hullabaloo that headed the animals before him into the undergrowth. Watching at the window, the two women were surprised to see him disappear into the darkness in pursuit. They called him back, but there was no reply and the barking of the dog grew fainter and finally ceased altogether, and there was only the swelling chant of the night insects. When he did not return after several minutes, they became alarmed; at the end of a half hour they were seriously frightened; and when an hour had passed, they were about to organize a searching party when suddenly the boy burst from the undergrowth and running across the moonlit lawn at top speed, rushed into the house. They found him at the door, eyes starting from his blanched face and his breath coming in gasps; but before any questions could be asked, he dropped at their feet unconscious. Finding that he was perfectly rigid and failed to respond to stimulants, the two women, frantic with fear, hitched a pair of mules to a cart, and lifting him into it, set off post haste to the house of a native doctor who lived near by. The doctor administered a hypodermic and signalled that they might safely take him home. Since neither Mrs. Crane nor her mother spoke Spanish, it was impossible to learn anything concerning the nature of the attack. The next day the boy was fully conscious, though still very ill; but since he volunteered no explanations, they thought best not to question him, expecting that when he was fully recovered the mystery would be solved. During the days and weeks that followed, however, he made not the slightest allusion to what had happened; and his mother, perhaps wisely, let the matter drop.

What actually happened that strange evening was never discovered. The only possible clue to the secret lay in a confidence that Crane made to his schoolmate, Wright, upon his return to Cleveland that summer. This was a dark mention of two attempts to commit suicide while on the island: once by slashing his wrists with a razor, and again, by taking as many of his mother's veronal tablets as he could find. The story itself sounds more like a morbid invention delivered for dramatic effect than an account of actual fact. But since Crane repeated it several years later in New York to another friend, it is possible that this incident concealed an impulse more serious than anyone suspected.

It was not long before Mr. Crane arrived to take his family home; and in the late spring of 1915 Harold left the island, not to return until eleven years later. During the summer in Cleveland his behavior was so moody and irritable that his parents were uncertain how to manage him. He railed bitterly at the prospect of returning to school in the fall, and shutting himself away in his rooms on the third floor, spent more and more time with his books and poetry. Once he was caught at the train in the act of running away to visit Elbert Hubbard, his only literary acquaintance, the quaint journey-man of American letters, who had made one of his "little journeys" to the Crane Chocolate factory. Although he finally had his way, he returned after a few weeks recalcitrant as ever, thoroughly disillusioned, it seemed, by his pilgrimage to East Aurora, but without having sacrificed his enthusiasm for poetry. On the contrary, everything he said and did convinced his father that he had no intention of following in parental footsteps. Fortified by his publication in *Bruno's Bohemia* and profoundly stirred by the recent months on the island, the boy openly declared himself a poet, and leaving no room for doubt, let it be known that he would devote himself to writing despite hell-fire. It was a shocking announcement. Poets, it is true, were nothing strange to Clarence Crane, for he had a genuine fondness for Whittier, Lowell, and the New England poets in general; but that a poet should appear in modern times and of his own flesh and blood was something he could neither countenance nor believe. Inevitably, he attributed it to a passing phase of adolescence; but, in the meantime, he was faced with a serious dilemma. Wishing sound advice on the proper procedure to take with such a son, he could think of no one who would be qualified to help him. No one, excepting, perhaps, a woman in Chicago who owned a catering establishment which he supplied with chocolates. Several times in business conferences, he recalled, she had mentioned artists and writers who were her friends and came to visit her. In her quiet manner there was something authoritative, yet sympathetic, which had impressed him. To her, then, he decided to turn for advice. Her name was Mrs. William Vaughn Moody.

Mr. Crane was not mistaken in his recollection that Mrs. Moody was the friend of artists and writers. The wife of one of America's leading poets, she was in her own right the intimate friend and counsellor of most of the important poets of that period. With the comfortable income from her catering establishment she entertained and sponsored them in Chicago and New York, visited them abroad, launched the younger ones with sympathy and subsidies, and brought to them all the rare insight and delicacy of her understanding. To the soirées over which she presided with her full, almost Buddha-like face and presence came Sandburg, Lindsay, William Butler Yeats, Rabindranath Tagore, and many others. It was a happy coincidence of fate that the one person of Mr. Crane's acquaintance who could help him should have been so eminently fitted to encourage the awkward unfolding talents of a young poet. When he finally sought her out with his troubles, she was true to her reputation, and Mr. Crane returned home with the injunction to give his son free rein in his desires, and an invitation for Harold to come to her during her next visit in Cleveland.

This message and the subsequent meeting, which took place some time during the fall, were a source of great encouragement to the boy in the midst of the dull routines of school-work. Still as solitary as ever, he was becoming more aware of his isolation. Even the big empty house—for his grandmother was again spending the winter on the island, and his parents were both constantly occupied in the management of Mr. Crane's shops—served as a hollow reminder of it. Though he was now in his third year of high school, his fellow students still represented an alien world. "They are so shallow over there at school," he wrote his grandmother, "I am more moved to disdain than anything else. Popularity is not my aim though it were easy to win it by laughing when they do at nothing and always making a general ass of oneself. There are about two out of the twelve hundred I would care to have as friends." But the fine scorn was only too transparent. It was he who felt disdained, rejected, cast out—an Ishmael skirting the pleasant oases of free and easy companionship, always fearful of the indifference or contempt that might greet his closer approach. He had been too cruelly exposed to the treacheries of human relations ever again to trust them completely. His reaction was to avoid betrayal by anticipating it and by fortifying himself within himself, to achieve a security which would exist independently of external factors and the uncertain quantity of affections. Only a year or so later he wrote his mother from New York that he was "beginning to see the hope of standing entirely alone." It was a paradoxical desire in one who craved companionship with such intensity. This dualism—the desire for affection and the fear of betrayal—gradually became one of the irreconcilables that distorted his life, the source of his monstrous egoism of later years, so intolerable to his friends, which was his only defense.

But if, as he wrote his grandmother, "it is surely lonely for me here, eating alone and seldom seeing anyone but in the darkness of morning or night," this at least gave him more freedom for his work, which, in turn, might bring him a more enduring recognition than popularity among his classmates. The hours outside of school he spent for the most part, like Yeats's young Platonist, in his tower room reading and writing. Among his books were Swinburne, the poet par excellence of adolescence, and the early Yeats himself, and the Georgian poets; but more important than all others, the *Dialogues*, where he read of that clear and radiant progression from the beauties of earth upwards to that other beauty, from all fair notions to the notion of absolute beauty and the final revelation of the very essence of beauty. He read, too, of the necessity of madness in a true poet, and this he thought true enough as observation or wise enough as precept to underscore doubly with red ink. Perhaps distorted recollections of this swarmed in his mind when, years later, he was seized by demonic rages, and typewriters cavorted through Connecticut windows and encyclopedias hurtled through quiet snow. Still another passage from Plato lurked in his memory in long gestation, gathering to itself new meanings and directions—the fable of Atlantis, sunk beneath the Western sea to a subterranean and esoteric peace.

Encouraged by his constant correspondence with Mrs. Moody, he devoted more and more of his time to writing. Working late into the night, he composed countless lyrics, symbolical allegories, long ambitious ballads, which he dispatched to her one after another. In reply he received letters of acute appreciation and sympathy, companionable and unassuming, full of exciting information about the literary

world, and occasionally bringing words of praise more refreshing than Hagar's well in the desert. In one letter she
wrote, "I have a deep conviction that you are following the
real right lead for you in giving all to poetry"; and again, in
criticism of a poem he had sent her, "the whole is beautifully
felt and delicately written. Love of your work, and work,
will give you your full voice." Her enthusiasm was genuine
and whole-hearted. She tried to arrange for the boy to visit
literary friends of hers in a New Hampshire village where he
could write in a more congenial atmosphere. She also sent
him invitations to visit her in Chicago, and news of the poets
of the day: of Sandburg, whose work, she wrote, "is good,
too, in a different way than yours and mine"; and of Padraic
Colum, who was bringing out an anthology of the young
Irish revolutionary poets. Doubtless from her, too, the boy
first heard of *Poetry*, *The Soil*, *The Seven Arts*, and all the
little magazines which were trumpeting the news of the
American Renaissance around the walls of Chicago and New
York. Before long he discovered these magazines for himself
at the bookshop of Richard Laukhuff in the Taylor Arcade,
which was a rendezvous for the Cleveland intelligentsia.
Thenceforth, he missed little in contemporary literature. It
must have been there that he first came across a copy of *The
Pagan*, a little paper similar to *Bruno's Bohemia*, published in
Greenwich Village by Joseph Kling, for in the October issue
of 1916 Kling printed a communication from Cleveland
which read:

"Dear Sir: I am interested in your magazine as a new and
distinctive chord in the present American Renaissance of
literature and art. Let me praise your September cover; it
has some suggestion of the exoticism and richness of Wilde's
poems.

H. H. C.
East 115th Street."

Evidently this formal and somewhat patronizing note was accompanied, or followed, by a poem, for the November issue of *The Pagan*, in addition to drawings by Auerbach-Levy and Robert Henri, a story by D'Annunzio, and other selections, published a lyric by Harold Crane, entitled "October-November," a slight cameo of seasonal imagism. He was reserving his better pieces for more important magazines. In a letter to a friend he wrote that "the poem came out in *The Pagan* but only succeeded in so doing by sacrificing its title and several lines. For compensation, though, I rec'd a fine acceptance from *Others*, Williams saying it was 'damned good stuff.'" The encouragement of Mrs. Moody and his own midnight devotions were bringing their first rewards.

With the closing of school for the summer holidays his literary activities were suspended for several weeks. With his mother he left Cleveland for a trip through the West on a conducted tour. Much to the boy's disgust the two of them shared a compartment together; and to express his emphatic disapproval of the arrangement, he would climb vigorously into his upper berth each night and, as he undressed, hurl his clothing down past his mother's berth with a special imprecation for each article. Then, evidently amused by his display of violence, he could be heard chuckling to himself, until, digging out whatever book he was reading, he settled down for an immersion in literature, which more often than not would last far into the night. Ignoring the other young people on the train, he did little but read during the day as well, excepting the hours he spent on the platform of the observation car, intently absorbed in the tremendous sweeps of sky and plain, the violent uprisen buttes, and the remote peaks; whence he would return again to his books thoroughly powdered with grey and yellow dust. Altogether, it was a pleasant and sometimes exciting journey. There were early morning coach-rides through Yellowstone Park when he and his mother rode up top with the driver, bundled against the chill mists that wavered horizontally across the vertical black gloom of the pine forests. In San Francisco there were visits to Chinatown and the large ball held at the hotel; and in Banff there were horseback riding and tennis and swimming in Lake Louise beneath the granite and snows of the Rockies. Gradually the boy was gaining some impression of the total vastness of the country, of its radical diversities of surface and life, and at the same time, of the common denominators of spirit, which, multiplied from coast to coast by those stubborn migrations his own forbears had taken part in, had somehow united the various territories in a native, homogeneous whole.

But there was no immediate opportunity to digest the raw stuff of these impressions, for upon their return to Cleveland towards the end of the summer a marital crisis once more disrupted the household. Beginning with the rumors of Mr. Crane's infidelities, which were flying up and down the counters of the Crane shops, there was a two-months' accumulation of quarrels, reconciliations, illnesses, and further quarrels, which painfully built up to the final climax in November when, one morning, it was discovered that Mr. Crane had secretly removed all his belongings from the house and disappeared. A few days later the newspapers printed the item that Clarence A. Crane, prominent clubman and candy manufacturer, was being sued for divorce on the grounds of "extreme cruelty and gross neglect." The next day in the midst of Mrs. Crane's preparations to leave for Chicago, where she hoped to find some peace of mind, Mr. Crane telephoned and begged her to see him for a few minutes, but she refused. Later, just before her departure, a large bouquet of roses and violets arrived from him with a note which is worth quoting for the light it sheds on his character.

" 'For *old* love's sake—Love sings a song
   Amid the ruins where the garden bloomed
      with beauty—when life was young and fair
   And in its broken statue's brow—a rosied
      wreath he binds
   Love isn't love that alters—when it alteration
      finds,'

"Surely no words of my own framing could express my heart as these do. Please wear this rose out of Cleveland and if my thoughts and true desires help at all—you'll find solace and health. I shall think of you each hour and pray for you each night.

As always,

Clarence

And I've opened this again to tell you that you're leaving with my heart and affections tucked away where it's been for twenty years."

It was with this token of her husband's enigmatic and moody temperament that Mrs. Crane left Cleveland.

Harold, in the meantime, had stood solidly by his mother throughout the crisis. Following the pattern established so firmly eight years before in Warren, he experienced her predicament as his own, and swept away by the general hysteria, ran the gamut of all her emotions—humiliation, resentment, self-pity. But he was not so exposed this time to the more subtle cruelties of the situation. Having learned not to look for security in the world about him, he was prepared for—possibly he even expected—this final foundering of his family. He was no longer a helpless child. He had tested certain spots of the unknown ground that had once terrified him—*Bruno's Bohemia*, Mrs. Moody, *Others*, *The Pagan*—and they not only stood firm, but offered promise of further support, even of eminence. As a poet, there was hope of independent strength, of facing the world down, perhaps of "standing entirely alone." In any case, now was the time to act. In the disruption of his family fate had challenged him to prove his mettle, and he accepted the challenge. As soon as his mother filed her petition for divorce, he dropped out of school, once and for all, and found a job in the city. The sudden mantle of maturity swung proudly from his shoulders.

"With pipe, solitude and puppy for company, I am feeling resplendent," he wrote Carl Schmitt, who was presently to be his guardian in New York. "After a day's work in a picture store selling mezzotints and prints, you may not think it, yet there comes a great peaceful exaltation in merely reading, thinking, and writing. For occasionally in this disturbing age of adolescence which I am now undergoing, there come minutes of calm happiness and satisfaction.

"I don't know whether or not I informed you in my last letter of the step mother and I have taken.—Next week mother files her petition in court for her divorce from father. In this I am supporting her. So the first thing to do was to secure some employment. Your poet is now become a salesman, and (it might be worse) a job at selling pictures at Korner & Woods has been accepted.

"I have had tremendous struggles, but out of the travail, I think, must come advancement. Working evenings will give me time for composing. And even should it not, I have been christened, I think, and am more or less contented with anything. Carl, I feel a great peace; my inner life has balanced, as I expected, the other side of the scale. Thank God, I am young. I have the confidence and will to *make* fate. Someday, perhaps next summer, I shall come to you and we may work together. You understand, I know."

He joined his friend much sooner than he expected. With his mother in Chicago, his father living at a club in the city, and no one left in the old home but his grandmother, there seemed to be no reason for him to remain in Cleveland. In the end, he had his way. It was decided that he should go to New York to live, where he might work at his writing and tutor privately in preparation for college under the guidance of Carl Schmitt, a young painter and family friend from Warren. The details of this new life being left to his own discretion, the plan suited Harold to the ground; and towards the end of December he boarded an eastbound train, brimming with high spirits and the determination to wrest a glorious fate from the future.

II

"Shoulder the curse of sundered parentage . . ."

Nᴇᴡ Yᴏʀᴋ in the winter of 1916–17 was an exciting place for any young man to live. As the principal port of embarkation for Europe, the central point at which munitions, supplies, and volunteers were gathered to be shipped across the Atlantic, it was much closer to the War than any other American city. Crowded with people who poured in from all parts of the nation, hoping to take part in the great cataclysm for love of money, ideals, or adventure, and bristling with a war fever that grew daily more hysterical, it was like an ancient city-state which independent of the rest of the country had already joined the hostilities. Citizens snatched at the latest editions of newspapers as though their own sons might be listed among the casualties; volunteers were public heroes; and the ships steaming out of the harbor were also heroic, for the German U-boats had only recently sunk three of them off the New England coast. Everywhere there was the electric tension of a national emergency. Resounding and splendid words could be heard on every street corner, words at which young men, in particular, took fire, and impatient with their own laggard government, rushed off to enlist in foreign ambulance corps and aviation units. The streets were full of uniforms of every description; and everyone sang, whistled, or stomped the marching tunes that were sweeping the country; everyone followed the bands and the brave parades. "Parades, parades," Harold wrote his mother from the midst of the tumult, "I am so tired of them. . . . There have been nurse parades, and dog-parades, and cat-parades, and all to that eternally rapturous and boresome melody, 'Over There.' "

It was not that he was actually bored, for life had never been so profoundly exciting. Nor was he insensible to the momentous events going on in the world about him, the epoch-making victories and defeats, the barbaric mechanical mass slaughters, the starvations and revolutions. But he hated war, and said so. Even more he hated the drunken patriotism which nourished it. If he had to go to the front, he would, but not to kill, not even in self-defense. For the rest, the less said about it, the better. He had come to New York to write poetry, to attend concerts and visit art galleries, to pursue a course of self-culture which might eventually liberate the powers he often felt surging within him; and with the single-mindedness that his friend Wright had remarked in Cleveland he was not to be distracted, least of all by street-corner orators. When the war invaded his own province—as it did in the case of *The Seven Arts*, which was forced to suspend publication because of its militant pacifism—he was eloquently enraged. And if, as sometimes happened, one of the endless parades made him late for a concert, he took it as a personal affront and cursed the War as he would a malicious enemy. Otherwise, he ignored it as much as possible, and turned his attention to another struggle, quite as epochal from his point of view and infinitely more stirring, in which he was determined to make his fame and fortune.

The colors of the American Renaissance were flying high in 1917. Victories reported up and down the literary front proved that for the time being God was on the side of poetry. Anticipating the shot at Sarajevo by two years, the first reverberation of the new poetry had been heard in Chicago in 1912 with the launching of *Poetry: A Magazine of Verse* and the publication of Vachel Lindsay's first poems. Throughout the following year it was echoed in other volumes of verse, and in 1914 further explosions occurred with the appearance of *Des Imagistes*, an anthology edited by Ezra Pound, and the founding of *The Little Review* in Chicago. In 1915 the redoubtable field-marshal, Amy Lowell, discharged the first of her annual blasts from Washington Square in another anthology called *Some Imagist Poets*. The same year saw the startling success of Edgar Lee Masters's *Spoon River Anthology* and the publication of Robert Frost's *North of Boston*. By 1917 the conquest of America by Imagism was signalled by the last of Amy Lowell's anthologies and the national recognition of a group of new poets: Lindsay, Sandburg, Masters, Frost, Lowell, Pound, and Fletcher. At the same time, as though in token of a further advance in American poetry, Ezra Pound, who had christened and launched the Imagist movement in London in 1912, transferred his allegiance as foreign representative from Harriet Monroe's *Poetry* to Margaret Anderson's *Little Review*, which had just moved from Chicago to New York. In the December issue of that year Pound confessed editorially to a long-discussed project of founding a magazine which would establish communication between New York, Paris, and London by publishing the best of contemporary English writing together with translations from the modern French poets. The best English writing of the time, according to Pound, was being done by himself, T. S. Eliot, James Joyce, and Wyndham Lewis, while the Frenchmen he wished to introduce to America were Rémy de Gourmont, Rimbaud, Laforgue, and Corbière. Thenceforth, this new cosmopolitanism with its especial cultivation of the French Decadents and Symbolists, both in poetry and painting, was sponsored by *The Little Review*, and later, after 1920, by *The Dial*.

There were also other, less purely aesthetic magazines, which, though participating in the spirit of internationalism, had as their principal goal the discovery of America with all its diverse traditions and unrelated phenomena as a cultural unity that, brought to vivid and active consciousness in American artists, might find expression at last in a national art. The new poets—Sandburg and Lindsay in particular—had again sounded the voice of the people, the sonorous chant and roll of the democratic paean which had not been heard in American poetry since Whitman; and those who had forgotten him recalled him with a thrill; those who had never heard of him—and there were many such in 1916—bought his books, and reading them, felt the surge of the many-blooded, many-landed nation of which they knew so little. The spirit of Whitman was the presiding genius among the group of men—James Oppenheim, Waldo Frank, Van Wyck Brooks, Paul Rosenfeld—who in 1916 founded *The Seven Arts*. Clear echoes of it could be heard in their first editorial:

"It is our faith and the faith of many that we are living in the first days of a renascent period, a time which means for America the coming of that national self-consciousness which is the beginning of greatness."

From France Romain Rolland wrote his encouragement, for in war-riddled Europe America seemed even more to be the torch-bearer of democratic civilization:

"I rejoice in the founding of a magazine in which the American Spirit may seek and achieve consciousness of its nature and of its role. My faith is great in the high destinies of

America. . . . This is my dream. . . . You must harmonize all of the dreams and liberties and thoughts brought to your shores by all your peoples. You must make of your culture a symphony . . . express your brotherhood of individuals, of races, of cultures, banded together. . . . Behind you, alone, the elemental Voice of a great pioneer, in whose message you may well find an almost legendary omen of your task to come,—your Homer: Walt Whitman."

Such was the mission of *The Seven Arts*. By its resurrection of the Whitman spirit, by its search for a "usable past" in American culture and its examination of traditions, so acutely carried on by Van Wyck Brooks, by its demand for a synthesis in art of the complete America, *The Seven Arts* in its one short year of life gave a permanent direction to American letters of the first quarter of the century.

Another magazine, which was the *enfant terrible* of the same platform, was *The Soil*, edited by R. J. Coady, the aggressive red-headed Irishman who had founded the Washington Square Gallery. Devoted chiefly to art forms, it printed reproductions of Cézanne, Picasso, Rousseau, and primitive sculpture, with critical and descriptive comments. But following a Van Gogh or a Matisse one might find a photograph of Toto, the clown at the Hippodrome, or Jesse Stahl, the bronco-buster, of Bert Williams or Charlie Chaplin. There was a camera study of Annette Kellerman in her abbreviated black swimming tights, and another of the huge Negro heavyweight champion, of whom it was claimed that "after Poe, Whitman, and Emerson he is the most glorious American." In an article on American art Coady listed its diverse forms with a profusion and vigor that Whitman might have envied:

"Skyscrapers, colonial arches, East River, the Battery, Bridges, Docks . . . Annette Kellerman, 'Neptune's Daughter' . . . Jack Johnson, Charlie Chaplin, Bert Williams, Rag-Time, Buck and Wing, and the Clog. The Crazy-Quilt and the Rag-Mat . . . Coney Island . . . *Others, Poetry, The Police Gazette* . . . Krazy Kat . . . Nick Carter, Deadwood Dick, Tom Teaser, Walt Whitman and Poe . . ."; and so on for a page and a half, to conclude succinctly: "This is American Art. It is not a refined granulation nor a delicate disease—it is not an ism."

The "barbaric yawp" of such manifestoes as this served to counterbalance the scholastic and sometimes rather precious eccentricities of the Imagists and Ezra Pound's new cosmopolitanism.

With the literary scene divided fairly equally between these two groups, with an unprecedented freedom for poetic experimentation, and with numerous little magazines open to all newcomers, it is little wonder that Crane was intoxicated by the prospect of living in New York. The cold, poorly lighted room he had rented at number 308 East 15th Street, near the ragged patrician dignity of Stuyvesant Square with its summer remnant of green and its ancient church, was only a few minutes' walk from the center of these activities. One block south lay Fourteenth Street, clotted with strange rich odors, and stranger sounds, one of the city's melting-pots; a few blocks west Fifth Avenue stretched its granite magnificent length northwards in a haze, and southwards presently issued into Washington Square, where every spring the old red brick and brass knockers and white porticoes of the colonial houses became pristine and bright with the greening of the trees. Here were the front-line fortifications of the American Renaissance. From the quiet square a network of jumbled streets and alleys branched out through the Village, like veins from a central artery, in which the poetic blood of the century ran high. Nor was the boy entirely a stranger to the neighborhood. From the garret across the square a blond Bohemian by name of Guido Bruno had first introduced him to the literary world in an issue of *Bruno's Bohemia*. And not far distant was the establishment of Joseph Kling, whose magazine he had hailed as a "new and distinctive chord" in American poetry. There was also Mrs. Moody's apartment in Waverly Place where he soon went to dine with his distinguished elders. And there were names he knew by reputation: the Washington Square Bookshop, where the Boni brothers had published the first of the Imagist anthologies; the Washington Square Gallery; the renovated stable in Mac-Dougal Street where the Provincetown Players were establishing Eugene O'Neill's reputation.

Among the first acquaintances he made at Mrs. Moody's parties was Padraic Colum, the Irish poet and dramatist, who was so favorably impressed by his verses that he assured him he should have no difficulty in having a book of poems published within two years, and even offered to write a preface for it. There was also Alfred Kreymborg, the founder of the magazine *Others*, which was printing the most important Imagist poets and the early work of T. S. Eliot. Although Kreymborg as an experimenter in new forms of *vers libre* found Crane's first poems somewhat conventional and thin, he was nonetheless generous with his encouragement. One of the assistant editors of *Others*, Maxwell Bodenheim, the loquacious and morose poet from Tennessee, found more to admire in the boy's short lyrics and promised him publication in the next issue of their magazine. Bodenheim also carried away some of the poems to show to his friend James Oppenheim, the editor of *The Seven Arts*. The praise and interest of such well-known poets of the day were a heady intoxicant to Crane. "Success," he wrote his mother, "seems imminent now more than ever." It did not evidently occur to him that other young men from all parts of the country were pouring into New York, each with his little notebook of poems, and that in the indiscriminate camaraderie of the Village each of them found a welcome and much

praise. The truth was that to his more distinguished contemporaries Crane appeared simply another young man of
some talent, good-natured and eager, but with no touch of
genius in his rather heavy face and conventional manners.
He had not yet emerged from adolescence, and both his
personality and poetry showed many adolescent characteristics. As for his premonition of a high destiny, his will to
make fate—these were interior matters apparent only in his
letters.

"O if you knew how much I am learning!" he wrote his
mother. "The realization of true freedom is slowly coming
to me, and with it a sense of poise which is of inestimable
value. My life however it shall continue, shall have expression and form. Believe me when I tell you that I am fearless,
that I am determined on a valorous future and something
of a realization of life. The smallness of hitherto large things,
and the largeness of hitherto small things is dawning. I am
beginning to see the hope of standing entirely alone and to
fathom Ibsen's statement that translated is, 'The strongest
man in the world is he who stands entirely alone!'"

Throughout the inevitable moments of doubt he was fortified from within by a sense of his own growth, for which
the first exciting months in New York provided a constant
stimulus.

"I realize more entirely every day," he declared to his father,
"that I am preparing for a fine life: that I have powers,
which, if correctly balanced, will enable me to mount to
extraordinary latitudes. There is constantly an inward struggle, but the time to worry is only when there is no inward
debate, and consequently there is smooth sliding to the devil.
There is only one harmony, that is the equilibrium maintained by two opposite forces, equally strong. When I perceive one emotion growing overpowering to a fact, or a statement of reason, then the only manly, worthy, sensible thing

to do, is to build up the logical side, and attain balance, and in art,—formal expression."

His most constant companion during these days was not one of the literati, however, but the painter, Carl Schmitt, who had been made his guardian at large. A young man some eight or ten years older than Crane, Schmitt had been born and brought up in Warren, Ohio, where his considerable talent had been noticed and encouraged by Harold's aunt, Mrs. Zell Hart Deming, a person of influence and means, who owned and published a daily newspaper. With her help he had pursued his studies abroad and travelled extensively on the Continent, a fact which lent him glamour and interest in the eyes of his young charge. The boy was further delighted by his dry sarcastic wit, his excellent taste in poetry, and his long discussions of the artist's problems. Since Schmitt's rooms were only a few doors removed from his own dingy quarters, he sought him out on all occasions. Almost every evening they had dinner together, possibly at Strunsky's Stuyvesant Restaurant just around the corner from East 15th Street, where between courses one could examine on the walls the latest French influence on the younger American painters. Thence they would return to Schmitt's rooms for long hours of talk. Harold spent much of his time there during the day as well. Indeed, he devoted more attention to Schmitt than his friend could well appreciate, so that often enough he arrived only to find him locked in his studio, deaf to all persuasions. Never suspecting for a moment that Schmitt could really be engrossed in his painting, the boy would imagine that he had in some way offended him, and would return later with some small gift to leave outside his door.

Aside from discussions of art in general, their talk was mostly about Harold's poetry; and there is little doubt that he benefited by the painter's sensitive responses to rhythm and movement. It was particularly in these respects that his early poems were most deficient. More often than not they were written in a sing-song anapaestic meter with awkward stops at the end of each line. Had it not been for their brilliant imagery and color, one might well have dismissed them as unfortunate efforts of no importance. But Schmitt seems to have sensed the growing power in the poems, for he spent no little time with Crane in going over his work. It was agreed that the latter should compose a certain number of poems a week simply as technical exercises with the purpose of breaking down formal patterns. These he would bring to his critic as he wrote them, and the two would read them over together, Schmitt illustrating with pencil on paper the rising and falling of cadences, the dramatic effect of caesural breaks, and the general movement of the poem as a whole. This was meat and drink to Crane who had never before had any detailed criticism of his poetry. He was furthermore learning a great deal about painting, which thereafter became a rich source of stimulation and new direction for his work. Altogether, it was a very profitable discipline and one that bore quick fruits, as the poems he carried down the street to the offices of *The Pagan* testified. Surprisingly enough, this conscious experimentation with verse forms did not lead him, as it might well have done during those flourishing days of *vers libre*, to abandon meter and rhyme. With a sound instinct for the value of mastering the traditional forms of English verse, he observed the conventions, with very few exceptions, until he felt secure in the control of his craft.

In March a visit from his mother brought this casual bohemian life to an end. Returning from Palm Beach, where she had passed most of the winter, and expecting daily to be awarded a decree of divorce, Mrs. Crane was eager to establish a home once more where she could be with her son. Harold, for his part, was overjoyed at the reunion and her plan to take an apartment in New York. Despite his preoccupation with his new life, his letters to her had been full of anxiety for her state of mind and health; again and again he begged her to forget his father and take an interest in her own future. "How I do long for your ultimate and complete happiness," he had written her in January. "You are a queen, and you shall have it, too. Often I have come across the most charming old apartments in my walks and I like to think of you calmly happy in one of them, happy with me and Grandma in a few clean rooms." Now that his desires were about to be realized, it seemed to him that perhaps the past years of torment had been only a necessary preparation for this new beginning, and a preparation, too, of the fallow earth of his creative spirit. Possibly he showed his mother the poem he had just written, called "The Hive," which was published in the March issue of *The Pagan:*

Up the chasm-walls of my bleeding heart
Humanity pecks, claws, sobs and climbs;
Up the inside, and over every part
Of the hive of the world that is my heart.

And of all the sowing, and all the tear-tendering,
And reaping, have mercy and love issued forth;
Mercy, white milk, and honey, gold love—
And I watch, and say, "These the anguish are worth."

Early in April, when his mother finally received her divorce and what he hoped would be a complete liberation from the past, he moved from his rooms on East 15th Street to the delightful apartment she had leased in the old brownstone house at 44 Gramercy Park.

Once established there, he yielded to his mother's insistence that he hire a tutor who would prepare him to enter

Columbia University in the fall, and presently engaged a Monsieur Tardy who instructed him daily. Although he had honestly intended to pursue a regular course of studies after his arrival in New York, actually he had done nothing about it, conceiving a cultivation of the arts to be a more pleasant and important obligation. Now, with only a few months left in which to make ready for the entrance examinations and presented by Monsieur Tardy with an impossibly heavy curriculum, he found scholastic discipline even less desirable than before. Doubtless it seemed downright madness to him to be memorizing the irregularities of verb forms or working over the chill hieroglyphs of algebra when poems by William Butler Yeats were appearing in *The Little Review*. What music had the declensions of the gerund to compare with that of "The Wild Swans at Coole"? As the weeks passed, college became an increasingly remote possibility, and once more he could devote his hours of reading to the little magazines and his books, and, in particular, to the works of William Blake, which his mother had recently given him.

Most of his time, however, he devoted to his mother, who, unable to rid herself of depressing recollections, needed constant companionship and diversions. Together they attended the few plays and concerts available during the summer season; and Harold, eager for his mother to share in his own exciting life in New York, introduced her to as many of his new acquaintances as he could find in the city. They also discovered friends in Charles Brooks and his wife from Cleveland, fellow-tenants at 44 Gramercy Park, who spent a part of each year in New York where Mr. Brooks, an established author of light essays, could find new material and stimulation. While Harold championed the cause of the "new" poetry against Mr. Brooks's professional cynicism, his mother was renewing her interest in Christian

Science, a faith that she believed had made possible the re-union with her husband and the few succeeding years of harmony after the crisis in Warren. With the help of Mrs. Brooks, who was a member of the church, and of Mrs. Spencer, another Cleveland woman, who was a practitioner, she was again trying to restore her health and nervous equilibrium by an active observance of its teachings.

Harold, too, was a frequent visitor at the Spencers' home; not, however, from an interest in Christian Science, though he pretended to believe in it for his mother's sake, but to call on Mrs. Spencer's daughter, Claire, with whom he had struck up a close friendship. Drawn together in the first place by a common hatred of Cleveland, they soon discovered more lively interests. In the long walks and intimate confidences of summer evenings, they began to exchange plans and ambitions and personal problems. Before long, Claire Spencer realized that her friend was suffering violent spiritual reactions to the turmoil of his family life. With the penetrating sensibility which lent a peculiar distinction to the novels she was later to write, she was the first of Crane's friends, and for several years the only one, to recognize the pathos of his interior life and the incipient growth of that pattern whose final mazes offered no exit but tragedy. More than grateful for this understanding, the boy formed a deep attachment for her, which lasted throughout his life. But their relationship, however distorted it later became in the drama of his imagination, was no more than a solid friend-ship based on a community of interests and mutual sym-pathy.

Despite the pleasant social life at 44 Gramercy Park and the ministrations of Mrs. Spencer, Mrs. Crane remained rest-less and unhappy, and towards the end of July returned to Cleveland to visit her mother, leaving Harold in charge of the apartment. It was a journey that filled the boy with apprehension. He knew that her divorce, far from bringing her freedom and reassurance, had left her with a sense of desolate estrangement and loss. In separating from his father, she had also had to separate herself from a comfortable home, her mother, and friends of long acquaintance—from almost everything necessary to her well-being. Often it seemed to him that the melancholia from which she suffered was little more than simple regret; and underneath her resentment against his father he sensed a longing for reconciliation. Furthermore, he knew that his father, too, was unhappy. On the very day the divorce had been granted he had been heard to say that he would remarry his wife within a year. And Harold himself had discovered evidence that he was employing private detectives to keep him informed of his wife's activities in New York. Given these indeterminate factors and his father's enigmatic temperament, almost anything might happen during his mother's visit in Cleveland. As the days passed, his mind swarmed with speculations of all sorts, and after several weeks he was prepared for either the best or the worst, when a wire summoned him home. Upon his arrival he found his parents completely reconciled: his father, impetuous as a young suitor, boisterously insisting upon an immediate marriage, and his mother once more swept away by her husband's dominance. Apparently the best had happened. A few days later Harold returned to Gramercy Park where, it was planned, his parents, after a quiet civil ceremony, would join him to celebrate the beginning of a new life. But he waited at the apartment in vain. Shortly before the proposed ceremony his father disappeared, leaving a curt note for Mrs. Crane to say that he had changed his mind and definitely abandoned their plans for remarriage. There was no further explanation.

Again a period of mental anguish followed for Harold

and his mother. When she returned to New York under the care of her mother, who dared not leave her alone, the boy's indignation flared into rage at the sight of her suffering. During the succeeding weeks all their efforts to achieve an ordered and happy life at the apartment were futile. Despite the distractions and amusements Harold and his grandmother contrived, she could not shake off the obsession with Mr. Crane's last injustice. Incessant brooding aggravated her condition, so that much of the time she was confined to her bed. There, as in years before, Harold again took up his post, sitting beside her in the darkened room for hours, his spirit once more wrenched from the pattern of its own growth and inflamed by the old wounds of humiliation and resentment. That his father had again shattered their prospects of stability and happiness seemed to him a gesture of deliberate malice; and his offer of remarriage now appeared to have been a diabolical plot to bring about their present mortification. In the face of such maneuvers his own efforts to maintain a just balance of affection between his parents seemed naïve, and thenceforth he made no attempt to control or conceal his true feelings. In a letter written a few weeks later, after the apartment in Gramercy Park had been abandoned and his mother had returned to Cleveland to live—only to suffer some new outrage at the hands of Mr. Crane—his attitude towards his father was bitterly apparent:

"My dear sweet Mother," he wrote, "I have just read your letter and find it hard to express my rage and disgust at what you say concerning C. A. Crane's conduct. 'Forget him,' is all I can say. He is too low for consideration. I am only quietly waiting,—stifling my feelings in the realization that I might as well get as much money as possible out of him. Why be scrupulous in one's dealings with unscrupulous people, anyway?"

The question of accepting his father's money after this crisis presented an embarrassing problem. Although both Harold and his mother felt he was justified in the hypocrisy involved, excuses did not help him play the part any more comfortably. With the extravagant hope of being able to earn his own living by writing he turned all his attention for a time to prose. Once settled in new quarters in a boarding house at 25 East 11th Street, he began what he hoped would be a popular novel, the romance of two young Americans in a colorful Caribbean setting. When this failed to progress, he undertook short stories that could be sold to *Smart Set*, and scenarios for the movies. He was especially eager to establish a source of independent income because he feared that when his father learned he was not really preparing himself for college, he would be less disposed to support him. The terms of the divorce, it is true, had stipulated that Mr. Crane should be responsible for his son's education and living expenses until he was of age; but Harold was well aware that the two items were practically synonymous in his father's mind and that by refusing one he would probably sacrifice the other. Since he had already turned his back on college by dismissing Monsieur Tardy after his mother's departure in September, he now stood in danger of losing his allowance. The fact that he continued to study French under the instruction of another tutor scarcely concealed his real indifference to a formal education. In view of this, the explanation he offered of his failure to matriculate was hardly exact:

"You speak quite emphatically in your letter about my education," he wrote Schmitt, who had returned to Ohio. "I must explain to you that on twenty-five dollars a week, Columbia is out of the question. This is all I am to get,—clothing and everything. While it will do for decent living, it really is too meager for any college. I understand that my male parent has spoken of me to several mutual friends as being a weakling, and totally incapable of anything at all. Knowing this, I can understand a great many more of his actions than I have heretofore. However, I am not going to seek work and drudge at completely foreign tasks as long as I can help it, and I am pursuing the old course of self-culture with reading, etc. I don't want to have to go to court, but if any more pressure is brought to bear, I'm afraid it will be inevitable."

It was obviously not true that he was expected to pay for his education and living expenses out of his weekly allowance. The court action which he mentioned in the letter was in itself proof of this, for it was a suit his mother had brought against his father for several hundred dollars' worth of bills, incurred in purchasing clothing for him, which Mr. Crane had originally promised, and finally refused, to pay. The litigation itself was short and the decision was awarded to his mother; but the incident illustrated the way the maladministration of his financial needs still further complicated the family relationships, and stood as a presage of the bitter conflicts and recriminations over money matters which harassed him throughout his life.

This law suit might also have provoked the cruel gesture Mr. Crane made several weeks later, which created another painful scene, and convinced mother and son that they were being persecuted in the literal sense of the word. Some time in November Mrs. Crane returned to New York to be with Harold for the Thanksgiving holidays. During her visit he was taken seriously ill, evidently with one of his obscure nervous disorders, for the attending physician could find no recognizable symptoms. Fearful lest some unforeseen crisis arise and find her helpless, she telephoned his father in Cleveland to ask him to come East and take charge of the situation. Mr. Crane replied flatly that he would not come to New York even if his son were dying. The shock of this brutal rebuff proved too much for Mrs. Crane, and that evening as she was about to retire, she was seized by a sudden attack and lost consciousness. For two days she lay in a curious state of coma, insensible to what was going on about her; and even when this condition passed, her state of mind was so dangerous that Harold, recovering from his own illness, found it necessary to send for some member of the family to come to his aid.

"I am holding on to health and sanity with both hands," he wrote to his one confidant, Schmitt. "You will excuse me for writing you in this state of mind and in such words, I know, when I tell you that in a measure it is a relief. Mother is in a worse state than I have ever had to cope with. Indeed, I have had to telegraph Zell this morning to come here immediately, though by her orders, for I would expire before I would trouble Zell so to leave her pressing duties. What course things will take after her arrival I am resigned to accept as best. The hardest thing for me to bear is the blame that Mother puts on me as being in a major way responsible for her present condition. You know how hard it has been for me, and was last summer. This trouble will never, never end, I'm afraid, or if it does, it will be in insanity. I no longer anticipate, there is enough, it seems, in the present.

"Your letter came yesterday when I was sick in bed, and has done me a lot of good. I'm very glad to hear how loaded with commissions you are, and that you will be back again in March. How I shall enjoy an evening a week with you. There is no one in the world whom I have to explain things to but you. One cannot explain to any but those who have understanding. So do not be too critical of my confessions."

He was right, it seemed, in thinking the trouble would never end. Already a year had passed since his parents' divorce, and the prospect of a happy readjustment and consequent freedom, which he had anticipated on leaving Cleveland, appeared more remote than ever. In the meantime his nervous system was being constantly distorted by hysterical tensions, and his spirit was suffering wounds that eventually, from incessant probing, became incurable cancerous growths. With each new cataclysm it seemed as if at last the remaining ties which bound his mother and father would be severed. But there was always some form of partial reconciliation, some impulsive gesture of kindness from his father, which again aroused his mother's hope of an ultimate reunion. Only three weeks later, when Harold and his mother had returned to Cleveland for the Christmas holidays, Mr. Crane invited them to be his guests of honor at a New Year's Eve party, and throughout the evening showed them only the greatest courtesy and sympathy. But his son could not forgive him on such slight evidence of good will, and his letters to Carl Schmitt during that winter were signed "Harold Hart," as though to announce his complete alienation from him.

Despite the painful turmoil of his family life, he had not entirely neglected his writing during the fall and winter. In October *The Pagan* had printed a poem entitled "Echoes" by Hart Crane. This name, suggested to him by his mother on the grounds that his maternal forbears should take equal credit with the Cranes for his poetry, he adopted permanently. But publication in *The Pagan* no longer brought him a sense of achievement; its pages were open to almost any poem he chose to submit. The editor, Joseph Kling, was said to consider him the equal of any American lyricist of the day. Reporting the rumor to his friend Schmitt, Hart wrote soberly, "I don't trust Kling's criticism very far judging by the 'tone' generally prevalent in the magazine. But I *am* improving and would just as soon be deceived a little as not." He would have given the accumulated praise of all the editors in the country, however, for a single publication in *The Little Review*, which set a permanent mark of distinction on its contributors. At one time he had thought this distinction was to be his, for the editors were considering his poem "North Labrador"; and anticipating their acceptance, he wrote Schmitt in high spirits of the prospect of appearing in print beside Pound, Symons, and Yeats. But in the end the poem was rejected. It was not until January, when he and his mother returned to 25 East 11th Street after the holidays in Cleveland, that he joined the distinguished company. In the December issue of *The Little Review*, then on sale, he discovered his poem "In Shadow," a delicate piece of imagism:

> Out in the late amber afternoon,
> Confused among chrysanthemums,
> Her parasol, a pale balloon,
> Like a waiting moon, in shadow swims.

He was improving indeed; such stanzas showed a great stride from the ragged anapaests he had carried to Schmitt a year before. Margaret Anderson, the enterprising editor of the magazine, who had rejected so many of his poems, was enthusiastic in her acceptance. "Dear Hart Crane, poet!!", she wrote, "I'm using 'Shadow' in the December issue, now going to press. It's the best thing you've sent yet: I'll tell you the details of just why when you come. It's quite lovely. Hurrah for you!!" But Ezra Pound, her foreign editor and self-constituted arbiter at large of contemporary poetry, evidently did not agree with her, for in due time Crane received an "Easter sonnet" from him remarking that "Beauty is a good enough egg, but so far as I can see, you haven't the ghost of a setting hen or an incubator." This damnation, however, was taken in good part by Crane, who undoubtedly himself recognized the thinness of the poem; and having some knowledge of Poundian pronouncements besides, he only commented that it was "too good a douche to waste on one novice." He added in the same letter, more-over, that he considered Pound second only to Yeats among living poets writing in English.

December had also seen the publication of another poem, "The Bathers," in *The Pagan;* and when he returned from the holidays "Modern Craft" was in the press for the January issue. By this time he had become such an inveterate contributor to Kling's magazine that in March he was made an associate editor. "Such a burst of trumpets," he wrote Schmitt in great elation, "cannot fail to arouse the relatives of a slim, sleek youth of eighteen, I am sure." His relatives probably respected his new position less than they had his brief employment in the basement of Brentano's bookshop, where for a time he had sold books "on wet nursing, care of mothers during pregnancy, the Montessori method, and how to know the wild flowers." For *The Pagan*, like all the other little magazines, led a hand-to-mouth existence and could pay its contributors and editors in nothing but psychological coin. Nonetheless, Hart's duties in his new capacity were far more pleasant than clerking. They consisted, for the most part, simply in contributing more material to the magazine. In the April-May issue of that year he was responsible for "The Case Against Nietzsche," a valiant defense of the poet against the current anti-German sentiments of war propaganda; two short poems; and a column called "The Last Chord," which was a critical commentary on the concerts, exhibitions, and drama about town, as seen and heard by "A. Pagan Knight." The drama in particular was in full flower during the spring of 1918 in the Village. Besides the Provincetown Players, there were also The Greenwich Village Theater and the Other Players. The latter group under the direction of Alfred Kreymborg, its founder, was experimenting with poetic drama and pantomime, including Kreymborg's "Manikin and Miniken" and "The Two Slatterns and a King" by Edna St. Vincent Millay, the girl poet of a few years past. The concerts, alas, were all tagged by the national anthem, even in the case of the Boston Symphony Orchestra conducted by Dr. Carl Muck, who was himself a German. And as for the Academy Exhibition— "well, turnips are turnips; one season a little bigger,—or a little smaller." Listed as "tragi-comique" among the Pagan Knight's observations about town was the fact that the most artistic war poster on Fifth Avenue had been created by a pacifist. And a patriotic poem in the same issue carried an editorial note by "H. C." to the effect that it was printed with reservations of approval.

The War in its fourth year was at last penetrating to the very heart of the Village. With the increasing pressure of propaganda many of its inhabitants began to disappear: Maxwell Bodenheim fled to Boston to escape the military authorities; Padraic Colum returned to Ireland; and Carl Schmitt wrote from Ohio that he had been drafted into the government employ. In May Hart received a letter from his mother, who had returned to Cleveland a month earlier, begging him to come home for the summer and pointing out that the government required all young men of eighteen years or older to be occupied in some helpful employment. But there were also other reasons for her urgency.

"You have within your grasp," she continued, "the privilege of making me very happy by having you with me for a while during a time which may be very trying and hard for me to bear. . . . It may be that your father has selected a wonderful woman for his second wife—or at least one who will make him happy. I am not going to say that I am glad that he is to be married so soon because I had thought that some day with the necessary separation and time to view things more broadly we might all three again be happily reunited. But it doesn't look that way now. However you have no quarrel with your father over that any more than if I should take the same step. So please write him a good letter to that effect very soon. I know he does care for you and you for him."

It was clear enough that whether or not the government demanded his presence in Cleveland, his mother most certainly did; and towards the end of May he returned once more to his old home.

The first employment he found in Cleveland was at a munitions plant, where he had the task of tightening bolts on machine parts as they passed in endless file before him on a conveyor belt. It was a monotonous and maddening kind of work for a young man accustomed to regulating his own time and activities, and a far cry from *The Little Review* and Ezra Pound's *canzoni*. Outside the factory he found little to interest or amuse him. Alone in the house after his mother and grandmother had left for a motor trip through New England, he could find nothing to replace the excitements of New York. Occasionally he spent an evening with his old schoolmate, William Wright, discussing poetry; but more often there were no available means of relieving his depression and irritability. The few duty calls he paid his father made him even more morose. Unable to forget his father's remarks and behavior in the past, he sensed cruel innuendoes and sarcasms in everything he said. Often he returned home scarcely recognizable because of the large red welts that broke out all over his body at moments of acute emotional stress. The obsession that his father was ridiculing him to his friends as a weakling and ne'er-do-well made life in Cleveland painfully self-conscious and uncomfortable. By the end of July his patience gave out. One day, having quit his job, he rushed to the drafting headquarters in desperation and tried to enlist as a volunteer, but was peremptorily rejected as being still a minor. Thwarted in this direction, he resigned himself once more to work, this time at a shipyard on Lake Erie where, employed as a riveter, he crawled about under the gigantic steel skeleton and epidermis of some modern leviathan. It was work even more strenuous than his first job, but in both capacities he was learning more than he realized about the machinery of high-powered industrialism, unconsciously absorbing its substance and spirit in a vivid hand-to-hammer relation, so that in later years he was able to use it in his poetry as a field of experience familiar and meaningful as the world of nature. When he wrote—

> Down Wall, from girder into street noon leaks,
> A rip-tooth of the sky's acetylene . . .

it was more than a brilliant decorative metaphor. By virtue of the qualities his personal experience lent it, it became a symbol of metropolitan America in the white heat of industrial activity.

Early in September, when the hay-fever from which he suffered reached its most excruciating stage, he left the shipyard at the doctor's orders. Before he could find other employment, the unexpected happened.

"I am included in the 18-45 draft," he wrote Schmitt, "and sincerely wish to be taken soon to be a 'rough . . . common . . . soldier.' I have skidded about at one thing and another most all summer and feel prepared and even enthusiastic. They say that all grouches stand excellent opportunities for promotion, so my ambition is becoming dreamily tickled at the prospect."

Actually he did not accept his summons with such pleasant equanimity. While his mother and grandmother hastened to muster the necessary clothing and accessories, Hart stormed about the house cursing the government. Only his disgust with the world in general made him feel kindly disposed at times towards his new profession. Fortunately, the violent epidemic of influenza, which swept the country that fall, closed the training camps to all new recruits for several weeks, and Hart was still at home in November when the news of the Armistice burst on the world in storms of confetti and shrieking whistles.

After three months of reporting for a Cleveland newspaper, *The Plain Dealer*, which had employed him on the strength of an Armistice sonnet he had written, Hart returned once more to New York. This time, however, he came not as a young man of leisure, to observe, to spend hours talking and writing and reading in the pursuit of self-culture, but as a young man in search of work. All plans for a college education had been definitely abandoned. He was now approaching his twentieth birthday, and he knew that by the ethics accepted in his family he would be expected thenceforth to contribute substantially to his own support. In recognition of the implacable laws of this code his mother had required him to pay her a small nominal sum for board and lodging while he had been gainfully employed during his stay in Cleveland. Furthermore, since his mother was now paying him his fortnightly check of fifty dollars, he was especially eager to earn his living, for he knew she considered her alimony no more than sufficient for her own personal needs. Acutely sensitive as he was to the slightest suggestion of inadequacy and tormented constantly by the fear of his father's ridicule, the challenge of these new responsibilities brought him back to New York with the strenuous intention of finding immediate work.

He finally found rooms at 307 West 70th Street, only a few doors from Riverside Drive and the tremendous reach of the Hudson River with its "oak-vizored" palisades and at night its beaded strings of lights and mournful fog horns. In

Alexander Baltzly, with whom he shared his quarters for a time, he found a congenial companion, well-versed in literature and music. If Baltzly, who was a Harvard graduate, was shocked to learn that his young roommate was reading certain of the Romantic poets for the first time, Crane for his part was no less distressed to discover in him a complete ignorance of Cézanne and the Post-Impressionists; and between them they carried on a kind of mutual instruction. There were also his old friends of Gramercy Park and the Village to see again; and there followed invitations to dine with the Colums, the Kreymborgs, and the Brookses. His most intimate friend of those days, Claire Spencer, had just been married to Harrison Smith, a young man of literary inclinations who later became a well-known publisher; and Hart was a frequent guest at their home. And not by any means to be forgotten were Joseph Kling and *The Pagan* of which he was still an editor, though he had contributed nothing but a few book reviews for several months. In April, he resigned his position with the magazine, and his name in the masthead was replaced by that of Gorham B. Munson, a newcomer to the Village, who became one of the important literary figures of the following decade. When the two first met at the offices of *The Pagan* and discovered in each other common excitements—Joyce's *Ulysses*, which was then appearing serially in *The Little Review*, the poetry of Pound and Yeats, the prose of Wyndham Lewis—they became close friends. Munson, who already looked up to Crane as a contributor to *The Little Review*, was the first to recognize in his brilliant enthusiastic talk about art and literature the genuine "excitability of a great poet," as he later wrote; and during the succeeding years he devoted to him a serious critical sympathy which played a considerable part in Crane's efforts to achieve a personal mode of expression.

When Hart finally came to look for work in all seriousness, he found to his dismay that the city was overrun with
soldiers recently discharged from the army, all in search of
jobs. Though he had not expected to meet with any com-
petition from them in the field of journalism, every newspaper office he visited was besieged by men whose age and
experience gave them certain precedence. Failing to get
work as a reporter, he tried to obtain assignments from the
Sunday feature syndicates, but with no greater success.
Padraic Colum sent him to Boni and Liveright, the publishers, to apply for employment as a reader of manuscripts;
rejected there, he tried other publishing houses; wrote and
dispatched scenarios to motion-picture producers, only to
meet everywhere with failure. Finally, in April, the editors
of *The Little Review*, knowing of his predicament, offered him the management of their advertising department
on a commission basis, doubtless thinking they might as well
turn over that hopelessly moribund office to their young
protégé for whatever he could possibly get out of it. Well
aware of its liabilities, Hart accepted nonetheless, having
calculated by some fantastic mathematics that he could earn
four thousand dollars a year in commissions. At the same
time, motivated by a desire to economize that proved he
did not put much faith in his great expectations, he moved
from his room on West 70th Street to the old brownstone house at 24 West 16th Street where William Cullen
Bryant had once lived. Ascending from the exterminator's
establishment in the basement through the malodorous stra-
tum of the embalmer's school on the ground floor, past the
gold and plum-colored offices of *The Little Review* to the
garret of the young poet, the building offered a rich cross-
section of life. Such a progression made easy game for a
polite essayist, who was not too genteel to indulge in ridicule, and Hart's elderly friend, Charles Brooks, having paid

him a visit in his new quarters, was quick to take advantage of it in an essay published in the volume *Hints to Pilgrims*.

These two rooms, for which Hart paid only ten dollars a month, were made available to him by the generosity of his friend Harrison Smith, who rented them as a workshop for writing, though he used them very infrequently. He and his wife, Claire Spencer, had already guessed Hart's financial distress, and with careful tact they not only rented him the rooms and furnished them for his convenience, but also invited him to dine with them several times a week. Once installed in his 'garret, Hart began to discover that he had grossly over-estimated the popularity of *The Little Review* as an advertising medium. An intensive canvassing of all the larger firms about the city yielded only one advertisement, and he soon became resigned to the failure of the project. He found an exciting compensation, however, in living on the floor above the offices of the magazine, where he acted as minister without portfolio to all artists and writers who arrived during the absence of its editors. It was in this capacity that he was terrified one day by the appearance of the magazine's most fantastic contributor, the Baroness Elsa von Freytag von Loringhoven, whose startling costumes and behavior provided a series of unparalleled sensations in the Village and the city's police force. Sometimes she appeared wearing her famous coal-scuttle hat and mustard-spoon earrings; at other times she dyed her hair green and decorated her face with postage stamps; and perhaps most memorable was the period when her shaved head was lacquered with vermilion and her body draped only with mourning crêpe. Whatever her costume that particular day, Crane turned and fled at her invasion of his quarters, and thereafter vanished into alleys and doorways at the very sight of her brilliant approach along the street. Another day, however, his habit of hanging over the stairwell brought him better luck.

In this way he first met Matthew Josephson, who was also eager for publication in *The Little Review*, and the long conversation which followed Crane's invitation to walk up another flight was the beginning of another friendship, like that with Munson, which offered him much critical encouragement during the following years. Josephson, who was then a student at Columbia University, by turns witty, scholarly, and acute in his perceptions, pointed out to Crane certain parallels and analogies in the history of English literature that extended his reading and led him more quickly to the discovery of his own tradition. It was in such vicarious ways that Crane was gradually receiving his own education.

During these months he was facing for the first time the knotty problem, which tormented him, like many another artist, throughout his life, of how to earn his living without sacrificing his art. There seemed to be a conclusive abyss between the small impoverished island of the arts in America and the vast mainland of its busy and prosperous life, a chasm which was bridged only occasionally by shaky contrivances of compromise from the one side and of uncertain sympathy from the other. Many lesser artists found this condition exciting and even stimulating, confirming, as it appeared, their philosophy of the antagonism between life and art. But for a poet like Crane, whose profound sympathies gave him a great hunger for life and demanded a living relation with its manifold reality for the right maturing of his genius, such isolation came as a serious frustration.

"The commercial aspect is the most prominent characteristic of America," he wrote William Wright, "and we all must bow to it sooner or later. I do not think, though, that this of necessity involves our complete surrender of everything nobler and better in our aspirations. Illusions are falling away from everything I look at lately. At present the world takes on the look of a desert,—a devastation to my eyes, and I am finding it rather hard at best. Still there is something of a satisfaction in the development of one's consciousness even though it is painful."

He was more positively inclined, however, to look for the cause of his difficulties in his own life. Looking back over the confusion of the past years, it seemed to him that its major events—his parents' divorce, his father's neglect, his interrupted schooling—all had collaborated in producing his immediate dilemma. The more pressing his troubles became, the more he brooded over these things; and his smouldering resentment flared forth at last in a bitter letter to his mother.

"What I wrote you about money," he complained, "still holds good. I have cashed the checks you sent as there is no use in my being foolish about such matters when I have only fifteen cents in my pocket and a very empty stomach. I do not ask you for more, however, I am very much against your sending me money from your personal allowance. It seems to me that it would not be very much trouble to go down and see Sullivan for a half hour for a few days and get sufficient results from the enactment of a perfectly just and practical contract so that I would not be due to hear within a few years the accusation of having made you economize and scrimp your own pleasures for my assistance during this trying time when I am making every effort to get started in something. You know, Mother, I have not yet forgotten your twitting me last summer at my not paying my board expenses when I was at home, and I don't welcome your generosity quite so much now on the possibility of a recurrence of such words at some future time. I don't want to fling accusations etc. at anybody, but I think it's time you realized that for the last eight years my youth has been a rather bloody battleground for yours and father's sex life and troubles. With a smoother current around me I would now be well along in some college, taking probably some course of study which would enable me upon leaving to light upon, far more readily than otherwise, some decent sort of employment. Do you realize that it's hard for me to find any work at all better than some manual labor, or literary work, which, as you understand, is not a very paying pursuit? My present job in connection with *The Little Review* possibly offers me an opportunity for experience in the advertising world, which is a good field for money,—but it's the hardest thing in the world to get worked up, especially with my complete inexperience in the work. I am looking for something else now every day,—anything that comes along,—with the intention of one way or another establishing my independence from all outside assistance. In the meantime I am carrying on with this job, and should it give enough promise, will continue in it. I have found out recently what it is like to be a beggar in the streets, and also what good friends one occasionally runs across in this tangle of a world. For some time after your letter I was determined not to write rather than compromise with hypocrisy or hurt your feelings. If this letter has wounded you, then I am ready to beg your pardon in apology with the understanding that I write no more, for I have discovered that the only way to be true to others in the long run, is to be true to one's self."

Needless to say, the prospects of his work with *The Little Review* did not improve, and under protest he continued to accept his mother's checks. Several weeks later he wrote her that he had once more made the rounds of all the advertising agencies and publishers, with no more success than before. "I can always find work," he continued, "in the machine shop and shipyard, but cannot help avoiding them as a last resort as they would merely suffice to keep breath in the body and get me nowhere in particular." Realizing only too well that his greatest drawback in applying for a position lay in his lack of any technical training, he had hoped to earn enough money to pay for a course in business and advertising at Columbia University during the summer. But when the time arrived for the course to begin, he was still without funds. It is absurd to suppose that his father, whose business at that time was grossing about three-quarters of a million dollars a year, would have refused to supply the necessary amount had he been asked for it. But Hart was too proud to admit his inability to pay his own way, above all to his father.

"I made no requests for assistance from C. A.," he wrote his mother, "in regard to the Columbia summer course which began the day before yesterday. In answer to his letter which announced his intention and *promise* to take an advertisement in *The Little Review* I thanked him and told him that his payment would help me in taking a course in business advertising which I was hoping to take at Columbia this summer. That was all there was said about it. He didn't mention the matter in his next (and last) letter, and has not even paid for the advertisement which he said he would do as long as I was associated with the magazine, and he has heard nothing to the contrary, I am positive. Of course, all my friends think his treatment of me is disgraceful and unaccountable. My own opinion is hardly less reserved, as you know, but I am trying my best to turn my thoughts to other channels as much as possible. It is only when hunger and humiliation are upon me that suddenly I feel outraged. . . . I don't know why C. A. hasn't answered my last letter of a month ago. It was certainly cordial, pleasant, and without a single feature that I can imagine anyone objecting to. Meanwhile no check for the ad. comes either. I suppose he had a quarrel with his wife and as a reaction felt kindly enough disposed towards me to write his first cordial letter in three years. I won't take him so seriously after this."

The dark prospect that faced him after the collapse of these plans was relieved once more by the generosity of his good angels, Harrison and Claire Smith. He wrote his mother that it had been a rather humiliating experience to have to depend upon them for so many of his needs, and that several times rather than ask their help he had gone for long periods without food. "They have been wonderfully thoughtful," he added, "and I haven't yet had to ask,—evidences seemed to be enough and better than words." The evidences in July were such that when the Smiths were preparing to leave the city, they dared not abandon him, and he received an invitation to spend the rest of the summer with them at Brookhaven, a charming village on Long Island not far from the sea. Although the long quiet days in the sun and salt air must have been a source of great relief to him, he was painfully aware of his peculiar position in the household. He suspected the slightest remarks and gestures of concealing criticisms and his irritability led him into provoking ridiculous quarrels with Mrs. Smith. One night the house was awakened by a tremendous thumping and banging. When Mrs. Smith rushed into the hall to investigate the uproar, she found Hart laboring down the stairs under his trunk, fully prepared to take his leave of them, having brooded half the night over some imagined insult. There were tears and a reconciliation, and Hart returned to his room to record in his diary the details of Mrs. Smith's behavior, her humble apology, and his own generous decision to remain as her guest out of kindness to her. This pathetic attempt to justify himself he left opened the next day on her dressing table where she might read it, the better to learn what sort of man she was dealing with. Naturally, other quarrels followed, and shortly afterwards Hart returned to the city, where for once certain employment was awaiting him.

The job he found on his return to New York was with the firm of Rheinthal and Newman, an agency for the reproductions of the Maxfield Parrish paintings that Mr. Crane had commissioned for the covers of his candy boxes. It was upon his father's recommendation that Hart obtained the work, and this gesture of good will signalized the commencement of a period of pleasant relations between them that lasted for some time. Hart had received the first evidence of his father's apparent change of heart with no little amazement. But with the quick responsiveness he always showed to any signs of affection, he immediately began to see his father in a more charitable light. That he genuinely wished to believe he had been wrong in his past estimation of him was clear from the letter which reported the news to his mother.

"Probably the truth consists more moderately in the estimate of him as a person of as many good inclinations as bad ones," he wrote. "Your feelings as a woman lover were bound to be dangerous in diverting you from an impersonal justice, and, however much I may have been blinded by my own relationship with him, I cannot deny having been influenced by your sufferings and outcries. . . . I am not building many air castles, as I have learned too much already for that,—but it is hopeful, at least, with present relationships prevailing."

During the next three months nothing occurred to destroy their accord, and when Hart finally resigned his position with Rheinthal and Newman, he did so with the comfortable knowledge that his father's support was behind him. Possibly he even took the step in deference to his father's wish, which, as he knew, was to bring him eventually into his own employ and train him in the candy business. With unflagging optimism and imagination Hart hoped that if he humored his father's wishes long enough, he might finally be rewarded with an independent income and the security to pursue his writing in peace. He had not yet fully understood that his father had no more objection to poetry as an avocation than to golf—as he later explained to Hart—provided that the greater part of one's time and interest was absorbed by a profitable business. What Mr. Crane for his part could not understand was that poetry could possibly constitute a respectable profession for a mature and moral person; and he persisted in believing that his son would recognize this in due time and conform to his wishes. This dangerous misunderstanding was the basis of their accord and of the arrangement they presently made whereby Hart was to begin working for his father as a clerk in one of the Crane stores in Akron, Ohio. Accordingly, in November Hart left New York with the impression that he had at last solved his dilemma: he would earn his own living, as well as his father's respect and affection, and at the same time be working towards complete freedom for his writing.

III

"*There is the world dimensional for
those untwisted by the love of things
irreconcilable . . .*"

Akron, "high place,"—
A bunch of smoke-ridden hills
Among rolling Ohio hills. . . .

The dark-eyed Greeks grin at each other
In the streets and alleys.
The Greek grins and fights with the Swede,—
And the fjords and the Aegean are remembered.

Above their jokes and contraband
Niggers dream of Kentucky melons,
Yellow as gold,—golden as money.
And they all dream of money.

It was such a town. Looking down on it from the surrounding hills, its few large buildings and the drab monotony of
identical roof tops multiplied away into obscurity under the
dark drift of smoke from the huge black stacks of the rubber factories. In the streets of the town one found the same

multiplication of industry in the continual shifts of rubber workers, pressing in grimy phalanxes through the downtown section on their way from work. It was a town becoming a city, typical of the violent growth of the twentieth century, drawing into the vast mechanism of its industry the new blood of foreign labor and creating a new wealth.

"A hell of a place," Crane wrote. "The streets are full of the débris from old buildings that are being torn down to replace factories etc. It looks, I imagine, something like the western scenes of some of Bret Harte's stories. I saw about as many Slavs and Jews on the streets as on Sixth Avenue. Indeed the main and show street of the place looks something like Sixth Ave. without the elevated."

This cultural desolation, however, had been anticipated and prepared for in his determination to sacrifice immediate pleasures for future benefits; and for the time being he was moderately content to be "Porphyro in Akron," pursuing poetry only as "a bedroom occupation" in one of the rooms of a downtown hotel.

It could be little else, for his duties behind the candy counter of his father's store demanded his presence from early morning to late evening. It was a long and wearisome schedule. His only consolation came during the slack hours of business when the store was almost empty of customers. Then he would sink out of sight behind his counter, and crouching cross-legged on the floor, light up one of his Cinco cigars and pull out from its shelf of hiding a copy of Pound's *Pavannes & Divisions*, the latest issue of *The Little Review*, the plays of Marlowe or Webster, or the poems of Donne. And there he would read absorbedly, the smoke from his cigar rising in a mysterious wraith above the counter until some bewildered customer coughed him back to reality, and he returned to his duties, the lines from Pound running through his head: "O helpless few in my country, O remnant enslaved! . . . You who cannot wear yourselves out by persisting to successes."

But he did persist, cheered on by his father's promise of a better position in Cleveland in the near future and his own confidence that such promotions would succeed one another rapidly until a permanent security and leisure were achieved. During the late evenings in his hotel room he returned to his reading and writing despite the "tumult of weariness from a basement cabaret" that clamored through his windows. His writing consisted mostly in correspondence. In poetry he composed only a few random verses of "Porphyro in Akron" and completed "My Grandmother's Love Letters," which he had begun before leaving New York. He was more than pleased by the latter, which, with its delicate, unrhymed cadences, achieved a further step in his poetic progress; and his pleasure was doubled by the praise it received from his friends, for both Munson and Josephson wrote him that it was the best thing he had written. The encouragement of these two men meant much to him in his industrial exile, and their letters, full of the literary news of New York, criticisms of new books, and suggestions for reading, assured him of continual contact with the world of letters. He was also corresponding with Sherwood Anderson, whose *Winesburg, Ohio* he had reviewed in the September issue of *The Pagan* with unreserved enthusiasm. "It constitutes an important chapter in the Bible of her consciousness," he had written. "America should read this book on her knees." He felt powerfully drawn to Anderson's writing not only because he saw reflected in it the problems of the artist against a Middle Western background, but also because in its poignant and obscure emotionalism he sensed a broad poetic impulse sympathetic to his own. And the letters he received from this itinerant correspondent pointed the direction of that impulse by suggesting that he turn his attention to a study of the national consciousness in such books as Waldo Frank's *Our America* and *The Ordeal of Mark Twain* by Van Wyck Brooks, both just off the press. The tradition of *The Seven Arts* had survived the magazine itself and was still coactive with the influence of *The Little Review*. Between the two forces, as between their exponents, Crane still maintained a pregnant equipoise, absorbing the stuff which he was later to fuse in his own work; but at times the period of preparation seemed to him nothing more than profitless suspension. In a letter to Munson that mentioned Anderson he wrote: "He and Josephson are opposite poles. J., classic, hard and glossy,—Anderson, crowd-bound, with a smell of the sod about him, uncouth. Somewhere between them is Hart Crane with a kind of wistful indetermination, still much puzzled."

Outside his correspondence his pleasures were limited to two or three new friends. In a tumble-down frame house in the center of the city he had discovered "a filthy old man" whose photographic portraits excited in him a lively admiration. H. W. Minns was not a new name in photography, for in his time he had received the Dresden and Munich awards; but caught in the backwash of time he had been almost forgotten and his work was practically unknown to the younger men of his profession. Fired with his usual enthusiasm, Crane undertook to rediscover him to the artistic circles of New York, and immediately began writing letters to editors and dispatching photographs for publication. But in spite of his admiration for Minns's work, he was discouraged from cultivating his society by his age and eccentricities. He found a more congenial companion in Harry Candee, a sophisticated and clever young man, brilliantly conversant with the things of literature and the world, who was also suffering a temporary exile in Akron. With him he spent much of his free time over jugs of the local raisin brew in the prohibition secrecy of a boarding house in the foreign quarter.

> I remember one Sunday noon,—
> Harry and I, "the gentlemen,"—seated around
> A table of raisin-jack and wine,—our host
> Setting down a glass and saying,—
>   "One month,
> I go back rich . . . I ride black horse . . .
> Have many sheep."
>   And his wife, like a mountain, coming in,
> With four tiny black-eyed girls around her,
> Twinkling like little Christmas trees.
>
> And some Sunday fiddlers, Roumanian business men,
> Came and played ragtime and dances before the door,
> And we overpayed them because we felt like it.

On such occasions Candee held forth with witty anecdotes about his experiences in Continental society and glib talk of his esoteric readings. Although he patronized and ridiculed Crane openly as the poet-son of the candy manufacturer, Crane with that pathetic lack of self-confidence and self-respect which throughout his life rendered him the easy victim of the malice and jibes of inferior persons, accepted this as possibly his due. From his earliest childhood, whether within his own home or outside of it, he had never experienced the security and unqualified affection that would have given him a sense of personal dignity and made him invulnerable to such attacks. Because of this there was something child-like and immature in his helplessness; for he was disarmed in advance by the too honest recognition that he had no conviction of his own worth. Characteristically enough, he was even grateful for what little genuine affection Candee showed him, as though he were receiving a favor he did not merit.

There was also another person in Akron, anonymously mentioned in his letters to Munson, who played an important part in Crane's life at the time and inaugurated one of its most tragic maladjustments. Early in December he had written to Munson: "I have lately begun to feel some wear from my surroundings and work, and to make it worse, have embarked on a love affair, (of all places unexpected, here in Akron!) that keeps me broken in pieces most of the time, so that my interest in the arts has sunk to a rather low station." There was no further mention of this new relationship until late in the month shortly before he returned to Cleveland to work in his father's factory.

"This 'affair' that I have been having," he wrote then, "has been the most intense and satisfactory one of my whole life, and I am all broken up at the thought of leaving him. Yes, that last word will jolt you. I have never had devotion returned before like this, nor ever found a soul, mind, and body so worthy of devotion. Probably I never shall again. Perhaps we can meet occasionally in Cleveland, if I am not sent miles away from there, but everything is so damned dubious as far as such conjectures lead. You, of course, will consider my mention of this as unmentionable to any one else."

This confession came as a distinct shock and surprise to Munson. Neither he nor any other of Crane's friends had had the slightest inkling that he was sexually abnormal. To all appearances he was a healthy and vigorous young man, extremely excitable, it is true, as was natural in a young poet, but without the least trace of physical or mental aberration, excepting, possibly, his morbid obsession with family difficulties. His sensibility, far from showing itself in effem-

inacy or any other apparent extremity, was an interior matter completely concealed from all but his intimate friends by
the conventional clothes and the rank smoke from his Cinco
cigars. It is more than likely that Crane himself had not recognized his homosexuality as such before the commencement of the Akron "affair," and that in confessing it to Munson he was more importantly declaring it explicitly to
himself, committing himself once and for all to a definite
status. For in spite of his implication that he had had other
"affairs," there is no evidence to show that his sexual activities had extended beyond the awkward and indiscriminate
experiences common to many adolescents. It is true that in
later years he spoke of having had a casual and unsuccessful experience with a cheap girl in Cleveland which had revolted
and terrified him; and again, he boasted defiantly of having
reversed the usual procedure of corruption by seducing a
tutor who had lived with him at his home. But since Crane
saw such incidents in a vividly dramatic light and described
them to his friends usually with the desire to create dramatic
effects, either by comedy or tragedy, the degree of their
authenticity must remain in doubt.

It was by his indulgence of this desire, by the violent exhibition of his most private experiences—holding them up to
the ridicule or sympathy of his friends and so playing upon
their emotions—that he compensated in large part for his
frustrations and tried to bridge the gap he felt between himself and others. The only serious attempt he made to locate
the cause of his aberration specifically was a pathetically
transparent example of this. In 1923 when he had returned
to New York and was beginning to confess himself defiantly
to his friends, he renewed his old friendship with Claire
Spencer, and immediately precipitated a quarrel with her by
charging that her husband's jealousy of him prevented his
coming to their home. When she pointed out the absurdity

of such a suspicion, he countered by overwhelming her with an admission of his homosexuality and accusing her of having been responsible for it. He insisted violently that she was the only woman he could possibly have loved and that by her marriage she had betrayed them both, leaving him no hope of a normal life. When faced with the reminder that their relationship had been one merely of friendship based on common interests, his insistence only increased and his violence threatened to collapse in tears. It was a painful attempt to justify himself in the eyes of his friend. Doubtless he thought that if Claire Spencer were involved in his predicament either by pity or participation, she would be morally unable to condemn or renounce him. This explanation itself would seem fantastic were it not that one of the most fearful obsessions of Crane's life, at times almost pathological in its exaggeration, was that his friends were only tolerating him and at any moment might repudiate him completely. In his letters the words "betrayal" and "humiliation" began to appear more and more frequently in the slowly increasing vocabulary of his suffering.

But whatever the causes of his homosexuality, certainly no single incident or person can be considered as anything more than contributory to it. The investigations of this field of sexual pathology are at best experimental, and have established only hypothetical relations of cause and effect, which, however rich they may be in suggestion, throw no conclusive light on the subject, especially in the case of infinitely complex individuals. The psychoanalytical explanation of Crane's homosexuality would probably be that it was due to an Oedipus complex, the fixation of the love impulse upon the mother with a correlative antipathy towards the father. His emotions since early childhood, it is true, had been involved with those of his mother to an unusual degree; and quite possibly his frequent exclamation that his mother was his only sweetheart echoed a more profound and less playful feeling in his subconscious nature. This view would also, very probably, assume from Crane's obsession with his father's sexual prowess, which he ranted about to his friends, that he felt a consequent impotence in himself, and that this only increased his aversion to the heterosexual relationship which he had already seen at its worst in the cruel light of his parents' quarrels. That there is much truth in such suggestions is undeniable. But it is more important here, and possibly more human, to consider the conditions rather than the causes of his aberration, and to understand clearly that when he arrived at the threshold of maturity, his nervous system was so inflamed by years of constant strain that he was probably incapable of sustaining any satisfactory relationship whatever, even of an abnormal kind. His emotional life, having been nourished on the most violent of adult fare, was unable to find gratification in any but the most highly pitched excitements and extremities of passion, which, when he could indulge in them, seemed to afford him the relief almost of a blood-letting. "I don't know," he wrote, "how much blood I pay for these predicaments,—but I seem to live more during them than otherwise. They give the ego a rest." In these relationships he also felt a characteristic gratitude, an almost fanatical humility which cried out a *non sum dignus* at each requital of affection. Somewhere in his writings about Walt Whitman, the eminent biographer Emory Holloway remarked that the unrequited love of Whitman's early years played an important role in his development and that a definite causal relation could be traced between it and such apparently diverse elements of his character as his narcistic egoism and his broad humanitarianism. If he had added a third term, mysticism, as he might well have done, the same statement would apply with equal truth to Crane's life. His letters show clearly that the religious intensity with which he experienced certain requitals of love was closely related by quality, if not by kind, to the "ecstasy" he often felt when composing poetry under the influence of music and alcohol. The why and how of this relation is one of the more obscure mysteries of psychopathology and art, but that it existed is certain; and it is because of this that the sexual life of an artist becomes a legitimate subject of study. In a letter to Wilbur Underwood in Washington, who was at that time the only person beside Munson to know of his homosexuality, Crane wrote:

"I am too happy not to fear a great deal, but I believe in, or have found, God again. It seems vulgar to rush out with my feelings to anyone so, but you know by this time whether I am vulgar or not (I don't), and it may please you, as it often might have helped me so, to know that something beautiful can be found or can 'occur' once in awhile, and so unexpectedly. Not the brief and limited sensual thing alone, but something infinitely more thrilling and inclusive. I foolishly keep wondering,—'How can this be?—How did it occur?' How my life might be changed could this continue, but I scarcely dare to hope. I feel like weeping most of the time, and I have become reconciled, strangely reconciled, to many aggravations. Of course, it is the return of devotion which astounds me so, and the real certainty that at least for the time, it is perfectly honest. It makes me feel very unworthy,—and yet what pleasure the emotion under such circumstances provides. I have so much now to reverence, discovering more and more beauty every day,—beauty of character, manner, and body, that I am for the time, completely changed."

This affair did not last any longer, however, than the one in Akron, which a few months after its beginning he had seen "go down through lust to indifference." A graph of any one of these relationships would show in each case the same line of declension, curving sharply from the first point of enthusiasm down to the final punctuation of disillusionment. But though he recognized the inevitability of this pattern, he continued for several years to idealize these attachments, seeing in them only the reflected features of his own desire and in his abandonment to this image blinding himself to everything else. It was not until much later, after years of painful experience had cleared his mind of such confusions, that he was able to see the appalling discrepancy between his desire and its gratification and to understand the impossibility of ever fulfilling his desires at their own level and in their own kind. It was then that he wrote in "The Visible the Untrue";—

> Yes, I being
> the terrible puppet of my dreams, shall
> lavish this on you—

in clear-sighted bitter recognition of this dualism and the ironic fate to which it committed him. And so he was forced to accept another frustration in his life, more final even than the original prohibition of a normal sexual relationship, since from this defeat there was no escape nor in it any reconciliation. He was too highly sexed to be able to achieve a sublimation of his appetites, and too rigorous in his honesty to make a pretension of normalcy. Life was not a thing to be deliberately tailored for the sake of comfort or safety, nor were the revelations of its nakedness to be concealed in the bed-chambers of hypocritical privacy, where the light might be switched off against the discoveries of too great an illumination, and sleep invoked to confuse realities protectively with dreams. Crane was incapable of such intellectual and spiritual cowardice. If a thoroughly honest experience of life brought suffering as well as beauty, and demanded of him the self-exposure which often met with ridicule and misunderstanding, one was as inevitable as the other, and their attendant cruelties equally valuable in his eyes with their exaltations. Whatever extremity of sensation he experienced, he accepted and even welcomed as the very stuff of life to which he submitted himself as to an initiation. He had no desire to master life by cautious calculation or the circumspect discipline of the golden mean; he wished simply to be possessed by its most essential forces and to be used by them as an instrument of expression, exercising his own will only in this function. "The true idea of God," he wrote, "is the only thing that can give happiness,—and that is the identification of yourself with *all of life*. It is a fierce and humble happiness, both at the same time." By his passionate and too literal practice of this principle he was able to idealize and endure many of his humiliations. What he could not endure was the absence of those violent emotions by means of which he experienced this identification. Consequently, happiness for him became inextricably involved with suffering. "Do not think," he once wrote to a friend, "that I am entirely happy here, or ever will be, for that matter, except for a few moments at a time when I am perhaps writing or receiving a return of love." During these moments his sense of separateness from the world dissolved in the sudden fusive heat of emotional intoxication; the impalpable barriers of irreconcilables melted down like wax to liquid and glowing reconciliations in which briefly, and unforgettably, he saw an image of transcendental unity shine. For him, then, any suppression of his emotional excitements, whether sexual or alcoholic, would have meant not only intellectual dishonesty and cowardice, but also a rejection of his most effective means of achieving the state of grace.

"I don't believe in the 'sublimation theory at all,'" he wrote to Munson, "so far as it applies to my own experience. Beauty has most often appeared to me in moments of penitence and even sometimes, distraction and worry. Lately my continence has brought me nothing in the creative way,—it has only tended to create a confidence in me along lines of action,—business, execution, etc. There is not love enough in me at present to do a thing. This sounds romantic and silly,— you understand that I mean and refer to the strongest incentive to the imagination, or, at least, the strongest in my particular case."

This letter was written from Cleveland in November of 1920, almost a year after the one reporting the Akron "affair." During the winter and early spring of that year the relationship had continued in spite of Hart's return to Cleveland, affording him not a little relief during week-end visits to Akron from the tedious hours spent at his father's factory. Beyond this he had no interest except his writing. He had been living in a cold, uncomfortable room in a boarding house at 11431 Euclid Avenue pending the return of his mother and grandmother from their winter visit to the Isle of Pines when his home would again be open to him. It was to this chill cubicle that he returned from a day's labor "with a head like a wet muffin" to work at his poetry. Early in January he had been greatly encouraged by The Dial's acceptance of "My Grandmother's Love Letters" for which he received a ten-dollar check, his first "literary money"; and with this distinguished seal of approval upon his latest effort he turned with fresh enthusiasm to a new poem he had just begun, entitled "Garden Abstract." He was also working sporadically over other poems: "Porphyro in Akron," "Episode of Hands," an unpublished impression of a factory incident, and "Auntie Climax," published in final form as "The Fernery." With each change or improvement made in one of the verses a new copy of the poem was straightway dispatched to Munson and Josephson and often to Anderson;

and as soon as the finished version was achieved it began the ungrateful rounds of the magazines.

This burst of creative activity, however, dwindled away to a period of recurrent bitterness against the conditions that wasted his time and energies day by day. His work at the factory, anticipated as a welcome change from his duties in the Akron store, consisted in unloading and storing barrels of sugar and cases of chocolate; but though he found physical labor more agreeable than the hours of boredom behind a counter, the demands of a ten-hour day left him too exhausted to do much writing during the evenings. Indeed, three months of the incessant lifting of heavy loads proved too great a strain and late in April brought on an incipient hernia which necessitated a week's rest at home, and made him "furious with resentment against all those concerned in the circumstances of its cause." His salary, moreover, had not been increased as he had expected. His father's insistence on "starvation wages," as he called them, colored his resentment with the suspicion that behind the gesture of giving him a job was the desire to break his spirit and curtail his independence. Certainly the work seems to have been unnecessarily strenuous and unpleasant; and quite possibly Mr. Crane hoped to drive the poetry nonsense out of his son's head by a rigorous discipline in practical living. But that he meant well became evident when he proposed at the end of the summer that Hart try his hand at salesmanship in the territory centering about the city of Washington.

"I must admit a happy surprise," Hart wrote to Munson, "at my father's recent appreciation of my efforts here during the last six months. He even made the unhoped-for concession of mentioning that he had chosen this territory for me on account of the better sort of business type that is in Washington, and also on account of Washington's literary and journalistic associations."

This first effort to climb higher on the slippery rungs of the business ladder proved a farcical failure. The chocolates shipped to Hart in sample boxes from Cleveland arrived grey and clammy from the September heat, discouraging what little hope he had of persuading anyone of their delicacy; and his few fearful displays of them to the Capital's buyers met with a complete and not surprising indifference. In the end he found more grateful employment in presenting the candy to the few acquaintances he had made in the city, and spending his time walking in the parks and cultivating the friendship of Wilbur Underwood, an elderly literary gentleman to whom he had been introduced by a letter from Harry Candee. Besides being a poet of slight but exquisite accomplishment, Underwood was also a connoisseur of literature, especially in its more esoteric periods and passages, and owned a fine library that supplied Crane with several new enthusiasms in his reading. The two spent many evenings together over the finely bound books, and among the titles that ranked with the Elizabethans in Hart's literary fare thereafter were Melville's *Moby Dick* and the works of Rabelais, particularly *Gargantua*, whose boisterous humor found a challenging echo in Crane's uproarious laughter during Underwood's selected readings. But in spite of such pleasant hours the sense of failure in his mission irritated him, and the city with its strange dignity and lack of industrial violence seemed ghostly to him and unreal. When his father summoned him back to Cleveland in October, he was only too glad to go.

"I am sure," he wrote, "I should not miss factory whistles in Pisa or Morocco, but I frankly did miss them in Washington. Anyway, they are more enlivening (and the people they claim) than anything or anyone that I saw in W. which seemed to me the most elegantly restricted and bigoted community I ever ventured into."

The following months brought him no further offer of advancement from his father. His work in the shipping department continued, its demands upon his time and energy increasing steadily as the Christmas season approached and the pace of production was accelerated to meet the holiday orders. Once more resentment returned to plague his imagination with bitter suspicions about his father's motives and intentions. The extra tasks required of him, the petty personal quarrels with other employees, growing out of the tension of over-work, he interpreted as humiliations instigated, or at least countenanced, by his father. He decided several times to make a clean and final break with him, but was always restrained by the fear of subsequent unemployment and the necessity of living at his mother's expense. In the end there seemed to be only one possible means of escape from his bondage; and he resolved again and again to save his meager salary with fierce and desperate parsimony until he should have enough to flee the country. "Literature and art be hanged!" he wrote, "even ordinary existence isn't worth the candle in these States now."

Such sentiments scarcely made for a closer relationship with his father. Occasionally Hart dined with Mr. Crane and his second wife, Frances; but his acquaintance with his stepmother was so slight that it only added to the guarded formality that both he and his father preserved at such times. The real issues between them were never mentioned until January, when they met face to face in all honesty. Hart then made it perfectly clear to his father that he would continue to work at the factory only as a temporary means to earning his living and that he had no intention of abandoning poetry. He pointed to his publication in *The Dial* and *The Little Review*, which had just printed his "Garden Abstract" together with his note on some Minns photographs, as tokens of success in his chosen profession. Mr. Crane, for his part, was equally frank. Conceding Hart's persistence in artistic directions, he still insisted that literary pursuits should be nothing more than an avocation and again prophesied dire consequences, should Hart elect to make them his only concern in life. Nevertheless, he was willing to give him employment until he could find work more congenial to his literary interests—at which time, it was understood, they would conclusively part company as far as business affiliations were concerned.

This interview cleared the air of animosities for the time being, and led to Hart's receiving a new and better position as the overseer of a warehouse, where he was his own master. For a time he was content with his new duties, which were to supervise the storage of bulk supplies and make inventories. Although it was monotonous work, it made no heavy demands on his energy and even offered occasional half hours for surreptitious reading. But in the spring he was transferred in the same capacity to the basement of the large Crane store and tea-room on Euclid Avenue, where the conditions were not so pleasant. The storeroom in which he worked was poorly lighted and ventilated and the heavy steam pipes that ran just below the ceiling made the air oppressively hot: Again resentment and suspicion began to fester in his mind. He felt ashamed of his position, and brooded over the fact that his father had discharged a Negro, who had formerly done the work, in order to make room for him. It became a certainty in his mind that his father wished to make a humiliating comparison by this move; and when he was forbidden to read during working hours, he took the prohibition as further proof that he was being deliberately persecuted. The only diversion left to him during the dark, monotonous days in the basement was the society of the Negro waiters and chefs in the kitchen, located directly across the corridor from the storeroom. He enjoyed their high animal spirits and rich humor and was in the habit of taking coffee and toast with them each morning during their breakfast hour, though he himself prepared his own breakfast at home before leaving for work.

One morning in April Mr. Crane, who was making an inspection of the establishment, descended to the kitchen and surprised Hart and his cronies in the midst of one of their hilarious meals. He reprimanded Hart and ordered him back to his own duties in the storeroom, adding that since he was living at home with his mother, he could also take his meals there. Whether this remark was meant as a malicious jibe or was simply a maladroit piece of humor on Mr. Crane's part is impossible to know. Hart, of course, interpreted it as another humiliation, too brutally direct this time to endure in silence. Turning on his father in a rage, he threw the keys to the storeroom at his feet and shouted that he was finished with him once and for all. Mr. Crane turned white with anger at the unexpected insubordination, and shouted in reply that he would disinherit him; but the threat brought no response from his son except a curse on him and his money. Hart left the store immediately and went directly home, where his mother was horrified to see him dash through the door and up the stairs to his tower room, his face swollen and inflamed almost beyond recognition with the large red welts that such excitements caused. Following him, she finally persuaded him to go to bed where he lay for several hours with the shades drawn against the bright morning light in an effort to quiet himself and rid his body of the burning inflammations.

Late that night when he had regained possession of himself, he began to reckon the consequences of his action and take stock of the future. With the necessity he always felt for communicating with sympathetic spirits in his emotional crises he wrote to Munson:

"I left my father's employ, yes—today, *for good*—nothing, I think, will ever bring me back. The last insult was too much. I've been treated like a dog now for two years,—and only am sorry that it took me so long to find out the simple impossibility of ever doing anything with him or for him.

"It will take me many months, I fear, to erase from my memory the image of his overbearing head leaning over me like a gargoyle. I think he had got to think I couldn't live without his aid. At least he was, I am told, furious at my departure. Whatever comes now is much better than the past. I shall learn to be somewhere near free again,—at least free from the hatred that has corroded me into illness.

"Of course I won't be able to get to N. Y. now for any summer vacation. You know what a privation that means to me. I have nothing in sight in the way of employment,—and as times are so bad,—I don't know when I shall. A job as copy-writer for an advertising house will probably be open to me about June 1st. And there is a newspaper opening out here soon,—perhaps that may yield me something. I have a roof over my head and food, anyway—here at home—and maybe I shall write something. The best thing is that the cloud of my father is beginning to move from the horizon now, you have never known me when it has not been there—and in time we *both* may discover some new things in me. *Bridges burn't behind!*"

Although the quarrel was conclusive and put an end to all communication between father and son for the following two years, the freedom Hart gained proved to be only nominal. In the discouraging quest for employment, which lasted for nine months until January 1922, he was haunted by the thought of his father's triumph in his failure to find work. Knowing full well the contempt his father would have for an able-bodied young man who lived at his mother's expense, he cringed at the possibility of meeting him on the street; and when he did find some temporary task—now distributing handbills, now selling books or real estate—he imagined the ridicule with which his father would consider such make-shift employment. The most important consequence of this quarrel, however, and its major significance extended far beyond any question of personal harmony with his father to the problem of his own orientation to life in society at large. There was no longer any possibility of compromise. In rejecting his father, he denied himself the comforts of an eventual position in his business which might have secured him the leisure and independence to devote himself entirely to writing. At the same time he accepted the dual responsibility of earning his livelihood without any help but what he might contrive for himself and of maintaining his creative activity and integrity. It had been the last step left for him to take before coming into his complete maturity. In 1916 he had "shouldered the curse of sundered parentage"; three years later he had honestly acknowledged, however blindly and prematurely, the terrible liability of homosexuality; and now in this last crisis of 1921 he accepted the full burden of his life. Thenceforth it was his to do with as he could. That is not to say, however, that he had achieved any freedom but that of his own will. It is significant that in each of these major responsibilities lay a profound and insoluble conflict, problems in irreconcilables, which throughout his life tormented him with endless frustrations and obligations. His only freedom consisted in having recognized them as part and parcel of his life, to be faced uncompromisingly, however bitterly he might complain, with the determination to maintain his own values in spite of them. It was a high resolve, and one that demanded much strength and courage. But it gave strength in return, the gift of sudden power and enduring fortitude that comes from accepting a large challenge; and in turning his attention and energy more toward the world, it enlarged the scope of his sympathies and imagination, and consequently of his poetry as well. The "will to make fate," which he had felt so prematurely as a boy, almost as though in reply to his urgent need for some weapon in the imminent struggle, had remained constant, and now continued on into his maturity. If it had thus far brought him little success and much suffering, it had also preserved him from the spiritual blindness and corruption of materialism. And in this there was much hope and a source of continual vigor.

⁓ IV ⁓

"You ought really to try to sleep, Porphyro,
even though in this town poetry's a
bedroom occupation."

During the year and a half Hart had worked for his father he had accomplished very little in his poetry. After finishing "Garden Abstract" in the spring of 1920, he wrote nothing of any importance until February 1921, when he composed the short piece "Black Tambourine." In the meantime, however, he had not lost contact with the magazines—*The Dial, The Little Review,* and the London *Egoist*—which he read religiously, comparing the language and technique of the moderns with those of the Elizabethans, of Donne and Vaughan and Blake. His enthusiasm for the modern French poets, which had been stimulated by the translations and essays appearing in the magazines, was doubled by the arrival of the books he had ordered from Paris—copies of Vildrac, Laforgue, and Rimbaud, which he studied painstakingly with the aid of a dictionary. In all this reading there was an acute critical effort to discover his own tradition, to establish his own hierarchy of values by the immediate touchstone test of his responses; and gradually clear facets of crystallization began to appear in the welter of his sympathies. Among his own contemporaries he found the poetry of Marianne Moore, William Carlos Williams, and Wallace Stevens too fastidious and intellectual, however admirable; and even the work of Pound he recognized as a genre antipathetic to his own temperament. He more than admired the poems of T. S. Eliot, who he had prophesied to Munson two years earlier would be the predominating influence in the "new" poetry, not excluding his own; but he could not accept the spirit of his work. Nowhere, except possibly in Rimbaud, could he find the rich-blooded language and largeness of spirit that drew him so powerfully to the Elizabethans or the purity of illumination that thrilled him in Blake and Vaughan. More and more he realized that if he were ever to express himself fully, he would have to create an idiom which would be not only peculiar to himself, but also "new" to poetry in general. It was already one of his strongest convictions that unless one could dignify the eternal themes and continue their long tradition by a new, intensely personal experience and recreation of their revelations, it would be better not to write of them at all.

His mind was flocking with possibilities and speculations. Germs of poems took root and put forth a line or two, only to be blighted by his lack of time or energy, or discarded because of an echo of Eliot's plaintive negations. In April just before leaving his father's employ he sent Munson a curious poem, called "The Bridge of Estador: An Impromptu, Aesthetic Tirade," which illustrated his state of mind. It included in a strange confusion many lines which later found their way into their own proper poems, as though for the time being Crane could no longer deny them their right to exist.

Since it was never published, it may be worth while to quote a few stanzas.

> Walk high on the bridge of Estador,
> No one has ever walked there before.
> There is a lake, perhaps, with the sun
> Lapped under it,—or the dun
> Bellies and estuaries of warehouses,
> Tied bundle-wise with cords of smoke.
>
> Do not think too deeply, and you'll find
> A soul, an element in it all.
>
> .   .   .   .
>
> But some are twisted with the love
> Of things irreconcilable,—
> The slant moon with the slanting hill:
> O Beauty's fool, though you have never
> Seen them again, you won't forget.
> Nor the Gods that danced before you
> When your fingers spread among the stars.
>
> And you others,—follow your arches
> To what corners of the sky they pull you to,—
> The everlasting eyes of Pierrot,
> Or, of Gargantua, the laughter.

But such lines had to wait for several months in dark gestation before they were fleshed with their complete form. As soon as Hart escaped from his father's storeroom to the dubious freedom of a depression unemployment, his most pressing concern was money. Unable to find any work, he began to dispatch the few poems he had on hand to various editors, eager for whatever meager remuneration they might bring. Even "The Bridge of Estador," which he did not in any way consider a finished poem, was sent off to *The Dial*, only to meet with the expected rejection. "Black Tambourine," which had already been refused by the same magazine, was the first to bring him a check, having at last been accepted for publication by *The Double Dealer*, a New Orleans paper. He also received from this paper an invitation to review Sherwood Anderson's *Poor White*, which had just been published, and this work netted him twenty dollars, the largest amount he had yet been paid for his writing. *The Double Dealer* seemed to appreciate his work, for a few weeks later they accepted "Porphyro in Akron," which had met with rejections from several New York editors, and also added Crane's ·name to the list of contributors they advertised.

Finding to his amazement that he could earn substantial rewards in the field of criticism, he undertook to write an article on Ezra Pound for *Shadowland*, a competitor of *Vanity Fair*, but when the subject proved too complex to be quickly dispatched, he turned to more concrete projects. From Villard's biography of John Brown, which had just appeared, he conceived the idea of writing a play about the striking figure of the abolitionist from Harper's Ferry which, he wrote to Munson, he was sure would be a great commercial success. Sporadically, he was also working on translations from the French: De Gourmont's *Marginalia* on Poe and Baudelaire, and poems by Vildrac and Laforgue. Even though he considered this a pastime and confessed to constant use of a French dictionary, still he felt that his strong sympathies with these poets qualified him as an interpreter. His translation of the three "Locutions de Pierrot," which he sold a few months later to *The Double Dealer* in order to buy a pair of shoes, was an extraordinary recreation in English of the Laforguian idiom. Remarkable as free translations, they were even more interesting for the advance they marked in Crane's technical progress. The French poets, particularly Laforgue, were proving to be a powerful catalyst in the formation of his mature style, both subtilizing his thought and sharpening his feeling for language to an important degree. The first of the three pieces alone, when compared with the French, demonstrates this beyond a doubt.

> Your eyes, those pools with soft rushes,
> O prodigal and wholly dilatory lady,
> Come now, when will they restore me
> The orient moon of my dapper affections?
>
> For imminent is that moment when,
> Because of your perverse austerities,
> My crisp soul will be flooded by a languor
> Bland as the wide gaze of a Newfoundland.
>
> Ah, madame! truly it's not right
> When one isn't the real Gioconda,
> To adaptate her methods and deportment
> For snaring the poor world in a blue funk.

With the exception of this piece and the Anderson review, however, none of his extra-poetical writings brought him any money; and he soon turned again to poetry, composing "Pastorale" and a slight unimportant poem called "Persuasion," both of which he sold in October to *The Dial* and *The Measure* respectively. During the same month he also wrote "The Bottom of the Sea Is Cruel," which appeared in *Secession* in 1923 as "Poster" and finally in *White Buildings* as "Voyages I." But the most important poem that these fertile weeks produced was "Chaplinesque," written after attending a performance of Chaplin's current film, "The Kid."

In this poem as well as in "Black Tambourine" and "Pastorale" Crane felt he was approaching the creation of a personal idiom which in its language and technique would be indubitably an expression of his own temperament. As a prophetic corollary to this sense of advance came the discovery that the friends to whom he sent the poem found it most difficult to understand. With his characteristic modesty, which amounted at times almost to apology, he replied by confessing that its technique was "virtuosic" and open to misunderstanding and that it failed to express its meaning to any but a very few readers. He already admitted to himself and his friends that his poetry would have only a small audience at best. And though he tried to eliminate unnecessary obscurities from his work—to "make my dark heavy poem light and light," as he copied into his notebook—still he refused to sacrifice his artistic integrity to a desire for popularity. He maintained his respect and liking for "Chaplinesque" because, he wrote, "I feel that I have captured the arrested climaxes and evasive victories of his gestures in words, somehow"; and this transposition was for him an important achievement.

> We make our meek adjustments,
> Contented with such random consolations
> As the wind deposits
> In slithered and too ample pockets.
>
> For we can still love the world, who find
> A famished kitten on the step, and know
> Recesses for it from the fury of the street,
> Or warm torn elbow coverts. . . .

When his friends did not understand such lines, he was only too willing to explain them, pointing out that the "we" expressed his feeling of identity as poet with Chaplin, the tragi-comic buffoon, and that poetry, or the human feelings, was symbolized by the "kitten in the wilderness." To Munson he wrote:

"I have made that 'infinitely gentle, infinitely suffering thing' of Eliot's into the symbol of the kitten. I feel that, from my standpoint, the pantomime of Charlie represents fairly well the futile gesture of the poet in U. S. A. today, perhaps elsewhere too. And yet, the heart lives on. . . . Maybe this is because I myself feel so particularly futile just now that I feel this pathos (or is it bathos?). *Je ne sais pas.*"

It was also significant for an understanding of the poem to know that while he was writing it, he was tramping about the streets of the city distributing handbills. With such explanations and information the poem usually became entirely clear to his friends—so much so, indeed, that they often wondered at their own stupidity. Gradually they discovered that upon longer acquaintance with his poetic idiom such guides to the meaning of his poems became less and less necessary. But Crane was not therefore encouraged to believe his poetry would achieve a wide recognition during his own life. That his work was destined to be read only by the vanguard of the contemporary intelligentsia was a bitter recognition for him to make on the threshold of his maturity, when he felt within him the power and portents of a major poet. Furthermore, it had the unfortunate effect of increasing that sense of isolation which hitherto he had felt mostly upon a social level. But in spite of such discouragements his faith in his poetry, however uncertain and intermittent, continued and was slowly strengthened as the mastery of his medium grew more sure.

Undoubtedly it was the "obscurity" of "Chaplinesque" that made it unacceptable to *The Dial* and *The Little Review*. In any case, it was not printed until December, 1921, when it appeared in *Gargoyle*, the first of the post-war magazines established in Europe by American expatriates. Founded in Paris in the summer of 1921 by Arthur Moss, formerly the editor of an obscure paper in the Washington

Square neighborhood called *The Greenwich Village Quill*, *Gargoyle* enjoyed the distinction for a few months of being the only literary clearing house for the work of young American writers newly arrived in Paris. Many of them served as members of its editorial staff at one time or another during its brief career, among them Gorham Munson, who was responsible for the publication of "Chaplinesque."

All through that summer from his tower room in Cleveland Crane watched his friends and contemporaries join the curious migratory movement of American artists to Europe which dominated the literary life of the "twenties." The first of his friends to write him from Paris was Sherwood Anderson, who with Paul Rosenfeld had sailed in May. A few months later Munson announced his departure, and from Maine Matthew Josephson wrote him that he and his wife were taking leave of America for two years. He heard also of the plans of Alfred and Dorothy Kreymborg and Harold Loeb, who were about to leave New York for Rome to found the magazine *Broom*. Singly and in groups they departed, on the one hand driven by the post-war depression in America and the country's oppressive indifference to the arts, and on the other, attracted by the rate of exchange, the cheapness and quality of European printing, and the lively interest of the French writers and magazines in things American.

By the autumn of 1921 the Parisian cafés were crowded with expatriates. In the letters and magazines he received from Josephson and Munson, Crane began to read the names of young unknown American writers who were later to become his friends in New York: Slater Brown, Malcolm Cowley, and Kenneth Burke. Members of the old expatriate guard were also there. Ezra Pound, acutely uncomfortable to find the younger Americans suddenly swarming through Europe very much out of hand, was there, editing the new

Little Review as a quarterly with Francis Picabia, and serving as foreign representative for *The Dial* under Scofield Thayer. Gertrude Stein was there issuing chastely engraved invitations in her spidery hand to the more interesting of the younger generation who went reverently to 27 Rue de Fleurus to sit with her and her Picassos. The pearl-grey envelopes bore a vermilion seal in which the impression showed a rose ringed by the inscription, "a rose is a rose is a rose is a rose." And Sylvia Beach was publishing from Shakespeare & Co. the final manuscript of James Joyce's *Ulysses* in book form, for a copy of which Crane sent Munson twenty dollars, imploring him to smuggle it into the country upon his return.

The newly arrived writers of the younger generation mingled freely with their French contemporaries, Tristan Tzara, Louis Aragon, Jean Cocteau, Philippe Soupault, and others, drinking in the intellectual intoxications of Dadaism together with their Pernods and Hennessys. Their talk over the marble-topped tables of the Dôme and the Rotonde was a continual and bizarre excitement over the gods of the Dadaist movement: skyscrapers, American jazz, aeroplanes, vaudeville, machinery, advertising methods, and Walt Whitman. The Americans saw their country anew through the eyes of their European friends, and having fled from its industrial oppression, sat down in Paris bedrooms to write praises of its mechanical marvels. It seemed a far cry from the pre-war Greenwich Village, and yet the crazes of Dada were not entirely unlike the violent manifestoes of *The Soil* in 1916 which had proclaimed the art of the buck-and-wing, the crazy-quilt, Bert Williams, skyscrapers, and the *Police Gazette*. Down in the South of France at Montpellier a French production was being given of Kreymborg's "Manikin and Miniken," which Crane had reviewed for *The Pagan* in 1919. But Paris in 1921 seemed to them another world, almost another century that had been born in the years after the Armistice. With it had come a new freedom, a post-war psychology of irresponsibility and futility, which liberated them from the routine of moral and practical obligations into the endless and pleasant ether of aesthetic speculation. They wandered up and down the Continent, from Paris to Rome, thence to the Tyrol or Venice, from Vienna to Munich, from Munich to Berlin, haunting the bars and cafés and discussing personalities, founding groups and magazines, dissolving them, and quarreling over quarrels. Everything they did and said showed tremendous energy. There was a great stir in all their activities, a bustling back and forth as though in attendance at a momentous birth in the world of literature. But the cause they had espoused in Dadaism was a barren one: its réclames of revolution were little more than manifestoes of spiritual bankruptcy, and even its startling iconoclasm appeared pitifully unimportant after the great image-breaking of the War. They were, as they soon realized, a lost generation fumbling for convictions and values among the spiritual ruins of post-war Europe.

It was a token of Crane's temperament and his increasing sense of his own stature that, however much he envied the cosmopolitan freedom of his friends, he had little respect for the movement they had adopted. When Matthew Josephson, one of the most brilliant of the young expatriates, advised him to abandon the usual formulas of poetry for experimentation in original models, supposedly after the manner of the Dadaists, his reaction was to "work away from the current impressionism as much as possible," as he wrote to Munson. "I mean such 'impressionism' as the Cocteau poem (trans.) in the *Little Review*, which you have probably seen. Dada (maybe I am wrong, but you will correct me) is nothing more to me than the dying agonies of this movement, *maladie moderne*." His own interests were in establishing a solid continuity with the traditions of English literature and in expressing the positive forces of living. Thus as the influence of Dada on his friends gained impetus, sweeping them to new hysterias and enthusiasms, he felt himself more and more apart from them, increasingly alone in the direction he had chosen for himself.

"All this talk from Matty on Appollinaire," he wrote Munson, "about being gay and *so* distressingly and painfully delighted about the telegraph, the locomotive, the automat, the wireless, the street cars and electric lamp posts, annoys me. There is no reason for *not* using them—but why is it so important to stick them in. I am interested in possibilities. Appollinaire lived in Paris, I live in Cleveland, Ohio. These quotidian conveniences so dear to him are not of especial pleasure to me here. I am not going to pity myself—but, on the other hand, why should I stretch my face continually into a kind of 'glad' expression. Besides,—sadness (you will shrink in horror at this) has a real and lasting appeal to me.

"I am stubborn—and grow indifferent at times about all this mad struggle for advance in the arts. Every kind of conceivable work is being turned out today. Period styles of every description. Isn't it, after all, legitimate for me to write something the way I like to (for my own pleasure) without considering what school it harmonizes with? I'm afraid I don't fit in your group. Or any group, for all that."

He was particularly jealous of his integrity since he felt that he had reached a crucial point in his poetic evolution, where it would perhaps be fatal to make a wrong choice in the question of spiritual allegiance or technical imitation. The Elizabethans, as always, claimed his most profound devotion; even his admiration of T. S. Eliot was founded almost completely on the way in which he had adapted their language and technical devices.

"I don't want to imitate Eliot, of course," he wrote to Munson, "but I have come to the stage now where I want to carefully choose my most congenial influences and, in a way, 'cultivate' their influence. I can say with J. that the problem of form becomes harder and harder for me every day. I am not at all satisfied with anything I have thus far done, mere shadowings, and too slight to satisfy me. I have never, so far, been able to present a vital, living, tangible,— a positive emotion to my satisfaction. For as soon as I attempt such an act I either grow obvious or ordinary, and abandon the thing at the second line. Oh! it is hard! One must be drenched in words, literally soaked with them to have the right ones form themselves into the proper pattern at the right moment. When they come, as they did in 'Pastorale' (thin but rather good) they come as things in themselves; it is a matter of felicitous juggling; and no amount of will or emotion can help the thing. So you see I believe with Sommers that the 'Ding an Sich' method is ultimately the only satisfactory creative principle to follow."

It was a sound instinct that led him to avoid the critical feuds and aesthetic affectations of the literary world in favor of concentrating on his medium. But it proved difficult for him to find the time or the patience to cultivate the slow maturing of his powers.

It was now November and he had had no steady employment since April. The consequent leisure, which had at first been welcome to him in many ways and had resulted in the burst of writing during the summer and early fall, finally became irksome. For the time being he had written himself out. He had composed nothing since "Chaplinesque" in October with the result that his conscience, so deeply impressed by the utilitarian morals of his family, tormented him constantly with a sense of guilt. After two years of comparative financial independence it was especially painful for him to be again reduced to the status of a dependent on his mother's generosity. However gladly she offered him his livelihood, he could not accept it with any comfort or complacency. Realizing that some specialized training was necessary if he were ever to be able to support himself, he enrolled towards the end of the month for a course in advertising. The instruction, which was given two nights a week to a large class in the basement of an office building in the city, was to extend over a period of eight months until the following May, and offered as a dubious reward a certified diploma. Once having chosen this means of earning his living, Crane set himself to master its mechanics with the tense, concentrated enthusiasm that characterized all his actions. His tower room at home was gradually cluttered with books, magazines, folders, and all the various propaganda of advertising methods, which he studied intently, even to the neglect of his Elizabethans. Meanwhile, he continued to seek out odds and ends of temporary employment to relieve his sense of guilt and earn a little pocket money. During November he tried his hand at selling real estate, mapping out in great detail a sales plan which brought him in the end nothing but a profound conviction that he would never make a salesman. Shortly afterwards he secured a position selling books during the Christmas season at Korner and Woods, the shop where several years earlier he had obtained his first employment. Five years, in fact, had passed since that time, during which he had worked in many different capacities, and now as a young man of twenty-two he was back where he had started from with no more hope of financial security and with no more training, excepting his new venture in advertising, than he had had as a boy of seventeen. "There is nothing but gall and disgust in me," he wrote Munson, "and there is nothing more for me to tell you but familiar, all-too-familiar complaints. I wish I could cultivate a more graceful mask against all this."

If the pressure of circumstances made it difficult for him

to devote much time to poetry, still he received a definite compensation for this loss in psychological toughening. Whatever slight lacquer of "artiness" he had carried away with him from the days near Washington Square had been worn down to the sheer grain of the wood by the incessant friction of the succeeding years. This sand-paper process in which he rubbed up daily against all sorts of wage-earners from truck-drivers to clerks scoured away the glaze of literary attitudes and left him with a clear sense of human values. It was hardly strange that he should find the transatlantic effusions of his friends from the Rotonde and the Dôme somewhat unreal and irrelevant. Even when Munson wrote him of his plan to start another little magazine in Europe, Crane could not conceal his impatience.

"Don't waste your time with it all, is my advice," he wrote. "Much better sit down and pound on your typewriter, or go toting mss around to stolid editors. Listen,—there is now *some* kind of magazine that will print one's work however good or bad it is. The 'arty' book stores bulge and sob with them all. I pray you invest your hard-earned money in neckties, theatre tickets or something else good for the belly or soul,—but don't throw it away in paper and inefficient typography. Don't come home three months sooner for the prospects of that rainbow. No one will especially appreciate it and it will sour your mouth after all the vin rouge you have been drinking. By all this you must not think that I have joined the Right Wing to such an extent that I am rollicking in F. Scott Fitzgerald. No,—but by the straight and narrow path swinging to the south of the village DADA I have arrived at a somewhat abashed posture of reverence before the statues of Ben Jonson, Michael Drayton, Chaucer, and sundry others already mentioned. The precious rages of Matty somehow don't seem to swerve me from this position. He is, it strikes me, altogether unsteady. Of course, since Mallarmé and Huysmans were elegant weepers it is up to the following generation to haw-haw gloriously! Even dear old Buddha-face de Gourmont is passé. Well, I suppose it is up to one in Paris to do as the Romans do, but it all looks too easy to me from Cleveland, Cuyhoga County, God's Country."

In January the long period of unemployment and anxiety came to an end. The intense interest he took in the night classes, which he had attended regularly, coupled with the lively pieces of copywriting he had submitted, singled him out as one of the most promising pupils in the course; and after only two months of instruction he was recommended by the instructor to the advertising firm of Corday & Gross, which immediately employed him. They soon discovered that in Crane they had a young man of considerable talent whose lively imagination and flair for striking word combinations made him a valuable writer of advertising copy. Within a few weeks they were dispatching him to neighboring cities and towns to investigate the products of their clients and draw up catalogues for them. Crane, for his part, was happy in his new job, finding his employers surprisingly affable and the work interesting. The novelty of inventing metaphors for water heaters and sundry household conveniences proved great sport during the first few months. It was not until later when his inventive faculties began to flag under the incessant demand for copy that the work became burdensome. Then, under the necessity of seeking relief, he discovered that a few long drinks of wine or liquor revived his imagination to an extraordinary degree and stimulated him to do some of his best work. Indulging in this device more and more, he soon established the beginning of that curious collaboration between music and alcohol which eventually became almost indispensable to his writing of poetry.

The most immediate effect of his employment, however,

was to give him a tremendous sense of liberation. His small salary of twenty-five dollars a week freed him not only from the feeling of guilt that had tormented him while living at his mother's expense, but from the fear of his father's contempt as well. It also allowed him to make a few purchases for his "ivory tower": a set of Webster's works, which he had long wanted, a few records for his portable victrola, and prints of Gauguin, Vlaminck, and Toulouse-Lautrec for the grey-papered walls. He felt more free, too, to join his few friends in such social diversions as the city offered. Life seemed generous once more, and the future somewhat secure.

"I pass my goggle-eyed father on the streets now without a tremor!" he wrote Munson. "I go on mad carouses with Bill Sommers wherein we begin with pigs' feet and sauerkraut and end with Debussy's 'Gradus ad Parnassum' in the 'ivory tower.' Around Ernest Bloch at the Institute of Music here are gathered some interesting folks from all over everywhere. There is even a French restaurant here where the proprietress stands at the cashier's desk reading *La Nouvelle Revue Française* and where wonderful steaks with mushrooms are served—alas, everything, including garçons, except vin. The place looks like a sentence without punctuation, or, if you please, this letter."

The friends Crane had made since leaving his father's employ were few, and he had discovered them slowly; but by the winter of 1922 they formed a small group of painters and writers with whom he spent much of his free time. It was, in fact, the first group of friends he had ever had, for up to this time the few people whom he had been able to call friends he had known only singly. This fact had been a curious anomaly in his life, for his natural instincts were extraordinarily social and communicative; and he loved the gaiety and conversational excitements of a group. In later years he often spoke of his social appetites as a weakness which devoured the best part of his time. Consequently, this first company of friends, who met together once every week and whom he saw much of individually at other times, was a continual source of pleasure to him during his last year or two in Cleveland.

The first he came to know was William Sommers, whom he met in 1921. Sommers was an obscure painter of about fifty years of age who managed by working in a lithograph factory in Cleveland to earn a sparse livelihood and to support an unsympathetic family on a farm in Brandywine Valley not far from the city. Crane was drawn to the older man by his vitality, the Rabelaisian vigor of his spirits, which was reflected in his painting in what Crane liked to call his "dynamism." The two were soon in the habit of spending an evening together once a week when they would retire to the "ivory tower" to play records of Ravel, Scriabin, and Debussy; to read Heine's lyrics, or spar hilariously about the low-ceilinged room with an old set of boxing gloves that Hart had unearthed from a cupboard. More often they would spend hours talking of painting, and under this stimulation Crane began to do a few drawings and water colors for his own amusement. Although his talent in this field was undoubtedly slight, some of the caricatures he made of his friends in New York a few years later were surprisingly good, especially the one of Slater Brown, which was printed in *The Dial*. He also made drawings of Waldo Frank, Jean Toomer, Gorham Munson, and others, and was exhilarated when some of them won the approval of Gaston Lachaise, the sculptor, whom he so admired.

However slight the importance of his drawings as such, they served to sharpen and crystallize his awareness of the possibilities in his own medium. Throughout his life art had the power to stimulate him tremendously, even to focus and direct his imagination. He ordered many works from a well-known dealer in Germany, books on Egyptian and Greek art, African sculpture, and monographs on his favorite painters. The monograph he had on El Greco, in particular, was one of his most constant companions which he carried with him wherever he went. In 1926 he wrote Waldo Frank from the Isle of Pines, drawing his attention to the curious parallel in construction between his "Proem" to *The Bridge*, which he had just completed, and the "space and detail division" of Greco's "Agony in the Garden." There were also other paintings that bore a specific relation to his poetry, among them Joseph Stella's formalized composition of Brooklyn Bridge, which excited him deeply with its architectural patterns. Much of the excitement he derived from paintings may be seen at first hand in the poem dedicated to Sommers called "Sunday Morning Apples," which he wrote during the summer of 1922 after a visit to the painter's little white studio in the country.

> Beloved apples of seasonable madness
> That feed your inquiries with aerial wine.
> Put them again beside a pitcher with a knife,
> And poise them full and ready for explosion—
> The apples, Bill, the apples!

For Sommers's work he had unlimited enthusiasm from the first moment he saw some of his canvases. With the impetuous generosity that had characterized his attitude towards Minns's photographs and even towards the paintings of his old friend, Carl Schmitt, he immediately set himself to make Sommers's genius known to the New York critics and win him the recognition he deserved. The painter, himself, seems to have had a distaste for publicizing or selling his own work, however badly he needed funds, and turned the entire matter over to his young friend, even to the fixing of prices. Crane at once started writing letters to editors, dealers, and critics in New York, almost demanding that they recognize the work he sent them. He dispatched drawings, water colors, and oils to *The Little Review*, *The Dial*, *The Liberator*, and even to the almost extinct *Pagan*, which was at first the only one to accept any of the offerings for publication. He saved his money in order to have photographs made of them which he could send abroad for publication in *Gargoyle* and *Broom*. Communicating his enthusiasm to Munson, after the latter had returned to New York in the summer of 1922, he begged him to interest such people as Alfred Stieglitz, Waldo Frank, and de Zayas in Sommers's work. He sent off a folio of the best of the paintings to Sherwood Anderson, who had agreed to show them to a group of fellow critics and painters, including Paul Rosenfeld; and when he received an unfavorable comment from them, he flew into a rage of disgust. His own estimation of Sommers's work, however, remained constant.

"I can enjoy Bill's things," he wrote Munson, "regardless of their descent, evident or otherwise, from French and German artists of the last generation. He has certain perfections which many of the most lauded were lacking in. God DAMN this constant nostalgia for something 'new.' This disdain for anything with a trace of the past in it!! This kind of criticism is like a newspaper always with its *dernier cri*. It breeds its own swift decay because its whole theory is built on an hysterical sort of evolution theory. I shall probably always enjoy El Greco and Goya. I still like to look at the things Sommers makes, because many of them are filled with a solid and clear beauty."

Finally Crane's efforts were partially successful. Certain individuals of recognized taste and authority began to take an interest in Sommers's canvases. Sibley Watson of *The Dial* bought two or three pieces, and later printed several more in the magazine. William Carlos Williams made a purchase or two and wrote Sommers a letter to say that his paintings got "under his underdrawers" and that he thought him potentially greater than Marin. Stieglitz, too, the founder of the famous "291" gallery on Fifth Avenue, was favorably impressed. But Crane did not cease in his proselytizing until he left Cleveland in 1923.

It was through the painter that he met another of his friends of that period, Ernest Nelson, a man of Sommers's age and also an employee at the lithograph factory, who unlike the latter had not been able to preserve his art against the stringent demands of daily living. His painting, which had won him honors in his youth, and his poetry, which had merited publication in *Scribner's Magazine* many years earlier, had both disintegrated under the pressure of his poverty. Crane's friendship for the older man was tempered with a deep sympathy for his failure; and when, in the winter of 1922, only a few months after their first meeting, Nelson died, Crane wrote of him "a true Nietzschean—he was one of many broken against the stupidity of American life in such places as here." Both he and Sommers served as pallbearers at the funeral, which concluded with a cremation that stirred Crane very deeply by its simplicity and stark finality. A few weeks later he wrote "Praise for an Urn," dedicated to the memory of Nelson, a beautiful poem that one of his critics has called the finest elegy written by an American poet. In the first four stanzas several of the stray lines from "The Bridge of Estador" came at last to rest in the full perfection of their eloquence.

> It was a kind and northern face
> That mingled in such exile guise
> The everlasting eyes of Pierrot
> And, of Gargantua, the laughter.

His thoughts, delivered to me
From the white coverlet and pillow,
I see now, were inheritances—
Delicate riders of the storm.

The slant moon on the slanting hill
Once moved us towards presentiments
Of what the dead keep, living still,
And such assessments of the soul

As, perched in the crematory lobby,
The insistent clock commented on,
Touching as well upon our praise
Of glories proper to the time.

Another friend Crane discovered during the summer of
1921 was a young Swiss-French artist who had just arrived
in Cleveland from Paris, and whose exhibition of paintings
at one of the local galleries was causing no little excitement.
William Lescaze, who later became one of the most brilliant
architects in the country, was at that time completely unknown. But gifted with a vivacious personal charm that
functioned at its best in conversation, and with an intimate
knowledge of modern French literature, as well as of painting, he was eagerly welcomed by Sommers and Crane as a
charter member of the group. It was Lescaze who first instituted the weekly "salon," whither came not only its regular members, but also such composers and musicians as might
be visiting the Institute of Music, guest artists of the Opera
or the Cleveland Playhouse. The other habitués of the
"salon" were Charles Harris, a young engineer with a slight
talent for poetry; Samuel Loveman, a sensitive poet, who besides his own verse was writing fine translations of Baudelaire and a critique of Edgar Saltus; and somewhat later,
Richard Rychtarik, a young Czechoslovakian artist newly

arrived from Prague, who was soon designing sets for the Cleveland and Metropolitan Operas. With the last named came his wife Charlotte, a spirited and deeply sympathetic woman of considerable musical talent, for whom Crane formed a deep attachment.

This group of friends also met in Crane's "ivory tower" where the grey walls were hung with prints of the French painters and drawings and canvases by Lescaze and Sommers. Here they sat late into the night talking of the French Decadents, of modern architecture, of the strange anomalies of American life such as the exquisite Greek marionettes that Lescaze had discovered in a sagging tent down by the railroad tracks. The conversation usually described lively parabolas between Crane and Lescaze, who dominated the gathering with their enthusiasms. Many an evening passed while Crane plied the painter with questions about the French poets, in particular about Rimbaud, whose *Illuminations* and *Season in Hell*, as they had appeared in translation in *The Dial* in 1920, had aroused him to intense excitement. Often he discussed his own work, describing whatever poem he was working on at the time or the possibilities of some project he had in mind for future composition, always with the intoxicated absorption in his subject that characterized all his talk, emphasizing his points by violent animated movements of his body. It was probably during such an evening that Lescaze made the curious sketch of him in which the right eye is the focus of the composition by reason of the heavy emphasis with which it is drawn, an eccentric device that expressed very effectively Crane's concentrated energy. Crane, in fact, was delighted with the drawing, and before long had rationalized it after his own fancy, interpreting the prominence given to the right eye in accordance with a dictum of Jacob Boehme, the German mystic, to the effect that the right eye of a man looks forward into eternity while the left eye looks backward in him into time, and that until the eye of time is brought into the eye of eternity a man will not achieve unity of vision. From this Crane developed the half-fanciful, half-serious notion that a certain intensity and clarity of expression in the right eye betokened a person of mystic predisposition or power; and he was more than gratified to see in the drawing what he liked to consider an involuntary recognition of this trait in himself. The closing lines of the first part of "For the Marriage of Faustus and Helen" were an allusion to this portrait.

> Accept a lone eye riveted to your plane,
> Bent axle of devotion along companion ways
> That beat, continuous, to hourless days—
> One inconspicuous, glowing orb of praise.

This poem, however, was not written until the summer of 1922. In the meantime Crane often despaired of ever again finding time for writing. The depression, which for so long had held the country in the grip of apathy, was beginning to disappear; business was experiencing a revival of activity and was calling for more and more advertising. As Crane developed greater speed in his copywriting, his services were in greater demand, so that many of his evenings, which were usually devoted to his friends or his writing, had to be given over to his work. When Munson wrote him from Vienna in March asking for a contribution to the first issue of *Secession*, which was about to go to press, Crane had nothing to offer him except "Praise for an Urn," which had already been submitted to *The Dial*. He promised to do everything in his power to circulate the magazine about Cleveland as soon as Munson should send him the first copies.

"But," he wrote, "the worst is that most of my acquaintances are totally unfitted for enthusiasms of this sort. The indifference you will encounter when you return to these

States you must be prepared to face. Everyone is suddenly so enormously *busy*—making money, attending teas, motoring, starving—God knows what all. It makes me reel! Life is too scattered for me to savor it any more. Probably this is only on account of my present work which demands the most frequent jerks of the imagination from one thing to another, still,—the war certainly has changed things a lot here. The question in my mind is, how much less vertigo are we going to suffer in this latter whirl than we did in the first blows and commotion. If I am drifting into nonsense, it must be because I'm getting no time lately for anything but work."

It was fortunate, nevertheless, that he had found a regular job, for in the early spring of that year financial difficulties threatened his own family. The alimony his mother had been receiving from Mr. Crane came to an end in March. Thenceforth both she and her mother were forced to live on the income from the Hart estate which, though it had once represented a substantial capital, had dwindled away under the depression and mismanagement until it yielded little more than a comfortable allowance for the support of the two women and the old home at 1709 East 115th Street. There was even talk at the time of Mrs. Crane undertaking some sort of business to make their position more secure, a proposal that shocked Hart, who had been accustomed to think of his mother as permanently protected from such emergencies. He immediately felt that the responsibility of his mother's and grandmother's welfare lay partially with him, and exaggerating the seriousness of the situation, resigned himself to a further estrangement from his writing.

"I naturally shall henceforward be called upon not only to keep myself, but to lend as much of a helping hand as is possible in this predicament. So, it's hard work for some time ahead for me, I guess. My present wages *just* suffice for my own limited requirements. My pater is too much of a cad to really do anything for his former wife except what the agreement between them says. The fact that this was made when she was partially out of mind and very ill, makes no difference to him.

"However, I shall not resign myself to the proverbial and sentimental fate of the 'might-have-been' artist without a few more strenuosities. I will have to expect a certain tardiness of gait, however."

But the financial difficulties of his family did not prove as serious as he had anticipated, nor was the pace of his poetic production at all diminished. On the contrary he was standing on the threshold of a major achievement. The first work of his maturity, the fruit of his persistent struggle to arrive at a new and personal idiom, was at last ripe.

"*New thresholds, new anatomies! . . .*"

THE ten months extending from April 1922 to February 1923 were one of the most important periods in Crane's life. During that time everything he had learned from the French poets and the Elizabethans, the findings he had made in his own writing, every leisure hour, every creative impulse—all were absorbed in the composition of his first long poem, "For the Marriage of Faustus and Helen." Arranged in three parts, which he conceived as spanning a rising scale from the "quotidian" to the universal, this work was his first attempt to deal with the major problems of poetry. The parts as he described them were colorless abstractions: first, "Meditation, Evocation, Love, Beauty"; second, "Dance, Humor, Satisfaction"; and third, "Tragedy, War (the eternal soldier), Résumé, Ecstasy, Final Declaration." But the symbolism he chose provided a concrete, even a dramatic, framework. Once it is known that Helen is "the symbol of this abstract 'sense of beauty'—Faustus the symbol of myself, the poetic or imaginative man of all times," the action of the poem and its philosophical implications become perfectly apparent. Crane imagined the poem as a kind of prothalamion celebrating his pursuit and capture of the Platonic idea of beauty, and at the same time defining his relation not only to his art, but also to the world in which he was living and to the world of tradition in which beauty had sometimes lived as a vital principle.

In an unpublished essay, entitled "General Aims and Theories," * written in 1925, Crane clearly described the intentions of "Faustus and Helen."

"The evocation of this (to me) very real and absolute conception of beauty seemed to consist in a reconstruction in these modern terms of the basic emotional attitude toward beauty that the Greeks had. And in so doing I found that I was really building a bridge between the so-called classic experience and many divergent realities of our seething confused chaos of today, which has no formulated mythology yet for classic reference or for religious exploitation.

"So I found Helen sitting in a street car; the Dionysian revels of her court and her seduction were transferred to a Metropolitan roof-garden with a jazz orchestra; and the *katharsis* of the Fall of Troy I saw approximated in the recent world war. The importance of this scaffolding may easily be exaggerated, but it gave me a series of correspondences between two widely separated worlds on which to sound some major themes of human speculation—love, beauty, death, renascence. It was a kind of grafting process that I shall doubtless not be interested in repeating, but which is consistent with subsequent theories of mine on the relation of tradition to the contemporary creating imagination."

The ambitious scope of the poem was not without significance. It demonstrated the qualities of mind which soon identified Crane among the critics of the day as a "metaphysical" poet. It also reflected indirectly the problems that

* See *Appendix.*

dominated the art and criticism of the "twenties"—questions
of revaluation and reconstruction which the critic asked the
artist and the artist the critic in a vicious circle of bewilder-
ment. This state of affairs was the reaction not only to the
confusion of thought following upon the War, but also, in
the field of art, to the decay of values which, beginning in
the blind extremities of the French Decadence, continued on
through the post-war disillusionment to reach its fantastic
apogee in Dadaism. Any poet of major ambitions had, perforce, to wrestle with these problems and embody his solu-
tions, his victories and defeats, in his work. Thus, it was
hardly surprising that both Crane and Eliot, the two most
important younger poets of the day, should have attempted
the first statement of their positions during the same year.
In November 1922, when Crane was nearing the completion
of "Faustus and Helen," Eliot published in the first issue of
The Criterion, and simultaneously in *The Dial,* the whole of
"The Wasteland."

The letters quoted in the preceding chapter leave no doubt
as to Crane's feelings towards Dadaism, and the imitation of
French models. His reaction to Eliot's work, however, was
a much more complex matter.

"There is no one writing in English who can command
so much respect, to my mind, as Eliot. However, I take Eliot
as a point of departure towards an almost complete reverse
of direction. His pessimism is amply justified, in his own
case. But I would apply as much of his erudition and technique as I can absorb and assemble towards a more positive,
or (if I must put it so in a sceptical age) ecstatic goal. I
should not think of this if a kind of rhythm and ecstasy were
not (at odd moments and rare!) a very real thing to me. I
feel that Eliot ignores certain spiritual events and possibilities as real and powerful now as, say, in the time of Blake.
Certainly the man has dug the ground and buried hope as

deep and direfully as it can ever be done. He has outclassed
Baudelaire with a devastating humor that the earlier poet
lacked. After this perfection of death—nothing is possible in motion but a resurrection of some kind. Or else, as
everyone persists in announcing in the deep and dirgeful
Dial, the fruits of civilization are entirely harvested. Everyone, of course, wants to die as soon and as painlessly as possible! Now is the time for humor, and the Dance of Death!
All I know through very much suffering and dullness (somehow I seem to twinge more all the time) is that it interests
me to still affirm certain things. That will be the persisting
theme of the last part of "F&H" as it has been all along."

The difference in temper between the two men was clearly
indicated by the nature of their leading symbols: for Eliot,
the wasteland with its rubble of disintegrated values and desiccated spirits; for Crane, the bridge with its hope of spiritual harmony and order above and beyond the acceptance of
contemporary chaos. It can not be said, despite his philosophical optimism, that Crane was insensitive or blind to the
causes of despair about him, for certainly he had been exposed to them rather more than is the usual lot of the poet,
and had suffered proportionately. If one were to attempt a
definition of the difference between the two by the analogy
of religious convictions—which would not be entirely irrelevant—Eliot's attitude might be taken as being high Cal-
vinist and Crane's as Revivalist. Throughout his life Crane
rebelled against the psychology of despair, so contagiously
expressed in "The Wasteland" and predominant in the
thought of his time, without ever completely convincing
himself that the age was not foreordained to reprobation.

"The poetry of negation is beautiful," he wrote to Allen
Tate, a young poet in Nashville with whom he had just
opened a correspondence resulting from his admiration of
Tate's work, which was appearing in *The Double Dealer*,

"alas, too dangerously so for one of my mind. But I am trying to break away from it. Perhaps this is useless, perhaps it is silly —but one *does* have joys. The vocabulary of damnations and prostrations has been developed at the expense of these other moods, however, so that it is hard to dance in proper measure. Let us invent an idiom for the proper transposition of jazz into words! Something clean, sparkling, elusive!"

This was written in May when he was laboring over just such an idiom in the second part of "Faustus and Helen"— the first of the three sections to be composed—whose setting was the roof-garden of a metropolitan hotel.

> Brazen hypnotics glitter here;
> Glee shifts from foot to foot,
> Magnetic to their tremolo.
> This crashing opéra bouffe,
> Blest excursion! this ricochet
> From roof to roof—
> Know, Olympians, we are breathless
> While nigger cupids scour the stars!
>
> .   .   .   .
>
> O, I have known metallic paradises
> Where cuckoos clucked to finches
> Above the deft catastrophes of drums.
> While titters hailed the groans of death
> Beneath gyrating awnings I have seen
> The incunabula of the divine grotesque.
> This music has a reassuring way.
>
> The siren of the springs of guilty song—
> Let us take her on the incandescent wax
> Striated with nuances, nervosities
> That we are heir to: she is still so young,
> We cannot frown upon her as she smiles,
> Dipping here in this cultivated storm
> Among slim skaters of the gardened skies.

When it was finished in June, he had reason to be flushed with a sense of achievement. Although it was the least important section of the poem philosophically, it had presented him with the problem of catching in words the qualities of jazz, at once dynamic and insouciant, subtle and blatant, and he had solved the difficulties in a masterful way.

"I have been at it for the last 24 hours," he wrote Munson the day of its completion, "and it may be subjected to a few changes and additions, but as I see it now in the red light of the womb it seems to me like a work of youth and magic. At any rate, it is something entirely new in English poetry, so far as I know. The Jazz rhythms in that first verse are something I have been impotently wishing to do for many a day."

Thus confirmed in his intuition of the powers he had felt straining within him for so long, he could scarcely control his ambitions for the rest of the poem. Throughout the following weeks and months he labored under the greatest excitement, constantly discovering new possibilities in his material and glimpsing further technical resources in the idiom he was developing. During the same time he began to drink more heavily, and though he was limited to wine for the most part, his nights of spiritual intoxication soon became more or less identified with those of alcoholic inspiration. With a jug of red wine by his desk and the victrola playing constantly, often repeating the same record over and over, he was ready for an evening's work. After eight or ten hours of writing advertising copy on hot water heaters he doubtless needed such stimulants to arouse his sensibilities. But eventually music and liquor became almost indispensable aids to his writing, regardless of circumstances, as though he could achieve a kind of rhapsodic and visionary fervor by exacerbation of the senses which otherwise would have been beyond his reach.

The cultivation of such devices is peculiarly reminiscent of Rimbaud, who wrote that "the poet makes himself a visionary by a long, immense and reasoned derangement of all the senses," and who ended by considering sacred the disorder of his spirit. For that matter, it also calls to mind the various passages in Plato's *Dialogues* on the same subject, especially the one in the "Phaedrus," which is significantly and heavily underscored in Crane's copy, where Socrates maintains that the poet without madness is no poet at all and that the "poetry of sense fades into obscurity before the poetry of madness." Whether or not Crane justified his practice by these doctrines, one may be sure, at least, that once having read them, he would not be likely to forget them. But since his aesthetic theories were deeply rooted in the philosophical absolutism of the *Dialogues*, it is probably safe to assume that his practice derived from the same source.

Certainly an aura of Platonism, or better, Neo-Platonism, seemed to surround him during these months. As the summer wore on and his intoxications, both spiritual and physical, grew more frequent, Crane's sense of affinity with the visionary tradition of poetry began to emerge into the foreground of his consciousness. He began to interpret certain strange experiences in terms of revelation, and even, when drunk, to dare confiding them to his friends. A letter written to Munson in June shortly after he had completed the second part of "Faustus and Helen" was the first instance of such confidences. It was scrawled one Sunday midnight after he had returned to his tower room from an evening spent in wine and music at Simoni's, a prohibition rendezvous in the section of the city known as "Little Italy," where Crane and his friends used to foregather. "There," he wrote, "is the place to enjoy one's self in the family parlor of a pickslinger's family with chromos on the walls that are right in style of Derain and Vlaminck. Bitch dogs and the rest of the family wander in while the bottle is still half empty, and some of the family offspring." Evidently the music and the Chianti he had been drinking had aroused him to one of those states of exaltation that were becoming increasingly characteristic of his life.

"At times, dear Gorham," he wrote, "I feel an enormous power in me—that seems almost supernatural. If this power is not too dissipated in aggravations and discouragements I may amount to something sometime. I can say this now with perfect equanimity because I am notoriously drunk and the victrola is still going with that glorious Bolero. Did I tell you of that thrilling experience this last winter in the dentist's chair when under the influence of ether and *amnesia* my mind spiralled to a kind of seventh heaven of consciousness and egoistic dance among the seven spheres—and something like an objective voice kept saying to me— 'You have the higher consciousness—you have the higher consciousness. This is something that very few have. This is what is called genius.' A happiness, ecstatic such as I have known only twice in 'inspirations' came over me. I felt the two worlds. And at once. As the bore went into my tooth I was able to follow its every revolution as detached as a spectator at a funeral. O Gorham, I have known moments in eternity. I tell you this as one who is a brother. I want you to know me as I feel myself to be sometimes. I don't want you to feel that I am conceited. But since this adventure in the dentist's chair, I feel a new confidence in myself. At least I had none of the ordinary hallucinations common to this operation. Even that means something.

"You know I live for work,—for poetry. I shall do my best work later on when I am about 35 or 40. The imagination is the only thing that is worth a damn. Lately I have grown terribly isolated and very egoist. One has to do it in Cleveland. I rush home from work to my room, hung with the creations of Sommers and Lescaze—and fiddle through the evenings. If I could afford wine *every* evening I might do more. But I am slow anyway. However today I have made a good start on the first part of 'Faustus and Helen.' "

It is impossible to pass over this letter without considering the extraordinary experience which by Crane's own admission had such an important influence on him. It focuses beyond any possibility of evasion the question of whether or not Crane is to be considered a "mystic," a question that even during his own lifetime caused not a little contention among his critics. Having been born into a time and place where the actual experience of spiritual realities was almost unheard of, he was destined to meet with profound misunderstanding beyond the sympathies of a few individuals—a condition that militated strongly against a more clear understanding of himself. Even more unfortunately, he reached his creative majority during a period of violent experimentation in poetry when the extremities of style offered such confusion that the critics were able to ignore the profound and passionate sincerity of Crane's verse in favor of condemning his manner. Even after his death, he was identified by at least one critic as the leader, if not the originator, of the "decorative school" of poetry. Such gross misunderstandings may perhaps be cleared away by an attempt to define the spiritual stature of the man.

Certainly the experience he described must be considered by any established definition of mysticism as what is called a revelation. It has all the elements listed by William James in his *Varieties of Religious Experience* as characteristic of the mystic state. According to James's classification the incident would obviously come under the category of anaesthetic revelation, a field in which he did a great deal of experimental research, arriving at the conclusion that the

curious states of consciousness sometimes experienced under
such conditions were a genuine type of mystical illumination.

Although the incident of the dentist's chair was the only
case of revelation that Crane described specifically in his letters, there seem to have been at least two other instances
when the ecstasy of the mystical state was realized. There
were also continual references to states of intense exaltation,
inspirations of a power beyond the natural, and a consciousness of what might be called spiritual realities, as when he
wrote to Waldo Frank from the Isle of Pines that he felt "an
absolute music in the air again, and some tremendous rondure
floating somewhere." Though he often experienced such
states without the use of alcohol, even when they were
artificially stimulated, they must still be considered valid.
Only twice during his life did his indulgence in drink result
in the hallucinations common to alcoholic cases. For the rest,
his drinking was not so much the cause of these revelations
as it was a means to them—a liberator of immanent powers.
Professor James, in fact, in the book already mentioned,
testifies very definitely to the power of alcohol to stimulate
the "mystical faculties" of human nature. "Sobriety," he
writes, "diminishes, discriminates, and says no; drunkenness
expands, unites, and says yes. It is in fact the great exciter of
the Yes function in man. . . . It makes him for the moment
one with truth." There is an eloquent confirmation, almost
a poetic paraphrase, of this interpretation of the function of
alcohol in two verses from Crane's "The Wine Menagerie."

> New thresholds, new anatomies! Wine talons
> Build freedom up about me and distill
> This competence—to travel in a tear
> Sparkling alone, within another's will.

Until my blood dreams a receptive smile
Wherein new purities are snared; where chimes
Before some flame of gaunt repose a shell
Tolled once, perhaps, by every tongue in hell.

It is more by reason of the intense activity of this "Yes function" in Crane, than because of the sporadic states of "ecstasy," that he may well be considered a mystical poet. For the desire to expand the consciousness into higher levels of awareness and to achieve the ultimate reconciliation of universal conflicts is one of the chief characteristics and motivating forces of mysticism. In Crane's case this desire for an expansion of consciousness—for "new thresholds, new anatomies . . . new purities"—has too often been mistaken for a search for sensation. That it was much more than this is clearly proved by such letters as the one quoted in the third chapter where he wrote that the only happiness lay in the "true idea of God" or the identification of one's self with all of life. He seemed to feel that in such identification there were tremendous reservoirs of spiritual power that once released would supply the elect with the pure, enduring stream of a clairvoyant vision which would be the distinguishing feature of a new order of consciousness.

"I nearly go mad," he wrote, "with the intense but always misty realization of what *can* be done if potentialities are fully freed, released. . . . It is really not a projection in any but a loose sense, for I feel more and more that in the absolute sense the artist *identifies* himself with life."

Despite his more abstract speculations, however, his feeling itself remained in warm human contact with the life about him, taking its nourishment as much from his daily intercourse as from his imagination. "We must," he wrote, "somehow touch the clearest veins of eternity flowing through the crowds around us—or risk being the kind of glorious cripple that has missed some vital part of his inheritance." The crowds in the street were for him very much what they had been for Whitman—a source of continual inspiration and vigor; and though he suffered the inevitable reactions against the strain of metropolitan life and from time to time fled to the country for rest, he always returned to the massed motions of life. If they often represented the chaos and the materialistic madness of the world in which he lived, they also, and more importantly, represented the incalculable energy and spirit which fed the anatomy of his faith.

The numberless friendships he made during his life with people of all sorts—from bar-flies and taxi-drivers to eccentric spinsters—witnessed the abundant, almost promiscuous, affection for humanity, collectively and individually, which he shared with Whitman. But having a more violent nature than the older poet, his affections found more extreme expressions. At least one of his "cameradoes," a "beautiful rum-drinking, firewater wassailing friend of mine—a NY taxi-driver (independent!)," who used to drive him home in the early mornings across Brooklyn Bridge, found a curious immortality in Crane's poetry. His middle name, which was Maquokeeta in token of his descent from a Missouri tribe of Indians, Crane appropriated with great zest for use in the Dance section of *The Bridge* as the name of the tribal god to whom he prayed: "Lie to us,—dance us back the tribal morn!". There was also Mrs. T. W. Simpson, or "Aunt Sally" as Crane called her, his elderly housekeeper on the Isle of Pines, whose brown and wrinkled skin boasted the same resiliency as the scandalous profanity she lavished on her rheumatism and on her rooster, Ferdinand, Count Fathom, which she named after the Smollett novel Crane had been reading to her. She, too, took her place in Crane's work, not only as the "Aunt Sally" of the River section of *The Bridge*, but also in the short poem "Postscript" as the

> . . . paralytic woman on an island of the Indies,
> Antillean fingers counting my pulse, my love forever.

From such friendships as these Crane derived a reassurance of the fundamental goodness of humanity and its capacity for love. Lacking the heritage of any religious or intellectual system of thought, and the education necessary to create one, he turned to the individual relationship for confirmations of his faith. Thus, when one of his friends betrayed him by unkindness, neglect, or professional jealousy, it constituted an apostasy in more than a figurative sense, for it struck at the very foundations of the only faith possible for him, that of love. The bitterness with which he experienced such "betrayals" was token of the great value he placed on his friendships—the depth of his wound being a measure for the depth of his trust. After a quarrel with one of his closest friends in 1926, when he felt that his trust had been completely and maliciously violated, he wrote: "I doubt if I shall continue to write another year. For I've lost all faith in my material—'human nature' or what you will—and any true expression must rest on some faith in something." When such friendships failed him, he fell back with abandoned violence on his sexual relations, finding in them a gross substitute for the true affection that seemed always to founder beneath him, as well as an ironic commentary on human relationships in general.

"I treasure them," he wrote in the same letter, "I always can—against many disillusionments made bitter by the fact that faith was given and expected—whereas with the sailor no faith or such is properly *expected* and how jolly and cordial and warm the tonsiling *is* sometimes after all."

Once he had become involved in the literary life of New York, such "betrayals" were painfully frequent, for the decade of the "twenties" was notorious for its petty factional warfare, its mean jealousies and malicious backbiting; and Crane with his growing reputation and defenseless naïveté made a popular pawn and target. Most of his friends, even those closest to him, seem rarely, if ever, to have understood how completely he depended on them for his spiritual welfare, and were consequently careless in their treatment of him. That he suffered a great deal from this is certain. Many of his later poems testify to his slow and bitter recognition that he had too often placed his faith in repositories all-too-human.

> Friendship agony! words came to me
> at last shyly. My only final friends—
> the wren and thrush, made solid print for me
> across dawn's broken arc. No; yes . . . or were they
> the audible ransom, ensign of my faith
> towards something far, now farther than ever away?

But despite the long years of disillusionments and frustrations his belief in love as the transcendent force of life remained the steadfast lodestar of his imagination and work. And this alone—aside from his ecstatic "revelations"—justifies his being described as a poet of distinctly mystical temper. It was no more than this that gave the name of "mystic" to Whitman.

By the middle of the summer Crane was in a state of spiritual turmoil. At night the air in his tower room seemed to be teeming with influences of all kinds, hidden powers and fabulous secrets, waiting only to be plucked forth for the enrichment of his poetry. He felt a tremendous capacity for work and began writing on the first part of "Faustus and Helen," confident that the lines would come easily and clearly. But his impulses crowded upon him too fast; he was almost suffocated by inspiration. Meanwhile, there was no time to order and control his efforts, for his employers were pressing him for more and more advertising copy. Having sufficiently praised hot water heaters to thousands of American housewives, he was now expected to deliver matchless encomiums on Sieberling tires for the benefit of their husbands. But more than time and quiet he needed someone to talk with, someone to whom he could unburden himself of the excitements and speculations of the past months. His friends in Cleveland were painters, for the most part, who could hardly be expected to understand a poet's problems. He wanted someone whose intimacy with modern poetry was equal to his own and whose criticism might serve to clarify his ideas. The logical person to fill this need was Gorham Munson, who had fortunately just returned to New York from his expatriatism in Europe, and Crane lost no time in begging him to come to Cleveland.

The two weeks of Munson's visit in July proved scarcely long enough to give them a full measure of talk. Almost three years had passed since the two had last seen each other in New York, and in the interim the literary scene had been undergoing changes which concerned them both in an important way. The group of writers who had dominated the activities of the Village during Crane's early days in New York had now definitely become the older generation. The cause of rebellion which they had so fiercely espoused in the first years of the American Renaissance—the publishing of manifestoes and magazines—was now the concern of younger men, the post-war generation, who, having come of age on the Continent, found little to respect or admire in the platform of their elders. Munson, fresh from the café tables of Paris, had much to tell Crane of the activities of these younger writers. He also had exciting news to report of

Secession, the magazine he had founded in Vienna, which was still flourishing in Europe under the temporary supervision of Matthew Josephson. The very name of the magazine, as well as its platform, was a signal for rebellion against the literary generation in power: such men as Van Wyck Brooks, Mencken, and Dreiser, who were mainly concerned with the social aspects of art and criticism. The contributors to *Secession* on the other hand—Josephson, Cowley, Cummings, Burke, Yvor Winters, W. C. Williams—were primarily interested in aesthetic problems, questions of form and craftsmanship, which grew immediately out of creative activity and could be answered by experimentation. And it was for the express purpose of printing their work as that of a group with common directions that Munson was publishing the magazine.

All this held the greatest interest for Crane. Though he had originally written Munson against founding *Secession* and had later complained vigorously of its Dadaist tendencies, its program, when described in direct conversation, appealed to him strongly. He soon discovered, moreover, that there was little difference of opinion between him and his friend concerning the importance of Dadaism. The movement as such was rapidly disintegrating; and in any case Munson's sympathy with it, as he explained to Crane, had been primarily a desire to understand the directions of the "new" literature in order to clarify and organize his own ideas into some sort of critical synthesis. His efforts toward this end, in fact, were at last bearing fruit in the study of Waldo Frank which he was working on during his visit in Cleveland—a book whose influence on both "Faustus and Helen" and the conception of *The Bridge* Crane confessed to be considerable.

This study, which took Frank's *Our America* as its focal

point of reference, was an attempt to discover an integrated body of cultural criticism in which the younger American writers could take a positive and productive stand. Naturally, many of its theories were Frank's, and had in turn been originally held in common by Brooks, Bourne, and the *Seven Arts* group. Munson's own contribution seems to have been the insistence upon a positive creative attitude toward the machine rather than the negative one held by the older group, which rejected or evaded it. Briefly, he held that the spiritual life of man and his culture had now become dependent on three factors: man, nature, and the machine; that this had brought about an art of maladjustment rooted in a dangerous dualism; and that, finally, the only means of regaining an organic vital art lay in accepting the machine on the same level as nature, or, as he wrote, "to put positive and glowing spiritual content into Machinery." This was the dogma he had evolved and brought back with him from Dadaist Europe, and it was the section of his study suggesting ways of assimilating such new material as subject matter for poetry that Crane found so stimulating.

For the two weeks of Munson's visit this topic was their chief subject of conversation. It seemed curious that Crane, who but a few months earlier had written so impatiently of the machine-worship of the Dadaists, should suddenly become enthusiastic over the same phenomena. The explanation lay in the fact that where the Frenchmen and their imitators admired in the machine only its picturesque mechanical features, Crane had begun to see in it symbols and analogues of human life which would enrich and condense his art. Indeed, he saw even more than this. Carried away by verbal eloquence and the sweeping conception of a spiritual union between man, nature, and machine, both he and Munson seem to have had a utopian vision of a new order of humanity about to arise. The idea haunted his mind constantly; and when a few months later he read Ouspensky's *Tertium Organum,* he thought he had found impressive corroboration of it in the Russian logician's thesis of a fourth-dimensional order of consciousness emergent in the world. Given Crane's intense and lively imagination and his predisposition to mysticism, it was inevitable that such theories should have a powerful influence over his thought. But it was equally inevitable that they should ultimately confuse him.

Their immediate effect, however, was all to the good; and shortly before Munson's departure Crane was furiously at work again on the first part of "Faustus and Helen." Munson, in fact, found it impossible to do any writing of his own the last few evenings of his visit, for Crane, possessed by the "divine madness," completely monopolized their quarters in his creative frenzy. Without the slightest regard for his friend, he stomped up and down the room while the victrola played loudly, plunged to his desk to write a line, jumped up again to rewind the victrola and repeat the record, again rushed back to scrawl a verse, shut off the machine to declaim what he had written, and then once more returned to his fevered cycle of composition. But the inspiration was quickly spent. Worn out by the constant strain of writing advertising copy by day and poetry by night, he needed a complete rest; and in August he managed to collect enough money by selling some of his old books to take a vacation in the country. On his return to work he asked for a raise in pay, and failing to get it, transferred his services to another advertising firm which offered a better salary. Entangled in these changes, he found little time for writing, and it was not until the end of September that the final draft of the first part was finished—the closing lines declaring his immortal devotion to beauty.

The earth may glide diaphanous to death;
But if I lift my arms it is to bend
To you who turned away once, Helen, knowing
The press of troubled hands, too alternate
With steel and soil to hold you endlessly.
I meet you, therefore, in that eventual flame
You found in final chains, no captive then—
Beyond their million brittle, bloodshot eyes;
White, through white cities passed on to assume
That world which comes to each of us alone.

"What made the first part of the poem so good," he confessed to Munson with pardonable pride, "was the extreme amount of time, work, and thought put on it." Accordingly, he set to work on the third part with the determination to observe the same discipline; and throughout the fall and early winter the poem progressed slowly and painfully.

In the meantime he was unable to withhold the first part from circulation, or even publication. His eagerness to see it in print tempted him for a time to consider it a complete work in itself, letting the second part also stand as a separate poem and relinquishing the final section to its own independent evolution. Without having reached any decision in the matter, he submitted the first part to *The Dial*. When it was, amazingly enough, rejected, he sent it off on a transatlantic flight to Josephson, who was then acting as one of the editors of *Broom* in Berlin. Confusion followed. Josephson had already received a copy of the second part of the poem, then entitled "The Sirens of the Springs of Guilty Song," which Crane had sent him post haste upon its completion in June. This he had accepted for future publication, as he did also the first part when it arrived in November. But failing to understand the connection between the two, he printed the second part alone under its original title. By the time

Crane received a copy of the magazine in January he had finished the last part of the poem and had come to the definite conclusion that the three units formed an organic whole. Consequently, he was horrified to see one member of his aesthetic corpus appearing serenely in print in utter dislocation. Nevertheless, he dispatched the third section to Berlin, evidently hoping that editorial surgery might remedy the dismemberment, and so bewildered the editors of *Broom* that they could make nothing of the matter whatever.

The poem seemed fated to become an international waif of literature. In September 1923 another abortive attempt was made to print it in its entirety, this time by *Secession*, which was still in European exile under the supervision of John Brooks Wheelwright in Florence. Although Munson and Burke—the American editors—sent off a correct copy of the poem from New York, the magazine printed it in a sadly mutilated condition. The entire second part had been omitted, as well as single lines here and there, and appalling typographical errors had been made, the most painful of which was "blues in your breasts" for "bluet in your breasts." Crane was violently outraged. "Why don't you wire the consulate in Florence," he wrote Munson, "to stop W. from any further rape of S— . . . it is a positive elopement that seems to have no prospect of termination. I am thinking of starting abroad with the DIAL, calling it 'The Pile,' hemmorrhoid, or something like that!" In the end, the poem was excised from the magazine before its American distribution, and it was not until the winter of 1923 that it appeared as a complete and decorous organism in the seventh number of *Secession*, which had in the meantime immigrated to New York.

Despite the prolonged delay in getting the work published Crane was exhilarated throughout the winter by a sense of great achievement. Though "Faustus and Helen" fell short of the perfection of several of his shorter poems, it was furnished richly towards the future. Technically, it showed important extensions of craftsmanship: the long rhythmical lines approximating the pentameter without, however, committing themselves to any distinct pattern; the enrichment of language and music fused by syntax and assonance into an idiom unmistakably his own—these things brought him a sense of power and confidence. Furthermore, it stood as a milestone for him, marking the step from minor to major intention. Its subject matter indicated an expansion of consciousness, a shift of interest from the particular to the universal. He had achieved at least a partial realization of his long-standing desire to write of the "eternal verities" in a new and creative way, to ally his work firmly with tradition and still to express fully the spirit of his own times. There was, moreover, a strong accent of moral and spiritual vigor in the poem that sounded strangely, even marvellously, in the literary air where the overtones of Dadaism or despair predominated. In its closing lines there was an eloquent presage of things to come.

> Anchises' navel, dripping of the sea,—
> The hands Erasmus dipped in gleaming tides,
> Gathered the voltage of blown blood and vine;
> Delve upward for the new and scattered wine,
> O brother-thief of time, that we recall.
> Laugh out the meager penance of their days
> Who dare not share with us the breath released,
> The substance drilled and spent beyond repair
> For golden, or the shadow of gold hair.
>
> Distinctly praise the years, whose volatile
> Blamed bleeding hands extend and thresh the height
> The imagination spans beyond despair,
> Outpacing bargain, vocable and prayer.

For some time the poem did not receive any appreciable circulation; but the few who had the opportunity of an early reading recognized in it the arrival of a poet of primary importance. Munson's admiration for the whole was as unqualified as it had been for each part. Allen Tate in Nashville gave it his highest endorsement by hailing Crane as the greatest American poet living and by acknowledging him together with Eliot as a major influence on his own work. The praise that he treasured most, perhaps, was that of Waldo Frank, who was already recognized as an important figure in American letters. At Munson's instance Frank had read several of Crane's earlier poems with great interest, and when he received from Crane himself a copy of "Faustus and Helen," he answered with a letter of sensitive appreciation and encouragement. Crane's reply testified to the profound excitement that possessed him.

"Such major criticism," he wrote, "as both you and Gorham have given my 'Faustus and Helen' is the most sensitizing influence I have ever encountered. It is a new feeling, and a glorious one, to have one's inmost delicate intentions so fully recognized as your last letter to me attested. I can feel a calmness on the sidewalk—where before I felt a defiance only. And better than all—I am certain that a number of us at least have some kind of community of interest. And with this communion will come something better than a mere clique. It is a consciousness of something more than stylistic questions and 'taste,' it is a vision, and a vision alone that not only America needs but the whole world. We are not sure where this will lead, but after the complete renunciation symbolized in 'The Wasteland' and, though less, in *Ulysses* we have sensed some new vitality. Whether I am in that current remains to be seen,—but I am enough in it at least to know that you are definitely in it already. What delights me almost beyond words is that my natural idiom (which I have unavoidably stuck to in spite of nearly everybody's nodding querulous head) has reached and carried to you so completely the very blood and bone of me. There is only one way of saying what comes to one in ecstasy. One works and works over it to finish and organize it perfectly—but fundamentally that doesn't affect one's *way* of saying it."

Crane's stars seemed joined in beneficent conjunction during these months. Even his earlier poetry, which had appeared in magazines, was beginning to attract the official attention of established critics. Braithwaite, the conservative anthologist, wrote him for permission to print "Praise for an Urn" in his forthcoming collection. Louis Untermeyer, perhaps the most widely influential critic of modern poetry, wrote of him as a significant member of the younger group of poets, whom he styled the "New Patricians," and asked to see him during his next visit to Cleveland. And *Gargoyle*, the little magazine in Paris, besides printing his work, published a reproduction of the striking sketch Lescaze had made of him. Such general acclaim stimulated him to further efforts. During January and February, after finishing "Faustus and Helen," he composed "Belle Isle," which in a later much-altered form became "Voyages VI." "Perhaps this is an impossible 'story' to tell," he wrote of it to Munson, "but I think the last two or three stanzas achieve a kind of revelation." He also wrote a strange, compelling poem of childbirth called "Stark Major," which *The Dial* rejected with its usual aplomb.

But his imagination was concentrated most constantly on the conception of a new work, whose scope, as he began vaguely to conceive it, promised a fulfilment of all the possibilities he had glimpsed in the writing of "Faustus and Helen." He first mentioned it in a letter to Munson in early February, but it was not until the 18th of the month that he could describe it in any articulate fashion.

"Your summary of praises for 'F & H' was such a fine tribute," he wrote, "that it might account for my backache and confinement to the bed yesterday. But the more probable cause for that, however, is liquor and the cogitations and cerebral excitements it threw me into regarding my new enterprise, *The Bridge*, on the evening precedent. I am too interested in the *Bridge* thing lately to write letters, ads, or anything. It is just beginning to take the least outline,—and the more outline the conception of the thing takes, —the more its final difficulties appal me. All this preliminary thought has to result, of course, in some channel forms or mould into which I can throw myself at white heat. Very roughly, it concerns a mystical synthesis of America. History and fact, location etc. all have to be transfigured into abstract form that would almost function independently of its subject matter. The initial impulses of our people will have to be gathered up toward the climax of the bridge, symbol of our constructive future, our unique identity, in which is also included our scientific hopes and achievements of the future. The mystic portent of all this is already flocking through my mind (when I say this I should say 'the mystic possibilities,' but that is all that's worth announcing anyway), but the actual statement of the thing, the marshalling of the forces, will take me months at best; and I may have to give it up entirely before that; it may be too impossible an ambition. But if I do succeed, such a waving of banners, such ascent of towers, such dancing, etc. will never before have been put down on paper! The form will be symphonic, something like 'F & H' with its treatment of varied content, and it will probably approximate the same length in lines. It is perhaps rather silly of me to go on this way before more than a dozen lines have been written, but at any rate it serves to excuse my possible deficiencies in correspondence in the near future, should the obsession carry me much further. I hate to have to go to work every day!"

The more he thought about it, the more profoundly the conception gripped him. He spent night after night working out the pattern of the poem, scrawling down passages here and there to represent certain movements and sections of the whole, which steadily unfolded new reaches to his imagination. One excitement leading to another, liquor and music added their combined stimulus to the accelerated pace of intoxication. A letter written to Wilbur Underwood in February clearly revealed the dangerous pitch to which he had wrought his sensibilities.

"And we who create must endure," he wrote, "must hold to spirit not by the mind, the intellect alone. These have no mystic possibilities. O flesh damned to hate and scorn! I have felt my cheek pressed on the desert these days and months too much. How old I am! Yet, oddly now this sense of age—not at all in my senses—is gaining me altogether unique love and happiness. I feel I have been through much of this again and again before. I long to go to India and stay always. Meditation on the sun is all there is. Not that this isn't enough! I mean I find my imagination more sufficient all the time. The work of the workaday world is what I dislike. I spend my evenings in music and sometimes ecstasy. . . . I'm bringing much into contemporary verse that is new. I'm on a synthesis of America and its structural identity now, called *The Bridge*. I quote the last lines—

'And midway on that structure I would stand
One moment, not as diver, but with arms
That open to project a disk's resilience
Winding the sun and planets in its face.
Water should not stem that disk, nor weigh
What holds its speed in vantage of all things
That tarnish, creep, or wane; and in like laughter,
Mobile, yet posited beyond even that time
The Pyramids shall falter, slough into sand,—

And smooth and fierce above the claim of wings,
And figured in that radiant field that rings
The Universe:—I'd have us hold one consonance
Kinetic to its poised and deathless dance.' "

He found a further and peculiarly sympathetic stimulus to his imagination in his reading of Ouspensky's *Tertium Organum*, which he had just discovered. This work, whose thesis of a new order of consciousness was based on the main tenets of neo-platonic mysticism plus modern science in the form of relativity, could not but impress Crane deeply. Possessed as he was by the vision of a transfigured humanity, the learned arguments of the book convinced him that possibly an evolution toward such an end had already commenced. Furthermore, he recognized in its doctrines concerning "the world of many dimensions" many striking parallels to his own beliefs. Ouspensky's dictum that—"In that world the duality of our world does not exist. That world is the world of the unity of opposites"—was almost a paraphrase of the passage in his own "Faustus and Helen":—"There is the world dimensional for those untwisted by the love of things irreconcilable." He saw another parallel in Ouspensky's statement that "love is the motive force which drives the creative activity," which appeared simply another way of expressing his own belief that love was, for himself at least, "the strongest incentive to the imagination." But the section of the work which carried most weight with Crane was evidently that given over to long quotations from James's *Varieties of Religious Experience* describing in detail a wide range of mystical states; for after finishing the book, he wrote Allen Tate that "its corroboration of several experiences in consciousness that I have had gave it particular interest."

Before long the ferment of these accumulated excitements

began to show itself in a physical restlessness. With "Faustus and Helen" completed and *The Bridge* already under way, Crane felt that a definite period of his life had come to a close and a new one begun which demanded a larger environment than Cleveland. Now that he had attained his creative majority, his isolation weighed on him oppressively, and he longed to be in New York with Munson and Frank and the younger writers who were beginning to return from Europe. It was where he belonged, and so far as he could see there was nothing to prevent him from joining them. Certainly he had justified himself in the eyes of his father. By demonstrating his ability to earn his own livelihood in competitive business and by commanding at the same time the attention of the literary world to his poetry, he had won the fight on both fronts and could leave the battlefield covered with glory. Where before he had often reeled down the dark streets of Little Italy shouting "I am Christopher Marlowe" with a defiance worthy of Tamburlaine confronted by death, he could now, as he had written Frank, feel "a calmness on the sidewalk." The only real obstacle to his removal to New York lay in the question of supporting himself there; but this, he felt, was a problem that would solve itself when the time came. In any case, his daily work at the office had become such an intolerable burden that he was eager to escape from all business routine for a time, no matter what the cost. Early in March, he wrote to Munson complaining bitterly of his job as "a repressive fate" which was frustrating his further growth.

"To be stimulated to the nth degree," he continued, "with your head burgeoning with ideas and conceptions of the most baffling interest and lure—and then to have to munch ideas on water heaters (I am writing another book for house fraus!) has been a real cruelty this time, however temporary. The more I think about my Bridge poem the more thrilling its symbolical possibilities become, and since my reading of you and Frank (I recently bought *City Block*) I begin to feel myself directly connected with Whitman. I feel myself in currents that are positively awesome in their extent and possibilities. 'Faustus and Helen' was only a beginning— but in it I struck new *timbres* that suggest dozens more, all unique, yet poignant and expressive of our epoch. Modern music almost drives me crazy! I went to hear D'Indy's II Symphony last night and my hair stood on end at its revelations. To get those, and others of men like Strauss, Ravel, Scriabin, and Bloch into *words* one needs to *ransack* the vocabularies of Shakespeare, Jonson, Webster (for theirs were the richest) and add one scientific, street and counter, and psychological terms, etc. Yet I claim such things can be done! The modern artist needs gigantic assimilative capacities, emotion,—and the greatest of *all—vision.* 'Striated with nuances, nervosities, that we are heir to'—is more than a casual observation for me. And then—structure! What pleased me greatly about Frank's comment was the notice of great structural evidence in 'F and H.' Potentially I feel myself quite fit to become a suitable *Pindar* for the dawn of the machine age, so-called. I have lost the last shreds of philosophical pessimism during the last few months. O yes, the 'background of life'—and all that is still there, but that is only three-dimensional. It is to the pulse of a greater dynamism that my work must revolve. Something terribly fierce and yet gentle."

Before such an inspired sense of predestination obstacles became less than nothing. The letter was the last one Munson was to receive from Cleveland, for within two weeks Crane himself arrived in New York, thenceforth to make it, for better or worse, his home.

·· VI ··

"And this thy harbor, O my city, I have driven under,
Tossed from the coil of ticking towers. . . . Tomorrow,
And to be . . ."

Upon his arrival in New
York towards the middle of March Crane went directly to
Gorham Munson, who had invited him to stay with him and
his wife at their apartment at 4 Grove Street in the center of
Greenwich Village. Although his plans, as announced to his
mother before leaving Cleveland, proposed only a three
weeks' visit in New York with the purpose of estimating the
possibilities of finding work, actually he was determined not
to return home. With this in mind he had secretly packed all
his clothes and belongings before his departure, leaving them
ready for shipment in his tower room so that he could send
for them once he was established in New York. So certain
was he of finding a job with an advertising firm, that the first
week or two of his "visit" he made little or no effort in that
direction.

Life at 4 Grove Street proved too pleasant to be interrupted by practical considerations. There were hours spent

in stimulating talk with Munson, who was eager not only to listen to Crane's eloquent elaborations of his plans for *The Bridge*, but also to discuss his own work, a projected book of essays on contemporary men of letters. There were, too, many old friends and haunts to be revisited. He called frequently at the home of Claire Spencer and Harrison Smith who had extended him refuge during the summer of 1919. Another friend of that same year, whom he had not seen since then, was Matthew Josephson, now married and but a few months repatriated, who was editing the magazine *Broom* from West 12th Street. Everywhere he went about the Village he met acquaintances of his early days in New York, many of whom hardly recognized him as the boy who had quietly and sometimes awkwardly appeared at the meetings of the Poetry Society in 1917 and the literary gatherings at Mrs. Moody's apartment in Waverly Place. So changed were his appearance and manner that Padraic Colum and his wife could not for a moment place the young man who burst out of the Brevoort Café one day as they were passing and hailed them impetuously. The plaid topcoat, the cane swung with vigorous assurance, the hatless head and close-cropped hair already touched with grey at the temples, the highly flushed face and brilliant eyes, and the headlong, magnetic flow of talk—in all this there was little to recall to them Harold Crane who had diffidently brought them his first early lyrics.

But now he no longer turned to the older writers for encouragement and appreciation. The strides he had made in his own work, its modernity of content and technique, had created a gulf of misunderstanding between him and his elders.

"Most of them," he wrote to the Rychtariks shortly after his arrival in the city, "are very disagreeable, and don't talk the same language as we do, they are not concerned with the same problems. I read 'Faustus and Helen' to a group of people last evening, and very few of them, of course, understood anything that I was talking about. If it weren't for the praise and understanding I have received from people like Frank and Munson and Allen Tate, etc. I would begin to feel that I might be to blame. But this 'new consciousness' is something that takes a long while to 'put across.' "

Such rebuffs served only to swell his eagerness for friendship with members of his own generation, and especially with those few individuals whose work he felt similar in emphasis and direction to his own. Chief among these latter was Waldo Frank, in whose book *City Block* Crane had evidently sensed something of the spirit he conceived to be potential stuff for *The Bridge*. Their meeting took place shortly after Crane's arrival in New York at a luncheon which Munson had arranged. Although the circumstances that day prevented any intimate exchange of thought between them, there was a recognition of mutual sympathy leading to a friendship which was a source of moral and practical support for Crane in the following years.

During his stay with Munson he also met Jean Toomer, a talented young writer, whose first book, *Cane*, was soon to be published with an Introduction by Frank. Together with Toomer he saw much of Kenneth Burke, bristling with intellectual energy and personal charm, who as co-editor with Munson of *Secession* was a frequent caller at 4 Grove Street, and whose writing Crane had long admired. Still another visitor at the Munsons' was William Slater Brown, already known to Crane by his work published in the little magazines as well as by the role he had played as "B." in E. E. Cummings's war novel, *The Enormous Room*. Gentle, whimsical, and acutely sensitive to other people, he also had a capacity for hilarity and drinking equal to Crane's own. From their first meetings at Munson's Crane formed a deep attachment to him; and the friendship which followed was one of the few relationships in Crane's life which endured without quarrels, misunderstandings, and "betrayals." Through Brown he also met E. E. Cummings, somewhat but not altogether aloof and serenely sardonic, who was then probably the most widely known and published of the younger writers.

It was in such pleasant ways that the weeks slipped by and his circle of friends widened. At the end of three weeks, however, when his first few applications for employment had met with no success, he began to make strenuous efforts to find work. The little money he had saved to live on during the interim of pleasure had been exhausted, and he was reduced to borrowing money for his expenses. The Munsons' hospitality, extended with such eagerness, began to show signs of strain after the fourth week, for Crane with his drinking and late hours and ceaseless activity was not an easy guest to endure in a small apartment. But despite his host's increasing anxiety his resolutions, taken each Monday to find work by Friday, were continually undone by the distractions of the city. There were exhibitions at many of the galleries that were not to be missed; and there were performances and rehearsals at the Provincetown Playhouse, where he soon came to know Eugene O'Neill and the director, James Light, who with his wife, Sue Jenkins, often took care of Crane in later years. As the spring drew near, the very life of the streets was a seduction for him. "They have put lemon-yellow shades on all the lamps on Fifth Ave.," he wrote, "and it gives the street and everybody the color of champagne in the evening."

His intoxication continued well into May until his friends undertook to solve his problems for him. It was Frank who pieced together the interlocking chain of personal influence that finally secured him a position in the Statistical Department of the J. Walter Thompson Advertising Company. At the same time he left the Munsons' to stay with Slater Brown, where he lived until he could borrow enough money, pending his first pay-check, to rent a furnished room. Finally, by the first of June, he was established comfortably at 45 Grove Street in one of the square high-ceilinged chambers of the old house where he lived for the following year. He had been particularly fortunate in being able to sublet the room for a very modest sum from an acquaintance, for among its furnishings he discovered a fine new victrola, an article without which his muses might have become discouragingly inactive. "I can't tell you how fine I feel," he wrote the Rychtariks, "to get my feet on the ground again and put my nose up into the sky again for a few minutes with the 'Meistersinger' Overture."

Thus permanently settled in his new quarters and once adjusted to the mechanism of daily routine at the office, he could turn his attention once more to *The Bridge*. With the arrival of the summer season and the first blast of July heat the city lapsed into comparative apathy. The theaters closed, the exhibitions became more sparse, and one by one his friends left town for cooler retreats, leaving him to his own devices. One of his few companions during July was William Lescaze, his Cleveland friend, who had just returned from a visit to Paris and was casting about for employment in the city. Crane was especially glad to see him and the two spent many evenings together while he plied his friend with questions concerning the technical terms of engineering, speculated on their potentialities for metaphor, and read aloud the passages of *The Bridge* that he had already written. The stimulation of these evenings soon bore fruit, and after a week or two of intense work he sent the Rychtariks some fifty-odd lines "written verse by verse in the most tremendous emotional exaltations I have ever felt."

Although he seems to have had the general outline of the poem clearly established in its panoramic sweep from past to present, he still expected, surprisingly enough, that the entire work would not exceed twice the length of "Faustus and Helen," and that it would be completed within a year. Having thus far confined himself almost exclusively to the last section, he had not fully realized the quantity of material necessary to body forth his conception in its entirety. The fragment he sent the Rychtariks at this time was a further elaboration of this finale; but it approached much more closely to the spirit and language of the "Atlantis" of *The Bridge* than the brief passage he had written in Cleveland.

> To be, Great Bridge, in vision bound of thee,
> So widely straight and turning, ribbon-wound,
> Multi-colored, river-harbored and upborne
> Through the bright drench and fabric of our veins,—
> With white escarpments swinging into light,
> Sustained in tears, the cities are endowed
> And justified conclamant with the fields
> Revolving through their harvests in sweet torment.

This passage, in fact, with its brilliant animistic vision of city and field was an almost definitive version of the stanza in the finished poem. After this short period in July, however, composition of *The Bridge* flagged and finally ceased altogether. It would be two years before Crane again returned to its major scaffolding.

In the meantime he had another project in mind which he wanted to work on during the summer. This was a long essay on the photography of Alfred Stieglitz in which he hoped "to go very deep—into, perhaps, some of the most delicate problems of art in the future." The occasion for this was a profound admiration for Stieglitz's work and a belief that the famous photographer was in some mysterious way creating through his own medium the kind of communication he himself wished to achieve in poetry. This conviction had first come to him early in the spring, when he had attended an exhibition of Stieglitz's photographs. There he had seen a small and very simple print picturing two apples on a bare branch posed against the weather-worn and silvered end of a gable. Stirred deeply by its qualities of light and pattern as well as its rich, nostalgic suggestiveness, Crane was excited to a pitch of enthusiasm which soon became audible in the small gallery and attracted the attention of the artist himself. In the conversation that followed he was further aroused by Stieglitz's visionary philosophy of life and art, by the human, homespun "mysticism" which ran through his slow incessant flow of talk and with which he had fostered three decades of American art. When he left, it was with Stieglitz's expressed recognition that he had understood better than any other the nature and intentions of his photography. Fired by this encouragement, Crane had rushed back to his room to write several paragraphs which he immediately sent the artist as the "kernel" of his projected essay. Though the study never materialized, at least one of the paragraphs that were committed to paper sheds a further light on Crane's own aesthetic ideas.

"If the essences of things," he wrote, "were in their mass and bulk we should not need the clairvoyance of Stieglitz's photography to arrest them for examination and appreciation. But they are suspended on the invisible dimension whose vibrance has been denied the human eye at all times save in the intuition of ecstasy. Alfred Stieglitz can say to us today what William Blake said to as baffled a world more than a hundred years ago in his 'To the Christians':

'I give you the end of a golden string:
Only wind it into a ball,
It will lead you in at Heaven's gate
Built in Jerusalem's wall.' "

The metaphysics of this passage inevitably calls to mind the doctrines of Ouspensky, for whom the reality of things existed only in a spiritual fourth dimension. The *Tertium Organum* had not by any means been forgotten during Crane's transit from Cleveland to New York. Through his extravagant praise of it to his friends and his insistence that they read it, the book became a common bible for the small group which included, beside himself, Munson, Toomer, and Frank. Its conception of the spiritual decay of humanity under two centuries of scientific materialism and the imminent emergence of a new order of consciousness appealed strongly to their own sense of despair in the present and their hope in the immediate future. And its view of art as the beginning of vision and the artist as the visionary came as a splendid corroboration of their own beliefs. Related to this, was the claim advanced by Ouspensky for the analogical method of poetry as being the most efficient medium for the revelation of spiritual realities; and the correlative argument that language must be revolutionized and expanded the more directly to express such truths. This last idea interested Crane particularly, for he was enthusiastically sympathetic to any doctrine offering a rationalization for the deep-seated impulse which constantly drove him to revivify his medium. Very probably the obscurity of language that characterized many of the poems he wrote during the following year was due in part to the encouragement he received from these discussions of a more revolutionary use of syntax and metaphor.

However that may be, there is no doubt that he received an important moral support from this group of friends. For almost a year the four met frequently, tacitly recognizing a kind of spiritual brotherhood that bound them together in a unit distinct from the other factions of the artistic world. Their catch-words were "the new slope of consciousness," "the superior logic of metaphor," "noumenal knowledge," the "interior rapports" of *unanimisme*, the doctrine of Jules Romains, which had had a considerable influence on Waldo Frank. When in September Munson was invited to edit the fall number of the magazine *S4N* in homage to Frank, it was inevitable that the issue should be a brief of their common platform. Both Munson and Toomer contributed essays; Frank allowed extracts from his diary to be included; and even Crane, who evaded the responsibilities of an apologist, was represented by the sketch he had made of Frank.

But in spite of its appearance of complete harmony, the group dissolved into conclusive discord in the spring of 1924 when the Russian mystic, Gurdjieff, with whom Ouspensky had lately allied himself, arrived in New York with his troupe of dancers. Though Crane hailed their advent with great excitement, their first performance, which was held at the Neighborhood Playhouse and attended by a bizarre conglomeration of Greenwich Village leaders and patrons, completely smothered his enthusiasm. Distinctly repelled by the peculiar atmosphere of preciosity and fanaticism that pervaded the evening, he scoffed loudly to his companion; and at later and more intimate gatherings maintained a consistently hostile attitude toward the movement. Munson and Toomer, however, were swept off their feet by the experience, and definitely committed themselves to the discipline which Gurdjieff demanded of his followers. It was the insistence upon discipline, above all, that prejudiced Crane against the cult. In the end he was not interested in religious dogmas but in a faith, at once personal and universal enough to allow both the chaotic contradictions of his life and the inspired reaches of his imagination. He was primarily concerned with the faith of humanity in itself. And he had fought too long for the right to have faith in himself and his poetry to surrender it to any cause, or group, or person.

Though his friendship with Munson and Toomer survived this dissension, their common platform had foundered, and they met less and less frequently. His relationship with Frank, however, continued unchanged, for the latter was fortunately in Europe during the time of the "grand dissolution, birth control, re-swaddling and new-synthesizing, grandma-confusion movement," as Crane described it, and under no necessity to commit himself one way or another. But even when in America Frank remained quite aloof from social life and passed most of his time in country retreats outside the city so that Crane saw comparatively little of him.

As this group disintegrated, he became dependent for companionship upon his more recent friends: Brown, Cowley, Cummings, Burke, and Josephson. As early as the fall of 1923 he was already closely identified with them, even while a perfect harmony still prevailed in the former group; and in many ways he found them more congenial. They were his own generation. Many of them, just returned from Europe with their wives, were finding it difficult to get work and readjust themselves to the American scene. But their difficulties only served to unite them in a lively cameraderie. It was a life which satisfied Crane's intense craving for excitement, and offered him compensation, as it did them, for the long hours of frustration in business offices and the continual threat of insecurity. Whereas with his more serious friends he had been constrained to moderate his Rabelaisian humors and drunken rages, with these companions he could give vent to his most extreme impulse with immunity. They applauded, sympathized, or ignored him according to their own moods, repeating the observation of one of their Dadaist friends, "*Ce n'est pas un homme; c'est un ouragan.*" But they remonstrated with him only when he broke their furniture. Even then they forgave him when he telephoned the next morning, as became his invariable custom, to offer tentative apologies and inquire what damage he had done and whom he had insulted. Indeed, the sins of which his friends freely absolved him would, in a less tolerant society, have condemned him to eternal and exquisite damnation.

The activities of these friends during the fall and winter of 1923 centered around the magazine *Broom*, which Josephson and Cowley were struggling to nourish against the pernicious anemia of public indifference. Their platform insofar as they shared one in common was that which they had inherited from their Dadaist friends in Paris: a determination to plant bombs under the porches of American philistinism, to stick pins in the door-bells of dropsical critics, and to aim pea-shooters at the orotund periods of their elders. In short, their program was concerned more with the conditions of literature than its content. Consequently Crane had little interest in it aside from the social excitements it occasioned. The one official meeting he attended was the famous gathering, convened by Cowley and Josephson, of all the writers whom they considered in the progressive vanguard of American letters for the purpose of discussing and organizing a common program of action. Since Frank, Munson, and Toomer were unable to come, Crane was, as he wrote Munson, "the only delegate from the higher spaces" in attendance. This proved to be a somewhat delicate position before the evening was over; for when Cowley read aloud to the group the letter he had received from Munson, which consisted largely in a criticism of Josephson and his policies, Crane was under the necessity of defending Munson, who was at once violently attacked from all sides, without giving offense to the immediate company. By dint of much stomping about and waving of arms, however, and abetted by his own drunkenness and large affection for all concerned, he was able to keep faith with Munson without mortally insulting Josephson. But such quarrels caused him only amusement or distress, according as they were trivial or serious. In the end it was true, as he had written Munson two years before, that he did not, and could not, belong to any group.

In the meantime he was finding it almost impossible to continue to write and at the same time to fulfill the demands made upon him by his advertising work. Both were equally necessary, and the strain of trying to reconcile such incompatible conditions began to tell on his health. He was "forced to be ambitious in two directions," as he wrote the Rychtariks, ". . . like being put up on a cross and divided." Many of his letters during the summer and fall showed the despair he often felt in his life and that of his friends as well.

"The situation for the artist in America," he wrote, "seems to me to be getting harder and harder all the time. Most of my friends are worn out with the struggle here in New York. If you make enough to live decently on, you have no time left for your real work,—and otherwise you are constantly liable to starve. . . . Of course one's friends are worth it,—but sometimes, when you see them so upset by the fever and crowded conditions, the expenses and worries—you wonder whether or not there is much use in the whole business. I am, of course, rather tired out when I say these things. . . . I have been through the hardest summer in my life—the hardest year, perhaps, when you consider the developments I have been through and the material difficulties that I have encountered. I want to keep saying 'YES' to everything and never be beaten a moment, and I shall, of course, never be really beaten."

After August he was promoted from the Statistical Department of his company to the copywriting division, and was sent on a trip through the Middle West to gather sales facts about "Barreled Sunlight," a kind of paint that the firm was advertising. Upon his return the pressure of work increased. "Streams of 'copy' and ad layouts," he wrote, "course through my head all night sometimes until I feel like a thread singed and twisted in the morning." By the end of October he reached the limit of his endurance. His nervous balance was completely disordered; he had written nothing since July, nor had he any prospect of sufficient peace and detachment of mind to create in the future. Abruptly one day he resigned his position and began somewhat wildly to lay plans for the future. In the midst of his distraction he recalled the plantation on the Isle of Pines like a suddenly accessible Eden where he might renew himself and finish *The Bridge* and his essay on Stieglitz's photography. Having no money to finance the project, he determined to ask his mother and grandmother for assistance and "not to be sentimental about it." But his plans collapsed when his mother replied that it was impossible for him to occupy the plantation since it had been put up for sale and might at any moment be purchased. The only alternative left open to him was to seek refuge with his friend, Slater Brown, who with Edward Nagle was sharing an old house in the hills near Woodstock, New York, which had become a kind of sanctum and sanitarium for artists in flight from the city. When they learned of his predicament, an invitation was immediately extended; and having sublet his room on Grove Street to Kenneth Burke, Crane fled precipitately thither during the first week of November.

Though this alley of escape proved blind at its farther end, the respite it afforded him from the strain of life in the city was complete and delightful. The three men spent a large part of each day chopping down trees, sawing them into lengths, and laying in a supply of wood for the winter. Once or twice a week they walked into the village to buy food from which they concocted simple but enormous meals. During the evenings by the light of candles they read or wrote, or sat about the fireplace drinking hard cider and talking. Occasionally there were visitors: Gaston Lachaise, who was spending the winter in Woodstock, or William Murrel Fisher, the art critic; and once, during the week-end of Thanksgiving, a number of friends came out from the city and there was wine and a huge turkey roasted over the coals. It was a simple life of the kind Crane needed; and he responded to it quickly, regaining lost weight and color and nervous equilibrium. He also gained what he had not had before—a moustache, blond and of somewhat dubious cut, which he wore back to the city in January.

He also carried back to New York a bundle of five or six tattered notebooks, borrowed from their neighbor, Fisher, which were full of a strange scribbled poetry that excited him profoundly. These poems, which Fisher had shown him one evening, were the work of Samuel Greenberg, a poverty-stricken poet, uneducated, unpublished, and completely unknown, who had died in 1916 at the age of twenty-three in an institute for the destitute tubercular on Ward's Island. Fisher, who had taken an interest in the invalid over a number of years, inherited the notebooks through the indifference of the boy's relatives; and fascinated by the beautiful, almost unintelligible, poetry, he had preserved them from year to year in the hope of some day understanding the strange and tragic talent which produced them. When Crane read the poems, he was completely beside himself with excitement. He stomped up and down Fisher's small living-room muttering the lines to himself and declaiming them aloud; he compared them to the work of Rimbaud and Laforgue; and insisted, before he left, on borrowing the notebooks for the purpose of copying out the best of the verses. It was an important discovery, for the exotic visionary poetry with its curious entwined imagery of rainbow, sea, and flower exerted a distinctly traceable influence on Crane's "Voyages," which he composed during the same months that he was making transcriptions from the Greenberg Mss.

When he returned to New York about the first of January, however, he had little time to devote to the creation or appreciation of literature. Aside from his restored health and spirits, his situation was now infinitely worse than it had been before his flight, for he had neither pay-check nor capital with which to support himself. The little money he had for the rental of his room on Grove Street had been sent him by his mother and even she could ill afford it. In fact, she had written him that her resources were so low that she and his grandmother had decided to sell their old home with all its furnishings and move into a small apartment. Consequently he could not expect, or even wish for, much help from that quarter. The only offer of employment he received during the first anxious weeks of interviews and applications came, surprisingly enough, in the form of a letter from his father, suggesting that he return to Cleveland and accept a position with him.

Although all communication between the two had ceased in 1921 when Hart fled from his father's store in a bitter rage of indignation, it had been resumed in October just before he left New York for Woodstock. The brief note Crane wrote at that time was a gesture of defiance rather than of amity, a challenge to witness his complete and successful independence; but it betrayed, nonetheless, a longing for his father's approval and affection. The more or less constant correspondence that passed between them thenceforth was a pathetic one in which a genuine love for one another was apparent beneath the continued recriminations of old animosities. And it clearly acquits Mr. Crane of many of the charges that rumor brought against him in later years. In spite of the gross mistakes, the almost criminal misunderstanding, of which he had been guilty towards his son, he was neither deliberately cruel nor malicious; and contrary to report he did not deny Hart financial aid after 1924. Like many another American business man who had made his own fortune, he was simply a person of extraordinary power and determination with a pure and single devotion to one set of values, which made him preternaturally blind to all conceptions of life but his own. That in spite of this he tried to meet his son halfway in establishing a mutual understanding witnessed the sincerity of his intentions.

The letter Hart received from him in January was the first, however, to suggest any resumption of business relations between them, and came as a complete surprise, for he had not written his father of his unemployment. Incurably blind to Hart's real profession, Mr. Crane wrote with what he undoubtedly intended to be meticulous fairness that he did not wish Hart to return to his employ if it would involve sacrificing opportunities in fields more attractive to him. "In other words," he explained, "in later life I do not want you to feel that if your father had not been in the candy business that you might have developed into a real advertising success." Hart's reply was composed with great care and sincerity. He pointed out that it would be dishonest of him to accept his offer when his own interests were inimical to business; he mentioned his present financial distress "with less than two dollars" in his pocket as proof that he was willing to sacrifice comfort to attain his ends; he suggested with pathetic pride that the name Crane might some day stand for something in the world of literature, "not only in New York but in London and abroad." And in closing he made a moving plea for his father's understanding:

"Try to imagine working for the pure love of simply making something beautiful,—something that maybe can't be sold or used to help sell anything else, but that is simply a communication between man and man, a bond of understanding and human enlightenment—which is what a real work of art *is*. If you do that, then maybe you will see why I am not so foolish after all to have followed what seems sometimes only a faint star. I only ask to leave behind me something that the future may find valuable, and it takes a bit of sacrifice sometimes in order to give the thing that you know is in yourself and worth giving. I shall make every sacrifice toward that end."

The letter was convincing and effective, for it elicited not only his father's sympathy, but also what was more helpful for the moment, a check. Towards the end of the month he at last found work, only to be discharged after a week or two because of his employer's inability to pay him. At the same time he was forced to give up his room at 45 Grove Street to its original tenant. Without funds again he moved into another room, only to be evicted after a short time for being unable to pay his rent. There followed a month of desperate nomadic life. With his belongings divided into small bundles and stored here and there, he moved about with a suitcase of clothes, living by the hospitality and generosity of his friends, of whom Eugene O'Neill and James Light proved his most constant benefactors. Throughout March and the early part of April he was constantly unemployed. Advertising firms and publishing houses alike were indifferent to his previous experience and qualifications, and repeatedly refused him. His mother wrote begging him to come home where he would at least be provided with food and shelter; but he replied pledging her to secrecy concerning his plight, and continued to write lively letters to his friends in Cleveland describing the latest exhibitions and books as though he were happily and profitably employed.

Only once during this trying period did his despair threaten to undermine his pride and stubborn perseverance. This was when his father came to New York for a few days to investigate his branch offices and invited Hart one evening to dine with him at his hotel. Across the dinner table Mr. Crane again offered him a position in his company, and persuasively described the security, the comfort, even the possible wealth that would be his if he accepted. It was a difficult temptation to resist. The blandishments of good food, the solidity of his prosperous parent, the luxury of the immediate surroundings—all seemed marshaled in a conspiracy of fate to force his surrender. At the crucial moment, however, Mr. Crane betrayed his own cause by an irremediable error. Convinced that the victory was already his, he stipulated firmly and clearly that the moustache, which still decorated his son's upper lip, would have to be shaved before he returned to Cleveland. Hart's response was conclusive. He jumped to his feet, his face flushing suddenly and deeply crimson, and damning his father loudly and roundly for a tyrant, threw down his napkin and stomped violently out of the dining-room.

The episode was a fortunate one, for while it did not alienate his father, it left Hart free to benefit from a turn of fortune a few weeks later. Towards the middle of April Malcolm Cowley heard of an opening in the offices of Sweet's Catalogue Service Inc., where he was employed, and advised Crane to apply for the position. The application was made and accepted, and to his amazement Crane found himself once again a wage-earner, able to live in his own quarters and buy his own meals. By the end of April he was comfortably installed in a room at 110 Columbia Heights, Brooklyn, where John Augustus Roebling, the great engineer of Brooklyn Bridge, had once lived. There his window looked down on the brilliant or grimy mists of the East River with its continual turmoil and maneuver of shipping, and beyond it the granite towers, the steely spires of Manhattan, and rising symbolically above it the iron-black and powerful arches of the Bridge itself.

He was not alone there, for he had living with him a person with whom he had fallen deeply in love during the preceding weeks. This was a young man of his own age whom he had recently met through mutual friends and from whom he had received not a little help during the last weeks of his unemployment. He was quiet and retiring, but Crane soon discovered in him a sensitive knowledge and appreciation of music, which led to their attending a few concerts together. His almost bashful reticence in company, Crane learned, was due to the fact that he had grown up in the army and had subsequently taken to the sea to earn his living by making periodic voyages as ship's printer or checker of cargo. As their intimacy deepened, Crane found more and more to attract him in his new friend, until suddenly a relationship developed which for a time at least was of supreme importance in his life.

Though it is not necessary or even important to investigate Crane's sexual life in detail, in this one case exception should be made, for it must be considered as more than a casual "affair." Crane himself could not refrain from communicating his happiness in it to his friends and proclaimed it, however exaggeratedly, a profound influence in his life. In spite of the fact that he had originally intended to keep his homosexuality a secret in New York, it was already known among his intimate friends. "After all," he had, written Munson before leaving Cleveland, "when you're dead it doesn't matter, and this statement alone proves my immunity from any 'shame' about it. But I find the ordinary business of 'earning a living' entirely too stringent to want to add any prejudices against me *of that nature* in the minds of any publicans and sinners." These sentiments notwithstanding, Crane was temperamentally incapable of hypocrisy or dissimulation, and after his arrival in New York had gradually confessed himself to one after another of his intimates. Consequently there was no secrecy concerning the relationship in question, and it was accepted by his friends, if not with respect, at least with complete tolerance and equanimity.

Aside from the part it played in Crane's life the relationship was the source of much of the strange mystical exaltation that inspired the "Voyages," which must rank among his best work. Excepting the first and last poems of the group, they all bear eloquent witness directly or indirectly to the transcendent intensity of his love; and the fourth of the series was originally dedicated to his friend. Moreover, the title of these poems, which were written during the summer and fall of 1924, undoubtedly derived from the voyages his friend was making during that time, from which he periodically returned to Columbia Heights for brief visits. For the rest, it is useless to try to describe the significance of this relationship. More illuminating by far than any such effort are the "Voyages" themselves and the strangely moving letter to Waldo Frank written at the end of April 1924.

"For many days, now, I have gone about quite dumb with something for which 'happiness' must be too mild a term. At any rate, my aptitude for communication, such as it ever is, has been limited to one person alone, and perhaps for the first time in my life (and, I can only think that it is for the last, so far is my imagination from the conception of any-

thing more profound and lovely than this love). I have
wanted to write you more than once, but it will take many
letters to let you know what I mean (for myself at least)
when I say that I have seen the Word made Flesh. I mean
nothing less, and I know now that there is such a thing as
indestructibility. In the deepest sense, where flesh became
transformed through intensity of response to counter-
response, where sex was beaten out, where a purity of joy
was reached that included tears. It's true, Waldo, that so
much more than my frustrations and multitude of humiliations has been answered in this reality and promise that I
feel that whatever even the future holds is justified beforehand. And I have been able to give freedom and life which
was acknowledged in the ecstasy of walking hand in hand
across the most beautiful bridge of the world, the cables enclosing us and pulling us upward in such a dance as I have
never walked and never can walk with another.

"Note the above address, and you will see that I am living
in the shadow of that bridge. It is so quiet here; in fact, it's
like the moment of the communion with the 'religious gun-
man' in my F and H where the edge of the bridge leaps
over the edge of the street. It was in the evening darkness of
its shadow that I started the last part of that poem. Imagine
my surprise when E— brought me to this street where, at the
very end of it, I saw a scene that was more familiar than a
hundred factual previsions could have rendered it! And there
is all the glorious dance of the river directly beyond the back
window. . . . That window is where I would be most remembered of all: the ships, the harbor, and the skyline of
Manhattan, midnight, morning or evening,—rain, snow, or
sun, it is everything from mountains to the walls of Jerusalem and Nineveh, and all related and in actual contact with
the changelessness of the many waters that surround it. I
think the sea has thrown itself upon me and been answered,
at least in part, and I believe I am a little changed—not essentially, but changed and transubstantiated as anyone is
who has asked a question and been answered."

There was an unmistakable presage in the intoxicated and visionary intensity of this letter. Crane was again possessed by the "divine madness." Aroused to the utmost by the reciprocation and fulfilment of his love, his emotions had attained a tension of excitement which had inevitably to find release. "My eyes have been kissed with a speech that is beyond words entirely," he wrote; and added towards the end of the letter, "Just now I feel the flood tide again the way it seemed to me just before I left Cleveland last year, and I feel like slapping you on the back every half hour." As a token of what was to come, the letter enclosed two fragments he had recently composed—"Lachrymae Christi" and a "Sonnet," which during the productive months that followed became one of his most profoundly beautiful poems, "Voyages III."

"Let the same nameless gulf beleaguer us—
Alike suspend us from atrocious sums
Built floor by floor on shafts of steel that grant
The plummet heart, like Absalom, no stream."

Iᴛ seems strange that Crane, once again feeling the irresistible sweep of creative excitement, did not return to the composition of *The Bridge*. The anxiety of unemployment had been removed; his new position demanded only such attention to technical detail as would leave his imagination and energies comparatively free for writing; and he was again comfortably settled in a quiet room with his books, his drawings, and his victrola. Conditions were more than usually conducive to work, as the rich yield of poetry during the following months testified. That he turned to the writing of shorter pieces, however, instead of *The Bridge*, was largely because he was beginning at last to realize that the longer work would demand much more time and a more extensive elaboration than he had originally planned. As the conception slowly crystallized in his imagination, he saw that it would be necessary to postpone work on the poem until his materials were fully ripened.

There was a further reason for this postponement in the fascination he still felt for those unexplored potentialities of language which he had first sensed while writing "Faustus and Helen." Deeply excited as he had been by his achievement of a personal idiom of expression, he could not forgo the thrilling adventure of testing still further the resources of his medium and his power to exploit them. His attitude towards language was much like that of a painter to his pigments. He gloried in words aside from their meaning as things in themselves, prizing their weight, density, color, and sound; and gloated over the subtle multiplicity of their associations—"the so-called illogical impingements of the connotations of words on the consciousness"—very much as a painter would gloat over the "values" of certain textures. During his visit to the Isle of Pines two years later, when engaged on some of his best work, he wrote Frank of curious states of mind in which "sometimes words come and go, presented like a rose that yields only its light, never its composite form." On the other hand he was obsessed by a desire to approach poetry to the condition of music—not to describe but to recreate in full immediacy those "revelations" in the works of modern composers which he had reported to Munson as having stood his hair on end. Like Baudelaire, whose verse owed so much to Wagnerian music and Romantic painting, Crane wanted to enrich the province of poetry by poaching on the preserves of the other arts, to enlarge his own medium by assimilating or reproducing theirs. More exactly, perhaps, his desire was like that of Rimbaud, who had wished to invent a poetic language that would be "accessible to all the senses . . . to write silences, nights . . . to fixate vertigoes." But such ambitions involved a constant pursuit of sensation, an almost exclusive cultivation of subjective states of mind which would be scarcely compatible with the focus of attention demanded by the historical and social subject matter of *The Bridge*. For the time being, then, he was content to put off this long work in favor of pushing his explorations of language to the extreme frontiers of expression.

In view of these intentions it is not surprising that many of the poems written during this period were somewhat obscure. "Recitative," the first trophy of his explorations, was so difficult that it puzzled even such sympathetic admirers as Allen Tate. The version Tate had read was the one of four stanzas which was published in the spring issue of *The Little Review*.

> Regard the capture here, O Janus-faced—
> As double as the hands that crash this glass:
> Such eyes at search or rest you cannot see—
> Reciting pain and glee, you cannot bear.
>
> Twin shadowed halves: the second's glancing holds
> In each the skin alone, and so it is
> I crust a plate of vibrant mercury
> Borne cleft to you, and brother in the half.
>
> Resist this much-exacting fragment smile,
> Its drums and darkest blowing leaves decline
> In favor, only, of your tears—reserved
> Communicant to greet an ancient sign. . . .
>
> In alternating bells have you not heard
> All hours clapped dense into a single stride?
> Forgive me for an echo of these things,
> And walk through Time, yourselves, in equal pride.

Crane was always perfectly willing, however, to elaborate upon his poems for the benefit of his friends.

"Imagine the poet," he wrote in reply to Tate's queries, "say, on a platform speaking it. The audience is one half of Humanity, Man (in the sense of Blake) and the poet the other. ALSO, the poet sees himself in the audience as in a mirror. ALSO, the audience sees itself, in part, in the poet. Against this paradoxical DUALITY is posed the UNITY, or the conception of it (as you got it) in the last verse. In another sense, the poet is *talking to himself* all the way through the poem, and there are, as too often in my poems, other reflexes and symbolisms in the poem also which it would be silly to write here—at least for the present."

Certainly, the real complexity of this conception serves to substantiate Crane's often repeated statement that the obscurity of his work lay not in any desire on his part to mystify his readers but in the subject matter itself. Furthermore, Crane strove constantly to simplify his more difficult poems. This was undoubtedly the reason for the three stanzas and the minor revisions which he later added to the version of "Recitative" quoted above.

But in spite of his desire to be understood in his poetry he was unwilling, perhaps even unable for the time being, to abandon his quest for new idioms with which to express "the living stuff of the imagination." If his friends were bewildered by "Recitative," they must have been completely baffled by the poem "Possessions" that appeared with it in the same issue of *The Little Review*. For once even Crane was unable to give a rational explanation or paraphrase of what he had written. In the essay "General Aims and Theories," where he discussed much of the poetry written during this time, he confessed that "a poem like 'Possessions' really cannot be technically explained. It must rely (even to a large extent with myself) on its organic impact on the imagination to successfully imply its meaning." For a poet with less faith in the sheer intensity of his emotions and the magic power of words to recreate them, such an admission would have served as sufficient reason to return to more familiar modes of both expression and experience. But believing that it was "part of a poet's business to risk not only criticism—but folly—in the conquest of consciousness," Crane was not at all dismayed by the mystery of what seemed to many an impossible paradox. As long as a poem caused an "impact on the imagination" of the reader, he was satisfied that he had not entirely failed of successful creation.

Throughout the summer and fall his table before the window overlooking the river was strewn with the manuscripts of these poems, which later established his reputation among the critics as the most obscure and difficult of the modern poets. There was "Lachrymae Christi," probably the most esoteric of all, which, begun in the early spring of 1924, was not completed until April 1925. And with it there appeared for a time a short "Blakeian" piece, called "At Heaven Gates," which, since it was ultimately incorporated into the most arcane passage of the former poem, deserves to be quoted in part.

> At length the vermin
> and the rod
> blind thee at once,—
>
> .   .   .   .   .   .
>
> The sphinx upon the ripe
> borage of death clears
> with her tail thy tongue,
> and instantly shall dare
> ask from the embers of thy lungs
> a measure of full praise. . . .

There was also "Emblems of Conduct," constructed with amazing ingenuity and beauty from the fragments of several different poems in the Greenberg Mss. which he had brought back from Woodstock with him. And one day, after waking from a drunken sleep to the brilliant morning light with the impression that he was dead, a few scrawled lines of "Paraphrase" joined the other sheets. By October, "Legend" was finished. On all of these poems he was working simultaneously, focusing his attention upon this one or that according to his mood, and subjecting them with painstaking criticism to continual revision. But his imagination turned most constantly and intensely upon the "Voyages."

Of these the first, it will be recalled, had been written in 1921 as "The Bottom of the Sea Is Cruel," while the germ of the sixth and last had appeared in the poem "Belle Isle"; the remaining four and the final version of the sixth were all composed between April 1924 and April 1925. These alone with their incomparable music and imagery and their sustained intensity of vision would have constituted a rich return of poetry for a year's work. Possibly no other writer but Melville has ever been able to express the mysteries and terrors of the sea with such eloquence and imagination as Crane did in the "Voyages."

> And yet this great wink of eternity,
> Of rimless floods, unfettered leewardings,
> Samite sheeted and processioned where
> Her undinal vast belly moonward bends,
> Laughing the wrapt inflections of our love;
>
> Take this Sea, whose diapason knells
> On scrolls of silver snowy sentences,
> The sceptred terror of whose sessions rends
> As her demeanors motion well or ill,
> All but the pieties of lovers' hands.
>
> And onward, as bells off San Salvador
> Salute the crocus lustres of the stars,

In these poinsettia meadows of her tides,—
Adagios of islands, O my Prodigal,
Complete the dark confessions her veins spell.

Mark how her turning shoulders wind the hours,
And hasten while her penniless rich palms
Pass superscription of bent foam and wave,—
Hasten, while they are true,—sleep, death, desire,
Close round one instant in one floating flower.

Bind us in time, O Seasons clear, and awe.
O minstrel galleons of Carib fire,
Bequeath us to no earthly shore until
Is answered in the vortex of our grave
The seal's wide spindrift gaze toward paradise.

Much of the inspiration for these poems derived from
Crane's relationship with his sea-going friend, who seems to
have had a lively fancy and sensibility. Crane needed to hear
only the bare outline of such legends as that of the sunken
city off the island of San Salvador to be completely seized
by a "sea change," and to hear the tolling of water-muffled
bells in the towers undersea. And this and many other stories
he heard from his friend when he returned to spend occasional weeks of idleness at 110 Columbia Heights. But there
was another, less direct, contribution made to the "Voyages" by the poems of Greenberg. The imagery of these
almost unintelligible, but strangely affecting, poems offered
a confusion of rainbows, waves, shadows, and blossoms
which seem to have been used as symbols for the poet's
most obsessive theme: the conflict between spirit and flesh,
love and lust. It was a poetry which because of both
its subject matter and strangeness of expression could not
but fascinate Crane; and throughout the summer he spent
hour upon hour making copies from the original manu-

script. A quotation from one of these will illustrate the curious qualities of the verse.

> For lustre hath surmised
> Inpouring rainbows of satieties silhouette,
> Cosmies lotus shadowings and
> Lewd Satyr's passion sought
> Refuge, before their uprisen
> Luminous waves, all felt to
> The sensual net of lecherous
> Wounds, abiding from spiritual thought.

The influence of Greenberg's poetry on Crane's own work was inconsiderable, if one excepts the "Voyages" and "Emblems of Conduct"; but the way in which he assimilated certain lines into his own verse offers a striking illustration of his method of composition. In "Voyages II," for instance, quoted above, he borrowed phrases or metaphors from several different poems of the Greenberg Mss. and wrote them into his own lines, subsequently shifting them about from one context to another and gradually altering them until there remained of the originals only those qualities that had primarily attracted him. It was as though he sensed in such passages obscure elements or associations which had a significant affinity with his own work and which he could discover only by experimental juxtapositions, puzzle-fashion. One of the lines he borrowed was: "Silhouette set the sceptres roving." This first appeared in "Voyages II" as:

> Take this Sea then; enlisted by what sceptres
> roving wide from isle to isle have churned. . . .

It then appeared in the following successive variations: "Silhouettes of sceptres roving," "set with sceptres roving," "circled by their sceptres roving," "shadowed sceptres roving." A new phrase, one of Crane's own making, was then introduced into the poem: "in terror of her sessions." And thus in the next version the Greenberg line became completely assimilated into Crane's own poetry as:

> The sceptred terror of whose sessions rends
> All else than Deity's green crested Herb.

The second of these lines was also taken from one of the Greenberg poems, but shortly gave place to Crane's own line: "All but the pieties of lovers' hands," which rounded out the two lines as they appeared in the published version.

Although this method of composition was most clearly revealed in such pieces as "Voyages II" and "Emblems of Conduct," where he was borrowing deliberately from another poet, it was equally characteristic of all the poems written during this period. Many of his critics have discussed the method from a theoretical point of view. Allen Tate, who wrote the Foreword to Crane's first volume of verse, *White Buildings*, described it as the "oblique presentation of theme" which is "formulated through a complex series of metaphors" and whose meaning is implicit rather than explicit. From the more immediate view of practice Tate's somewhat abstruse definitions would seem to have been correct. Judging from manuscripts, Crane appears to have built up his poems in blocks of language which were cemented into coherent aesthetic form by the ductile stuff of complex associations, metaphors, sound, color, and so forth. This would account for the juggling about of lines from one context to another with what seems to have been a kind of creative opportunism. Actually he was doing no more than the painter or sculptor who strives for what has been called "significant form." His enthusiastic study of modern painting was having its own influence on these poems, for his attitude towards them was primarily plastic. He considered them not as vehicles of thought so much as bodies of the impalpable substance of language to be molded into aesthetically self-sufficient and complete units. Accordingly, Crane intended these poems not as descriptions of experience that could be *read about*, but as immediate experiences that the reader could *have*, very much like the ones he might have (also without benefit of rational explanation or description) in the sensitive subliminal interiors of his own consciousness. The reader was not necessarily expected to derive any more rational meaning from these poems than from those states of consciousness, experienced by everyone at some time, which forever elude the conclusive grasp of reasonable understanding and expression.

In the essay "General Aims and Theories," written in 1925 quite possibly as a reply to the complaints of bewildered friends, Crane gave a relatively complete statement of the aesthetic embodied in these poems. It was significant that he took Blake as his point of departure. After quoting him to the effect that:—

> "We are led to believe in a lie
>   When we see *with* not *through* the eye,"

he went on to develop his own conception of poetry.

"It is my hope to go *through* the combined materials of the poem, using our 'real' world somewhat as a springboard, and to give the poem *as a whole* an orbit or predetermined direction of its own. I would like to establish it as free from my own personality as from any chance evaluation on the reader's part. (This is, of course, an impossibility, but it is a characteristic worth mentioning.) Such a poem is at least a stab at a truth, and to such an extent may be differentiated from other kinds of poetry and be called 'absolute.' Its evocation will not be toward decoration or amusement, but rather toward a state of consciousness, an 'innocence' (Blake) or absolute beauty. In this condition there may be discoverable under new forms certain spiritual illuminations, shining with a morality essentialized from experience directly, and not from previous precepts or preconceptions. It is as though a poem gave the reader as he left it a single, new *word*, never before spoken and impossible actually to enunciate, but self-evident as an active principle in the reader's consciousness henceforward."

He continued by discussing the technical considerations of such poetry, stating that the "terms of expression" would be chosen more for their associational, than for their literal, meanings; and that:

"Via this and their metaphorical inter-relationships, the entire construction of the poem is raised on the organic principle of a 'logic of metaphor,' which antedates our so-called pure logic and which is the genetic basis of all speech, hence consciousness and thought-extension."

It was significant of the temper of Crane's mind and spirit that he instinctively derived his aesthetic and its vindication not from one of the various formulas of the art-for-art's-sake theory, but directly from the metaphysics of absolute idealism. The conception of the poem as having an "orbit or predetermined direction of its own" and as being a "stab at a truth" is closely related, in fact, to the aesthetics of Hegel whose ideas Crane may very likely have assimilated in his readings of criticism. Though he chose at times to deny any further significance to the "absolutism" that he admitted as a *modus operandi* in his writing, his judgments invariably betrayed a thorough philosophical idealism. Indeed, what is surprising in these poems is not their obscurity, but their constant preoccupation with moral and spiritual evaluations. Despite his pursuit of the esoteric extremes of language and consciousness, Crane had remained faithful to the precept he had written Munson from Cleveland: namely, that the "modern artist needs gigantic assimilative capacities, emo-

tion,—and the greatest of all—*vision*." In the end, it was these
moments of vision that gave the poems their final coherence
and power. Even in a poem as obscure as "Possessions" a
kind of clairvoyance predominates.

> I turning, turning on smoked forking spires,
> The city's stubborn lives, desires.
>
> Tossed on these horns, who bleeding dies,
> Lacks all but piteous admissions to be spilt
> Upon the page whose blind sum finally burns
> Record of rage and partial appetites.
> The pure possession, the inclusive cloud
> Whose heart is fire shall come,—the white wind raze
> All but bright stones wherein our smiling plays.

During these months Crane's capacities for assimilation
were being taxed to the utmost. Beyond the complex monotonous mechanism of his daily routine in the offices of
Sweet's Catalogues there was the city itself radiating a vicious heat through the "anvil weather" of the summer which
beat mercilessly on the humanity of its streets and tene-
ments. After the day's work came the long subway ride
back to Columbia Heights under the pounding floors of the
city and under the river, packed in the dense steaming
wedge of flesh homeward bound; to be regurgitated finally
into the long-drawn twilight of exhausted rooming houses,
whose stoops and windows were crowded with families
sprawled to the coolness. And beyond the worn life of its
people was the new metal-flashing life of its machinery and
buildings: the oblique electric stream of the Elevated scream-
ing upwards across the Bridge, the neon magnificence of its
nights, the "cloud-flown derricks" of its fierce incessant
industry, its overwhelming rise of stone and steel stepping
in shadows upwards to the flash of spire and pinnacle. Seem-

ingly without end in its extent, equally without limit in its variety, but having no purpose nor order, it was chaotic and meaningless, a monstrous hive of sound and fury. Yet it was the modern world and the contemporary poet had perforce to assimilate it, to express it, and, if he were a poet of Crane's temperament, to try to discover its meaning. Though Crane was not yet ready to undertake the writing of *The Bridge*, the materials for it were accumulating with headlong rapidity.

With the arrival of autumn many of his friends who had fled to the country for the summer began to return to the city. Among them were new arrivals, who joined the company of Crane's intimates during the following months. From Nashville, Tennessee, came Allen Tate in full flight from the provincial isolation of the South, very much as Crane had fled from Cleveland. After two years of stimulating correspondence the two were at last able to exchange ideas and criticisms of each other's work directly. Tate was immediately shown the "Voyages," then in process of composition, and with the same critical acumen which had led him to hail Crane's achievement in "Faustus and Helen" he now recognized the major importance of these poems. After they were finished in 1925 he proposed to write an essay on them for *The Guardian*, a literary paper edited in Philadelphia by Harry Alan Potamkin. Another stranger to the literary circles of New York that year was Laura Riding, a young woman whose poetry, which far surpassed Crane's in point of obscurity, was beginning to attract a small distinguished audience of fellow poets. In spite of very dissimilar temperaments, she and Crane became close friends: during the following year they saw a great deal of each other, sharing enthusiasms, depressions, money, and long hours of talk. For a time many people thought they were in love and plotted a romance between them; but this was a fiction which they enjoyed even more than those who reported it. With such new companions added to his old friends the winter passed quickly and pleasantly. Often they all met for dinner at the restaurant of John Squarcialupi in Perry Street, where they could spend the evening drinking and talking. Sometimes Crane and Cowley and Tate would each bring a poem or two to be read aloud, and in between serious discussions there was much laughter and nonsense.

The subject that caused the most argument and hilarity that winter revolved about the public feud between the critic, Ernest Boyd, and the younger writers, headed by Malcolm Cowley who acted as their most formidable champion. Cowley and Josephson had delayed too long their program of dynamiting the front porches of philistinism and exploding the literary scene into a turmoil of healthy intellectual fisticuffs. The philistines—for Boyd was a member of the elder generation already established—threw the first bomb in January 1924 with the inaugural number of the *American Mercury*, which printed an article by Boyd entitled "Esthete: Model 1924." This essay in impolite journalism, which set out to describe the career of the typical aesthete of the younger generation, took as material the characteristics of several of its better-known members. It caricatured their college life, their experience in the War, their subsequent Dadaist expatriatism, their return to New York to manufacture a reputation in the world of letters; and prophesied their eventual decline into mediocre journalism. It attacked them for an affectation of learning, for opportunism and insincerity, and in its innuendoes went so far as to impute to them a susceptibility to sexual aberrations. Like any pamphleteer Boyd had compounded a mixture of distorted truth and fiction calculated at once to enrage and humiliate his victims; and the phenomenal effect of his attack witnessed the success of his method. For a year or more the battle raged back and forth, dominating the news of the literary press and spicing literary gossip with rumors of violence and personal slanders. While Boyd's reputation soared on the wings of publicity, Crane's friends rallied such strength as they could muster under the banners of a counter-attack and finally published a pamphlet in reply, "Esthete 1925," which, coming almost a year later, was comparatively ineffective against the swollen tide of Boyd's journalism. Characteristically, there was no unanimity of opinion among the "esthetes"; some of them, in fact, reacting against the infusion of Dadaism in the others, found more truth than fiction in Boyd's caricatures. Crane, for his part, refused to participate in the polemics of rebuttal though he particularly resented Boyd's innuendoes of homosexuality and his ridicule of the "almost Swedenborgian mysticism" of the aesthete, which was clearly an allusion to the writings of Frank and Munson. But he had too much sense of humor and proportion to wish to dignify the quarrel by defending it. His only gesture of participation was made one night in the midst of a party when a group of his friends telephoned Boyd. When Crane, somewhat tipsy, took his turn and with considerable gusto introduced himself over the wire, Boyd asked him with sarcastic inflection where he could find his poems; to which Crane replied, "Oh, behind pianos and up chimneys."

The only value of this long feud lies in its description of the literary scene of those years. Making allowances for the distortions of invective, one may find in the series of attacks and counter-attacks a body of pertinent definitions of the vices of the older and younger generation of writers: the cliquishness, the pretense of learning, the susceptibility to cults of the latter; and of the former its intellectual inertia, its lack of artistic courage and vision, and its pandering to popular prejudice. The battle also served another purpose in marking the close of a certain period of development for the younger writers. In the spring of 1925, when the last frenzied philippics were but echoes and they paused to take stock of their gains and losses, they discovered that their groups had disbanded, gradually and unobtrusively, and that no new alignments had taken place. The French way of literary life, which they had looked to as a model, was not destined, it seemed, to be the American way. The rarefied air of aesthetic speculation which had intoxicated them in Europe would not sustain them in the too solid atmosphere of America where the dollar was still the dollar. Even their little magazines had died of suffocation and malnutrition: *Broom* in January 1924 and *Secession* a few months later. What had happened was that the young expatriates had at last become completely reorientated to their native country and the indigenous folk-ways of American culture. Although in their social life they were still banded together by old allegiances, after the spring of 1925 they shared no common program of intellectual purpose or endeavor.

With the first premature blasts from the imminent inferno of summer such considerations suddenly became unimportant. Those who were unemployed or able to commute to the city began to gather funds to join in the general exodus to the country. With the contagion of flight in the air Crane abruptly decided he could no longer endure the steady stultification of daily office work. He had finished a group of poems, it is true, which were later to win him wide recognition among contemporary poets, but he was unable as yet to estimate their real value. Furthermore, the strain of composing them in the shred ends of time left over from his daily work and social life had taken a decided toll of his health. He was exhausted mentally and physically, which further aggravated the uric-acid condition from which he was suffering. Forgetting the distress of his previous unemployment, and again without any capital with which to support himself, he resigned his position with Sweet's Catalogues at the beginning of June, and once more fled to the country. As for the future—he was willing, he wrote the Rychtariks, to "trust to fate for something for a change from this deadly office routine that I have been under for five years. It was either that—or a complete breakdown."

It was again Slater Brown who offered Crane asylum, this time, however, in the foothills of the Berkshire Mountains near Patterson, New York, where he and his wife had bought a small primitive farmhouse. This locality, like Woodstock, soon became a popular retreat for the writers and artists of Crane's circle; by 1927, in fact, it had been named "transition valley" after the famous magazine in Paris to which most of them contributed. Since Mrs. Brown was no stranger to Crane's recurrent need of refuge, having extended him protracted hospitality the year before when she was still the wife of James Light, she and her husband were equally hearty in urging Crane to stay with them. For several weeks the three found more than enough to keep them busy from morning until night: there was an incessant round of house-painting, gardening, renovating, and carpentry that Crane entered into with great zest. The delight he took in such homely activities reflected the singular, almost child-like, simplicity which underlay the violent, distorted conditionings of his spirit and needed only the proper environment and sympathy to show itself in its natural purity. He reveled in the planting and growing of things, especially of flowers, whose shape and color and texture he would elaborate upon at great length. The endless painting of the house he found infinitely amusing; and as the old weather-worn shingles soaked up the paint, as bucket after bucket mysteriously disappeared into the warped and wizened sides of the building, his laughter swelled to Gargantuan proportions. Particularly childish was the delight he took in stealing cookies from the counter of the village store, claiming for himself the distinction of being the most successful "biscuit-snatcher" in the valley.

In the middle of July, however, an urgent letter from his mother summoned him to Cleveland. Their old home at 1709 East 115th Street had at last been sold, and his mother and grandmother needed his help in packing and disposing of the accumulated belongings of two generations. Crane left Patterson at once, and for the next eight weeks was engulfed in the turmoil of dismantling the Cleveland house and moving his mother and grandmother into an apartment. It was a somewhat painful experience, for in spite of his years the sense of insecurity still had the power to unnerve him. The house in Cleveland was, after all, the only home he could recall and had consequently become a symbol of security for him. Possibly he felt faint pulsive overtones of the abysmal sense of loss and isolation that had overwhelmed him when his parents first separated in Warren, and his small patch of world threatened to founder. Certainly he found no reassurance for his apprehensions in his mother's plans, for he learned that as soon as the moving had been accomplished, she intended to leave for Florida with the purpose of establishing some source of income by means of the real-estate boom in progress there. Her capital, which was also her mother's, had dwindled to such small proportions that she was seriously concerned about their future. In view of the apparently complete dissolution of his family, the gesture Crane made upon his return to the Browns' in September was not altogether surprising. Although he had scarcely enough money to pay his train fare from New York to Patterson, he opened negotiations immediately upon his arrival for the purchase of a piece of property from Miss Flynn, who owned a substantial acreage in that vicinity.

The twenty acres of land he selected were situated on the top slopes of a hill overlooking the valley and because of their inaccessibility and uncultivated condition were being offered to him for two hundred dollars. It was a considerable sum for a penniless and unemployed poet, but Crane, having lost one home, was determined to own property where he might in time build another. It hurt him more than he would willingly admit to think of his mother and grandmother without a home of their own, particularly since he had become accustomed to think of himself, somewhat quixotically, as responsible for their welfare. And his way of relieving his sense of guilt and insecurity was to purchase land and to imagine, with a license transparently poetic, a simple colonial cottage set down in the desolate hills where he and his womenfolk might pass their declining years. The plan was fantastic, but Crane mustered his most business-like vocabulary and wrote to his aunt, Mrs. Deming of Warren, Ohio, asking for a loan of two hundred and twenty-five dollars at six per cent interest to be repaid within five years. He received a kindly refusal, which sensibly suggested that land selling at ten dollars an acre must be lacking in desirable qualities and that he had better not undertake obligations he could ill afford. The advice was wasted, however, for he applied to his friends, the Rychtariks, who immediately sent him the necessary sum. Needless to say, the bright mirage of the cottage in the hills never materialized, though he owned the property for some time. Fortunately for him, Miss Flynn proved to be a sympathetic and generous person, and eventually he was able to return her the land in exchange for his original investment. Even the Rychtariks were reimbursed in the end; and Crane's attempt to establish a permanent anchorage came to a close.

Meanwhile, as a landed proprietor, he felt he ought to amass sufficient capital to pay his debts and entrench himself beyond the reach of adversities; and he began to think of returning to New York to look for work. But for two or three weeks he lingered on as the guest of the Browns, walking for miles in the hills, which were already beginning to burn with the smoky haze and flare of autumn, and helping to make gallons of ale, which were set to "ripen" in immense crocks on the hearth, or jugs of apple-jack distilled in the shack behind the house. It was not until October that he returned to the city, penniless as ever, to reassume possession of his room at 110 Columbia Heights, which had been rented by friends during his absence. The confidence he had felt in the healthful quiet of the country that he would find immediate employment vanished almost overnight before the monstrous mechanical indifference of the city. In the offices, which he had imagined with his usual optimism would be eager to receive him, he met only with rejections; and once again the humiliating round of petty borrowings began. By November he had imposed on his friends as far as his conscience would allow, and finally, swallowing his pride with some difficulty, he wrote to his father for help. Evidently, even then, he could not entirely conceal his resentment at having to admit his failure, for his father's reply reproved him sharply for asking his favors and insulting him in the same breath. "You cannot catch flies with vinegar," Mr. Crane replied; but added after a page of admonitions: "Anyway it is a check you want so I am enclosing you $50.00." Hart wrote an apologetic letter of thanks in return in which his growing sense of insecurity was pathetically evident:

"I feel rather strange these days. The old house in Cleveland sold; Grandmother ill in Florida; Mother somewhere in Cuba or the Isle of Pines; and I not hearing from either of them for the past month. Altogether, it's enough to make one feel a little footloose in the world. But I'll have a job soon, and will probably be reassured in the mail that everything's alright. At such times, though, I realize how few we are and what a pity it is that we don't mean a little more to each other."

His mother's long silence preyed on his mind constantly, until he finally came to the conclusion that she had abandoned him. The fearful expectancy of betrayal and persecution always seething within him invariably surged to the surface whenever, as now, circumstances seemed inflexibly cast against him, so that the slightest personal affront sufficed to provoke a torrential eruption of defiance, abuse, or self-pity. Thus, for several weeks he was convinced that his mother, disgusted by his failure to provide for himself, had decided to ignore him; and though he later learned she had been ill in a Miami hotel, it was not until he had extricated himself from his difficulties that he was willing to write her a somewhat bitter and chilling note. In the meantime, he could hardly call upon her for financial aid; and since his father's check had been little more than enough to repay his friends, he was again reduced to a beggarly existence.

Throughout November his efforts to find work were in vain. The one opening of which he heard during those weeks —that of deck yeoman on a South American steamer— had been filled by the time he had rushed across the river to the docks; and he returned to the city with the meager consolation of an "O.K." sign on his slip of application. The only unpublished poems he had on hand were two he had written during the summer: "Passage" and "The Wine Menagerie," both of which had been rejected by T. S. Eliot's London *Criterion*, and the former by *The Dial* as well. The only remaining hope was that *The Dial* might accept "The Wine Menagerie"; and after polishing a phrase here and there Crane dispatched it with fervent prayers to Marianne Moore, who was then the managing editor of the magazine.

With the incredible editorial presumption for which she was notorious—incredible since she herself was a meticulous poet —she replied that she would accept the poem provided that Crane agreed to certain changes she had made in it. Crane was outraged to find that the changes she insisted upon included a new title and a wholesale excision of stanzas and lines which left about half of the original poem; but his need of money was too desperate to be denied, and in despair he accepted the terms.

He had no sooner sold the poem, however, than he rushed to Josephson's house to report the incident and ask if something might yet be done to save the poem from the editorial slaughterhouse. Throughout the recital his depression increased, and having at last unburdened himself of his full bitterness, he ran into an adjoining room and throwing himself on the bed, wept steadily until he fell into a sleep of exhaustion. Although Josephson offered to buy the poem for the same sum that *The Dial* would pay and wrote to Miss Moore proposing the transaction, he was covered with confusion for his pains. At the last moment Crane disclaimed responsibility for his friend's action and refused to go back on his word to Miss Moore, who thereupon castigated Josephson for an impudent meddler. Even Kenneth Burke, who was then secretary to Scofield Thayer, another of the magazine's editors, became innocently involved in the turmoil and for his friendship with the offending parties was suspected of being a spy. In the end, "The Wine Menagerie," sadly dismembered, was printed under the innocuous title "Again." As Burke concisely expressed it, Miss Moore had taken all the Wine out of the Menagerie.

One disaster followed another with overwhelming misfortune. The last and most crushing blow fell at the end of the month when Crane's manuscript of *White Buildings* was rejected by Horace Liveright.

Throughout the fall months Eugene O'Neill and Waldo Frank had been besieging the publisher with pleas to publish the book; and for a time it seemed they had been successful, for Liveright agreed to accept the manuscript provided that O'Neill would lend the publicity of his name by writing a Foreword to the volume. This stipulation, however, had caused delays, and in the interim Liveright reconsidered and withdrew from the agreement. For Crane the disappointment was conclusive; he had placed his last hope of retrieving his fortunes in the certainty of an advance payment for the book. Now there seemed no solution for him short of the most desperate measures.

On the third of December he came to a sudden decision, and dropping all concealments of pride, wrote his father a letter. It was not a plea for money; their correspondence of late had been too full of bitter recriminations and criticisms to allow Hart the gesture of such complete humility; it was rather a confession of the extremity of his defeat and the means he was taking to save himself.

"For the last six weeks," he wrote, "I've been tramping the streets and being questioned, smelled, and refused in various offices. Most places didn't have any work to offer. I've stepped even out of my line as advertising copy writer, down to jobs as low as twenty-five per week, but to no avail. My shoes are leaky and my pockets are empty: I have helped to empty several other pockets also. In fact, I'm a little discouraged. This afternoon I am stooping to do something that I know plenty of others have done whom I respect, but which I have somehow always edged away from. I am writing a certain internationally known banker who recently gave a friend of mine five thousand dollars to study painting in Paris, and I'm asking him to lend me enough money to spend the winter in the country where it is cheap to live and where I can produce some creative work without grinding my brains through six sausage machines a day beforehand. If he refuses me, I shall either ask Eugene O'Neill, who is now writing the Foreword to my book and won't refuse me for some help to that end, or I'll take to the sea for awhile —for I'm certainly tired of the desolating mechanics of this office business, and it's only a matter of time, anyway, until I finish with it for good."

On the same day he wrote Otto Kahn a long letter in which he cited his achievements in the past and plans for the future; described the impossibility of attempting to write *The Bridge* under "crippling circumstances"; quoted a few comments on his poetry; and concluded by asking for a loan of one thousand dollars "at any rate of interest within six per cent," offering as security the five thousand dollars he would receive upon his grandmother's death. It was a concise and convincing letter, and Kahn was well known for his patronage of the arts; but Crane scarcely dared hope for a favorable response. Two days later, however, the mail brought him a note from the banker's secretary asking him to call at his home within the week. In the interim Kahn communicated with Waldo Frank and Eugene O'Neill, both of whom he knew personally; and acting with surprising promptness was prepared in advance to make Crane a very generous offer. On the momentous day of his appointment Crane made an intoxicated exit through the impressive portals of 1100 Fifth Avenue with a thousand dollars in his pocket and a guarantee of a thousand more to come in five-hundred-dollar installments. Life seemed suddenly to renew itself, branching with infinite possibilities into the fine flower of freedom; the landscape of the future was revealed like a valley of Eden, serene and fruitful for the creation of new poetry. After a few days of frenzied purchasing, packing, and celebrations dedicated to the enduring glory of his benefactor, Crane left for Patterson in a whirl of excitement.

~ VIII ~

*"In dusk it is at times as though this island lifted, floated
In Indian baths. . . ."*

THE place in Patterson that
became Crane's haven of refuge on this occasion, and thenceforth served him as a more or less permanent headquarters
was a large gaunt frame house whose ugliness was relieved
only by its location high in the hills along the New York
and Connecticut State border. Standing in spare isolation at
the crossing of two rocky and grass-tufted dirt roads, it
dominated the wide valley below and was chiefly to be recommended for its accessibility to the lively company of
writers and artists scattered obscurely in the crannies of the
surrounding slopes. One of the roads jogged away towards
what eventually became the Cowleys' place; the other fell
away in gullies to the village of Sherman, a few miles
distant, passing "Tory Hill," where Crane had lived with the
Browns several months before, and still farther the old white
house of Eleanor Fitzgerald of the Provincetown Players,
which would also in time become one of his temporary
homes. Climbing a knoll, it ran by the little clapboard chapel

where the painter, Peter Blume, lived for a while, and finally dropping down through the village led to another back road where the Josephsons and Robert Coateses made their homes.

The house itself belonged to Mrs. Addie Turner, a wrinkled and toothless widow of uncertain age, who with her cats and superannuated aunt occupied one half of the building, which became known as "my Aunt's part." The other half had been rented by Allen Tate and his wife, Caroline Gordon, the novelist, who, thinking to aid Crane in his distress, had offered to share their winter quarters with him. Otto Kahn's generosity had in no way altered Crane's decision to accept the invitation; and by the middle of December he was busy installing himself in the bedroom and study which had been allotted to him on the second floor of the house. With the meticulous, almost fussy concern over his surroundings which characterized his occupation of any new domicile, he spent the first weeks at Patterson in arranging his rooms to suit his taste. Many of the belongings that he had shipped to the Browns from Cleveland were brought over the hill to add to the décor. On the walls he hung a bright knitted shawl of his grandmother's, Congo wood carvings purchased at an art shop in Brooklyn, paintings by Sommers, and prints of Japanese and modern French painters. The gigantic sleigh bed was covered with patchwork quilts; and before long the remaining wall space was occupied from floor to ceiling by a bookcase that he built to receive the crates of books he had brought with him from the city. Besides decorating his rooms, it was necessary to prepare for the winter. He ordered boxes of canned goods from the city, as well as a pair of snowshoes; he joined Tate in chopping wood for their kitchen stove; he bought a new typewriter lest his old one break down during the imminent siege of snow, and to insure his fingers against the cramp of cold, invested still more money in a fifty-gallon oil-drum to supply the stove in his study with fuel.

By the time these preparations were completed the sub-zero weather of January was already slicing about the rickety windows of the house. For the next two months Crane and the Tates had all they could do to keep warm; the need of self-protection proved far greater than that of expression, and their creative activities congealed as quickly as the water in the pump. Their only diversion aside from conversation and occasional visits back and forth with the Browns, who were also spending the winter in the country, was reading. Among the books Crane had brought with him were several volumes intended to furnish him with material for *The Bridge*. There were Prescott's *Ferdinand and Isabella*, a book on Magellan, *The First Voyage of Columbus*, Melville's *White Jacket*, books on whaling and whaling vessels, as well as merchant clippers, Whitman's *Specimen Days*, and Whitehead's *Science and the Modern World*. That he studied some of these books exhaustively may be gathered from the exactness with which he reproduced Columbus's voyage when he came to compose the Ave Maria section of *The Bridge*. Not only did he take from it the conception of Columbus as a mystic in search of the terrestrial paradise, but he also described in his poetry many of the factual details of the voyage such as the eruption of the Peak of Teneriffe. Sometimes even the language of the navigator's *Journal* was incorporated into the verse, as in the instance where Crane altered "They scudded under bare poles" to "under bare poles scudding." He made a less successful alteration when, in recounting the heaving overboard of a wooden cask which contained records of the voyage, he changed the crucial word to "casque," doubtless thinking that the word for a metal helmet was simply an archaic and more poetic spelling of the word for barrel. In Crane it was a mistake like many others he made, readily understandable in view of his slight education. But the oversight on the part of his critics, who never noticed the blunder, furnished an amusing commentary on the scholastic discipline that he himself lacked. Even the Latin epigraph of the "Ave Maria," a quotation from Seneca prophesying the discovery of a new world, was taken from this book, where it was cited (and translated as well) as witness that Columbus had fulfilled an ancient destiny. In later years this epigraph became a source of embarrassment to Crane when the critic Max Eastman, in a cheap, journalistic essay published in *Harper's*, ridiculed him for being unable to translate the passage into English and undertook to prove that Crane, like other modern poets, deliberately tried to be unintelligible.

Although his reading did not excite him to any great creative activity, it did stimulate him to work out in more articulate detail the interrelated sections of *The Bridge*. It served to crystallize his intentions and attitudes, which had hitherto remained comfortably nebulous, and forced him to consider conscientiously, perhaps for the first time, the full implications of his subject. The prospect was not completely encouraging. He realized only too keenly the discrepancy between his own philosophical affirmations and the negative skepticism of his contemporaries. At times the arch of his faith groaned heavily under the weight of the current despair; and had its keystone not been set deeply and obscurely in his emotional nature, it would very likely have collapsed before his major work had been spanned. Even shut off from the world by the snowdrifts of Patterson, there was no escape from the spirit of the times. Whenever Crane and the Tates and Browns spent an evening together, the conversation inevitably turned to the question of the modern poet's dilemma, and they discussed in the terms of T. S. Eliot's poetry and criticism the lack of an adequate faith or hierarchy of values in society, its spiritual drought and intellectual desiccation. Or in the terms of Spengler, the other great prophet of despair, they argued the imminent decay of Western civilization, letting the cultures of previous ages run with terrifying eloquence through the hourglass of their discussion. In the presence of such continual spiritual suffocation it is little wonder that Crane retired more and more, with what seemed to his friends an overweening egoism, to the insular rock of his personal emotions, whence he could defy the popular apostasies of his time. However much he might oppose this *mal de siècle*, its arguments demonstrated all too clearly the difficulties that he would face in his undertaking. It was significant that when he was but barely over the threshold of *The Bridge* he voiced some of the very remarks that his critics made years later when it was finished.

"However bad this work may be," he wrote Munson during the winter, "it ought to be hugely and unforgivably, distinguishedly bad. In a way it's a test of materials as much as a test of one's imagination. *Is* the last statement sentimentally made by Eliot,

> 'This is the way the world ends,
> This is the way the world ends,—
> Not with a bang but a whimper.'

is this acceptable or not as the poetic determinism of our age! "I, of course, can say no, to myself, and believe it. But in the face of such a stern conviction of death on the part of the only group of people whose verbal sophistication is likely to take an interest in a style such as mine,—what can I expect? However, I know my way by now, regardless. I shall at least continue to grip with the problem without relaxing into the easy acceptance (in the name of 'elegance, nostalgia, wit, splenetic splendor') of death which I see most of my friends doing. O the admired beauty of a casuistical mentality! It is

finally content with twelve hours' sleep a day and archae-
ology."

By the end of March, despite the cold and a defective
stove, he had struggled through to a comparatively complete
synopsis of the poem which he estimated would take him a
year to fill out. In token of good faith he sent the somewhat
meager fruits of the winter to his benefactor.

"Roughly . . . it is based on the conquest of space and
knowledge," he wrote Kahn. "The theme of 'Cathay' (its
riches, etc.) ultimately is transmuted into a symbol of consciousness, knowledge, spiritual unity. A rather religious
motivation, albeit not Presbyterian. The following notation
is a very rough abbreviation of the subject matter of the
several sections:

I—Columbus—Conquest of space, chaos.
II—Pokahantus—The natural body of America—fertility,
etc.
III—Whitman—The spiritual body of America.
(A dialogue between Whitman and a dying soldier in
a Washington hospital; the infraction of physical
death, disunity, on the concept of immortality.)
IV—John Brown
(Negro porter on Calgary Express making up berths
and singing to himself (a jazz form for this) of his
sweetheart and the death of John Brown, alter-
nately.)
V—Subway—The encroachment of machinery on humanity; a kind of purgatory in relation to the open
sky of last section.
VI—The Bridge—A sweeping dithyramb in which the
Bridge becomes the symbol of consciousness spanning time and space."

Although the last section, which he had revised and expanded to approximately one hundred lines, was the only

one completed, the process of crystallization which had been taking place made him feel that he was ready to begin work in earnest. He was comfortably settled, the drifts were beginning to dwindle away in streams of water, and he was free of any financial worries. In fact, a successful introduction to the "Ave Maria" had already been written, when calamity fell upon the house of Mrs. Addie Turner.

The disaster was not the less decisive for being domestic. The seeds of dissension had been automatically sown when three people, all with the intention of writing, had installed themselves in six rooms of a house completely empty of modern conveniences for the duration of a snowbound winter. For a time the arrangement had been a happy one, but as the sense of novelty began to give place to a desire for privacy, impossible to achieve under such circumstances, an unpleasant tension became evident in the air. Since Crane was the most restless and effusive of the three, he was inevitably the chief offender. Unable to stay for long in his own rooms when he was not working, he stomped in and out of the Tates' quarters full of unwelcome hilarity and distraction. Equally unable to conform to any schedule of responsibilities, he soon began to neglect his kitchen duties, which led to ill-feeling between him and the Tates over the division of labor. This led to Crane's withdrawing from the communal cooking agreement to hire Mrs. Turner to cook for him in the kitchen on her side of the house. But since he continued to use the communal pump for washing and shaving and so had to pass through the Tates' kitchen, his noisy invasions were simply reduced in number but not in kind. After a few hints on the part of his victims, however, he also withdrew his shaving utensils to Mrs. Turner's pump, and for a time the severance of social relations was complete and a formality as chill as the frozen landscape prevailed over the house. But the damage had been done; the silence was heavy with the lowering humors of outrage and resentment, which finally erupted in an open quarrel over some trifling incident. Not trusting the medium of speech to express their grievances, the Tates wrote Crane two letters which they slipped beneath his door that night. Although these notes were meant to effect a general reform rather than a further estrangement, they contained the fatal error of admitting compassion as the Tates' original motive in inviting Crane to Patterson. This tactical blunder was sufficient to arouse Crane's latent feeling of persecution and betrayal. In view of his rage and humiliation the letter he wrote in reply to announce his immediate evacuation was admirably restrained, and even admitted to serious deficiencies in matters of taste and consideration for others.

The letter written to his mother on the same day, however, was a more true picture of his state of mind. For three long pages he unburdened himself, violently and bitterly, of his despair. "The whole benefit of my patronage from Kahn," he wrote, "my year of leisure, my long fight with the winter, etc. out here is about to be sacrificed"; there were hints that he might "settle it with powder and bullet"; or again that he might flee "perhaps to the orient, even if I have just enough money to get there and no more." It seemed to him, and consequently was, impossible to effect a reconciliation with the Tates; and the prospect of returning to New York to live, where he would be hounded by rumors and reflexes of the quarrel, appeared equally insupportable. To make matters worse, he had already spent the thousand dollars he had been given in December in settling himself at Patterson, and had just applied for, and received, another five hundred dollars from Kahn. Even this sum was not entirely available to him, for the Rychtariks were in urgent need of the money they had lent him to purchase land; when he had discharged his debt to them, he would have only three hundred dollars with which to contrive an escape. There was only one practical solution: once again the tropical island in the Caribbean appeared to him as the one perfect haven of peace and security; and this time he was not to be denied. He demanded of his mother, he implored her by whatever affection she had for him, that she allow him to occupy her plantation on the Isle of Pines. "At least," he concluded bitterly, "I should not have to fear being put off the little land that is still ours in the world."

Although his mother did not thoroughly approve of the plan, she recognized the extremity of his desperation and gave her permission. The little resistance she might have offered was overcome by her excitement in her own affairs, for she was hesitating on the verge of another marriage. It was suddenly decided that she and her fiancé, Mr. Charles Curtis of Cleveland, would join Hart in New York, where he was staying temporarily at the Hotel Albert, in order to be married before his departure for the island. During the few days at the end of April when they were all together there was a continual turmoil of excitement, including the wedding celebrations, packing, and last-minute farewells, which, added to the strain of the preceding weeks, brought Hart to a dangerous point of nervous tension. One night at the theater, when his mother offered some slight objection to his plans, he flew into a rage which disrupted the performance for several moments, till he had made his furious exit up the aisle. But the next morning Mrs. Crane received a dozen penitent roses, and on the heels of the messenger who brought them, Hart himself, haggard from a sleepless night, who flung himself on her and wept for forgiveness. Finally on the first day of May, Crane and Waldo Frank, whom he had invited to accompany him for a short visit, boarded the *S.S. Orizaba* and steamed out of the harbor towards a more peaceful country.

The five-day voyage to the island proved a great relief. As the ship plowed southward, entering the Gulf Stream and later the great blueness of the Caribbean, where his imagination had so often dwelt, Crane's spirits rose and gloried in the superb sea-scapes and sky-vistas. "There were cloud epics," he wrote to Stieglitz, "great jeremiads and götterdämmerungs, and 'distances cascading to the gulf' as Rimbaud puts it." The French poet, together with Melville, was constantly in his mind during the months in the tropics. The approach to the island recalled to him vividly the archipelagic voyages of *Mardi*, the wild mountains darkening over the violent green foliage and the blond thatched huts, and the off-shore wind heavy with the perfume of oleanders and mimosas. Among the strange bird cries that filled the air with clamor he noted one that made him "stop and blush," like the bird of Rimbaud's *Illuminations*. But he also felt the latent power coiled in the heavy atmosphere, the "strange challenge and combat in the air—offered by 'Nature' so monstrously alive in the tropics—which drains the psychic energies."

This oppressive sensation coupled with the heat kept him from accomplishing any writing during the first two months on the island. Immediately after their arrival, of course, there was no question of work; the days passed quickly enough in settling themselves on the plantation, exploring the surrounding country, bathing, and above all, in making the acquaintance of their housekeeper, Mrs. Simpson, the "little wrinkled burnous wisp that can do anything and remembers so much." Despite her chronic rheumatism and racking cough, which her parrot, Attaboy, imitated with pitiless accuracy, "Aunt Sally" presided over the establishment with indomitable energy, day by day exercising her tart vocabulary and tireless body against the endless ravages of tropical decay. Crane was at once seized with an admiration for her tough-minded wisdom and humor and her infinite courage, which by the time of his departure from the island had become a genuine love. The rest of the household consisted only of an indefinite number of scraggly chickens, harried by a tattered rooster, the same who was later christened Count Ferdinand after the Smollett novel, and Pythagoras, a baby owl that Crane and Frank adopted. Beyond the confines of the plantation there were few distractions. The village of Nueva Gerona was a sleepy and slovenly place where one went only for the mail or a few solitary drinks; and the American colony was a small hard-working group of people, too busy with their groves to find social diversions necessary.

It might have been expected, then, that Crane would plunge into his work as soon as Frank left the island towards the end of May. He did, in fact, make an attempt to resume writing on the Ave Maria section,—"to mend the sails so beautifully slit by the Patterson typhoon," but in vain. Thereafter he busied himself with chores about the plantation, uprooting dead orange trees, planting young royal palms, repairing the rotted fences and posts. In June he made another effort to rouse himself from his creative lethargy, this time by taking a fortnight trip on a sixty-foot schooner to the island of Grand Cayman one hundred and fifty miles to the south, whose beauties he had heard praised excessively. In many ways the voyage might have been a success. There were: "acres of man-sized leaping porpoises (the 'Huzza Porpoises' so aptly named in *Moby Dick*) that greet you in tandems (much like M. & Mme. Lachaise if you have ever seen them out walking together) and truly 'arch and bend the horizons.' One enormous shark, a White-Fin, lounged alongside for a while." But Crane found that a more prominent feature of the trip was the thirty-five Negroes who crowded almost every inch of deck-space, making it impossible to find a place to be alone—"unless one could brave the stinks and fumes of a dozen odd sick and wailing nigger females below decks. Most of these never emerged from their hole there during the entire voyage, but pots, bowls, basins, fruit-peelings and a thousand shrieks and wails were raised up every hour of the day and night to be emptied on the deck, my nose and ears being kept busy, I can tell you!" The nine days on the island itself were a purgatory of savage mosquitoes, against which he had to keep "smudge fires burning incessantly in my room while I lunged back and forth, smiting myself all over like one in *rigor mortis* and smoke gouging salty penance from my eyes." Even the return trip, during which they were becalmed under a blazing sun for two days on "water like a blinding glassy gridiron," proved to be a nightmare. The only thoroughly enjoyable part of the adventure, ironically enough, was Melville's *Moby Dick*, which he read for the third time during the agonizing days in Grand Cayman.

The net result of his search for stimulation was that for the following three weeks he could do no work at all because of the painful abscesses which developed in both ears from the prolonged exposure to the sun. After a hasty visit to a doctor in Havana, he resigned himself to a period of convalescent reading. Unfortunately, he chose Spengler's *Decline of the West* as his chief intellectual fare, a book hardly calculated to arouse an artist to creative fervor. Significantly, Crane was immune to the philosophical pessimism of contemporary thought only when actually writing. During the interims of creative inactivity he was often engulfed in an abysmal void of uncertainty which undermined even his belief in his past achievements; at such times not one tenet of faith nor a single line of poetry was proof against the overwhelming corruption of doubt. It was hardly surprising that after a week or two of immersion in the baths of Spenglerian despair Crane should write Frank letters which read like admissions of complete defeat.

"At times," he confessed, "it seems demonstrable that Spengler is quite right. At present I'm writing nothing—would that I were an efficient factory of some kind! It was unfortunate in a way to have been helped by our friend, the banker,—with my nose to the grindstone of the office I could still fancy that freedom would yield me a more sustained vision; now I know that much has been lacking all along. This is less personal than it sounds. I think that the artist more and more licks his own vomit, mistaking it for the common diet. He amuses himself that way in a culture without faith and convictions—but he might as well be in elfin land with a hop pipe in his mouth. . . . No, the bridge isn't very flambouyant these days."

The next day, overcome by remorse at the violence of these sentiments, he composed a second letter, apologizing for his "crudity" and analyzing the reasons for his state of mind with considerable restraint. It was but the more incriminatory, however, for it exposed the dangerous conflict in him between a rational skepticism and an inspired idealism upon which his life and work were so precariously poised.

"Emotionally I should like to write the Bridge," he wrote in summary; "intellectually judged the whole theme and project seems more and more absurd. A fear of personal impotence in this matter wouldn't affect me half so much as the convictions that arise from other sources. . . . I had what I thought were authentic materials that would have been a pleasurable-agony of wrestling, eventuating or not in perfection,—at least being worthy of the most supreme efforts I could muster.

"These 'materials' were valid to me to the extent that I presumed them to be (articulate or not) at least organic and active factors in the experience and perceptions of our common race, time, and belief. The very idea of a bridge, of course, is a form peculiarly dependent on such spiritual convictions. It is an act of faith besides being a communication. The symbols of reality necessary to articulate the span may not exist where you expected them, however. By which I mean that however great their subjective significance to me is concerned—these forms, materials, dynamics are simply nonexistent in the world. I may amuse and delight and flatter myself as much as I please—but I am only evading a recognition and playing Don Quixote in an immorally conscious way.

"The form of my poem rises out of a past that so overwhelms the present with its worth and vision that I'm at a loss to explain my delusion that there exist any real links between that past and a future destiny worthy of it. The 'destiny' is long since completed, perhaps the little last section of my poem is a hangover echo of it—but it hangs suspended somewhere in ether like an Absalom by his hair. The bridge as a symbol today has no significance beyond an economical approach to shorter hours, quicker lunches, behaviourism and toothpicks. And inasmuch as the bridge is a symbol of all such poetry as I am interested in writing it is my present fancy that a year from now I'll be more contented working in an office than before. . . . All this does not mean," he concluded in a grim postscript, "that I have resigned myself to inactivity. A bridge will be written in some kind of style and form, at worst it will be something as good as advertising copy. After which I will have at least done my best to discharge my debt to Kahn's kindness."

In view of such devastating analyses of the very essence of his poem it is little less than amazing that Crane could resume work on it within a few weeks with all his old gusto. The explanation lay in the fact that believing poetry to be ultimately a kind of revelation, he could ignore the most convincing arguments of logic once he was possessed by the divine madness. Fortunately for him the moment of "possession" was almost at hand. It was hastened undoubtedly by the arrival of news from Frank, so much more effective than spiritual sympathy or advice, that Horace Liveright had at last accepted *White Buildings* for publication. Though the publisher had rejected the book the preceding autumn, Crane's friends had not despaired of winning him over. Both O'Neill and Frank, as well as James Light, who had just directed the famous production of *Hamlet* in modern dress at Liveright's invitation, besieged him with persuasions throughout the winter and spring. Again Liveright's stipulation that O'Neill write a Foreword to the book almost thwarted their hopes a second time, for the playwright, despite his intense admiration for Crane's poetry, could not produce intelligible criticism. The impasse was finally resolved when Tate, who had heard of the difficulties, sent word from Patterson that he would gladly write the Foreword and allow it to be published under O'Neill's name. The offer was accepted and Liveright announced himself content if O'Neill would simply write a "blurb" for the cover jacket of the book. Needless to say, the Foreword appeared under the author's own name, and when Crane eventually heard of the fine generosity of Tate's original suggestion, he was deeply moved and wrote him a delicate note of gratitude, which tacitly relegated their quarrel to the limbo of unpleasant accidents.

Enclosed with the letter from Liveright accepting the book for publication in the fall was an advance payment of one hundred dollars, which came as a great relief to Crane's dwindling resources. His anxiety over his financial condition had already driven him to write Miss Flynn in Patterson asking her to return him the two hundred dollars in exchange for the land he had bought from her. His capital was further swelled not only by this sum, which was remitted to him with admirable graciousness, but also by the sale of several poems. Four of the "Voyages" had been published in the spring number of *The Little Review;* Edgell Rickword, the English biographer of Rimbaud, had accepted "Praise for an Urn," "Passage," and "At Melville's Tomb" for publication in the London *Calendar;* and Marianne Moore had printed "Repose of Rivers" in *The Dial.* Knowing Miss Moore's fondness for animals of all kinds, Crane had written the poem with an eye to pleasing her in particular, and had achieved eminent success. "This time," he wrote Brown, "she didn't even suggest running the last line backward."

With such good fortune and a complete restoration of health to stimulate him, all the nightmarish doubts of the preceding weeks melted away before a new radiance. "I feel an absolute music in the air again, and some tremendous rondure floating somewhere," he wrote Frank towards the end of July, and enclosed with his letter the final version of the "Proem" to *The Bridge*, which he had just completed. Two days later he dispatched another letter to Frank along with the greater part of the "Ave Maria," to which he had at last returned.

"My plans are soaring again," he wrote, "the conception swells. Furthermore this Columbus is REAL. In case you read it—(I *can't* be serious)—observe the water-swell rhythm that persists until the Palos reference. Then the absolute and marked intimation of the great *Te Deum* of the court, later held,—here in the terms of C's own cosmography."

In Columbus's prayer at the close of the "Ave Maria" Crane achieved the full organ-like diapason of some of his greatest poetry.

O Thou who sleepest on Thyself, apart
Like ocean athwart lanes of death and birth,
And all the eddying breath between dost search
Cruelly with love thy parable of man,—
Inquisitor! incognizable Word
Of Eden and the enchained Sepulchre,
Into thy steep savannahs, burning blue,
Utter to loneliness the sail is true.

Who grindest oar, and arguing the mast
Subscribest holocaust of ships, O Thou
Within whose primal scan consummately
The glistening seignories of Ganges swim;—
Who sendest greeting by the corposant,
And Teneriffe's garnet—flamed it in a cloud,
Urging through night our passage to the Chan;—
Te Deum laudamus, for thy teeming span!

  . . . . . .

White toil of heaven's cordons, mustering
In holy rings all sails charged to the far
Hushed gleaming fields and pendant seething wheat
Of knowledge,—round thy brows unhooded now
—The kindled Crown! acceded of the poles
And biassed by full sails, meridians reel
Thy purpose—still one shore beyond desire!
The sea's green crying towers a-sway, Beyond

And kingdoms
    naked in the
        trembling heart—
 Te Deum laudamus
      O Thou Hand of Fire

Within a week another letter: "I feel as though I were
dancing on dynamite these days—so absolute and elaborated
has become the conception. All sections moving forward

now at once! I didn't realize that a bridge is begun from the two ends at once. . . ."

Throughout the month of August one poem followed another, later versions tripped on the heels of earlier ones, in breathless and magnificent haste. After revising "Atlantis" once more, he composed the three short pieces: "Southern Cross," "National Winter Garden," and "Virginia," which he later sold to the *Calendar*. Then he plunged into one of the long sections of the poem and one of the most impressive, "The Dance," in which he became identified with the Indian life of the continent and anticipated the conquest of the race by the white man. "Lie to us," he cried, "—dance us back the tribal morn!"

> Spears and assemblies: black drums thrusting on—
> O yelling battlements,—I, too, was liege
> To rainbows currying each pulsant bone:
> Surpassed the circumstance, danced out the siege!
>
> And buzzard-circleted, screamed from the stake;
> I could not pick the arrows from my side.
> Wrapped in that fire, I saw more escorts wake—
> Flickering, sprint up the hill groins like a tide.
>
> I heard the hush of lava wrestling your arms,
> And stag teeth foam about the raven throat;
> Flame cataracts of heaven in seething swarms
> Fed down your anklets to the sunset's moat.
>
> O, like the lizard in the furious noon,
> That drops his legs and colors in the sun,
> —And laughs, pure serpent, Time itself, and moon
> Of his own fate, I saw thy change begun!
>
> And saw thee dive to kiss that destiny
> Like one white meteor, sacrosanct and blent
> At last with all that's consummate and free
> There, where the first and last gods keep thy tent.

At the same time he was working on "The Tunnel," recalling vividly and strangely in his Caribbean exile the violent phantasmagoria of the metropolitan life he had known so well. "It's rather ghastly, almost surgery," he wrote Frank;—"and, oddly almost all from the notes and stitches I have written while swinging on the strap at late midnights going home." With an amazing dexterity of imagination he was able to skip from one section to another, "like a sky-gack or a girder-jack," evidently without experiencing the slightest difficulty in shifting his attention through a series of widely disparate subjects. He was also writing "Cutty Sark," a derelict sailor's drunken fantasy of clipper ships in a waterfront dive, which was arranged as a fugue of two parts: the voice of the world of time and that of eternity.

"The Atlantis theme," he wrote, "(Eternity or the Absolute) is the transmuted voice of the nickel-in-the-slot piano, and this voice alternates with that of the derelict sailor and the description of the action. It is into this Absolute that the finale to the whole poem (Atlantis) projects at the close of the book."

> Rose of Stamboul O coral Queen—
> teased remnants of the skeletons of cities—
> and galleries, galleries of watergutted lava
> snarling stone—green—drums—drown—

> Sing!
> "—that spiracle!" he shot a finger out the door. . . .
> "O life's a geyser—beautiful—my lungs—
> No—I can't live on land—!"

> I saw the frontiers gleaming of his mind;
> or are there frontiers—running sands sometimes
> running sands—somewhere—sands running. . . .
> Or they may start some white machine that sings.

Then you may laugh and dance the axletree—
steel—silver—kick the traces—and know—

> ATLANTIS ROSE *drums wreathe the rose,*
> *the star floats burning in a gulf of tears*
> *and sleep another thousand—*

By the end of August he had written three-quarters of
The Bridge in comparatively final form, as well as several
shorter pieces: "O Carib Isle," "The Idiot," "The Air
Plant," "Royal Palm," and others included in the section of
his *Collected Poems* entitled "Key West." The production
of poetry during the single month seems almost incredible,
not only in its quantity, which was sufficient in itself to be
startling, but also in the rich variety of subject and style
and the sustained energy of inspiration. The "Proem," "Ave
Maria," "Cutty Sark," and "The Dance" must all be considered among the most perfectly conceived and executed sections of *The Bridge;* in them Crane was more completely the
master of his subject matter than in any other part of the poem
excepting "The River." Such a brilliant achievement had
not been attained, however, without complete exhaustion. In
September he abruptly stopped writing; the period of "possession" had run its course, taking heavy toll of his energy.
The tension of creative excitement had been so great that for
several weeks he had been unable to sleep for more than a
very few hours each night. Even then he could not sink into
complete unconsciousness, but remained in a state that wavered like water-changes between sleep and waking while his
imagination incessantly spun gossamers of words, textures
of language scarcely more palpable than light, and more
elusive. Added to the insomnia of the nights was the intense
unbroken heat of the day, which the natives calculated to be
the worst in several years. Such annoyances had gone un-

noticed in the intoxication of writing; but now they proved intolerable.

In search of relaxation and physical comfort he left the island for Havana with the improbable idea that after a short time he would be able to resume writing with the same success. For a week he abandoned himself to the pleasant diversions of the gay and colorful city, enjoying the bathing, the fine wines and food, the rich cigars, and not least, the bawdy performances at the Alhambra, Havana's equivalent of the National Winter Garden Burlesque in New York, where he had spent so many hilarious nights. But his funds were not proof against more than a few days of such indulgences, especially since the companionship of a Cuban sailor during much of the time doubled the already heavy expenses. Upon his return to the plantation, in fact, his little capital was so depleted that he wrote at once to Kahn asking for another five hundred dollars, which would complete the payment of the two thousand dollars originally promised him. Early in July when he had been so despairing of his work, he had resolved not to apply to his benefactor for the rest of the subsidy unless a renascence of activity should justify it. Now with the greater part of *The Bridge* finished, he was able to make application for it with a clear conscience. "I can warn you," he wrote, "albeit with no excess of modesty, that the poem is already an epic of America, incomplete as it is. And it is well worth the faith which you have so kindly volunteered,—a little of which on the part of my father, who still stubbornly sulks, would also be welcome." Kahn, however, was traveling about the country, and did not receive the letter until the middle of October.

In the meantime Crane's elation gradually suffocated under the persistent heat. For several weeks he waited for his inspiration to return, hoping to be caught up again into a creative excitement that would carry him through to the completion of the poem. But there was no "absolute music" to be heard throughout the heavy oppressive air, only the maddening monotone of innumerable insects shrilling day and night like the incessant crazy pulse of a fever. At first he passed the time in reading and studying Spanish; but as his restlessness grew on him, he was unable to remain quiet despite the heat, and wandered about the house, now pounding out the few tunes he knew on the old piano, now playing his victrola records, finally to rush into the town to spend the afternoon drinking beer and talking with the bartender. Soon his insomnia returned to deprive him of what little relief he found in sleep from the heat and the torments of impatience. Even the veronal powders he took were only partially effective, and left him limp the following day. With the second week of October he reached the limit of his endurance and determined to quit the island as soon as possible despite his original plan to pass the winter there. In desperation he wrote again to Kahn begging him to cable the money at once if he had not already done so.

"You can see the situation is a little harrowing," he wrote, "especially as I am ill, entirely without funds, and need to get to a cooler locality. The summer here according to the natives has been the hottest in twenty years. With my work on my mind (of which I have done considerable) and the pestilence of heat and insects, I'm completely exhausted."

Before there was time for the mails to bring a reply to the letter, a howling cataclysm of wind and rain broke loose over the Caribbean. As though Nature itself were no longer able to endure the heat or contain the sullen accumulation of its resentment, there came a pause pregnant with profound anger and malevolence, a sinister silence in which the elements withdrew in coils of electric rage to generate the extreme voltage of insane violence. The hurricane struck with the impact of a solid wall of water, as though the ocean had been upended to the sky and again hurled down. Gigantic palms hurtled like tenpins before the wind, chicken-coops and roofs whirled like dervishes through the air, animals were flattened out or impaled on broken walls; nothing withstood the fury of the storm. The Hart plantation was no exception. When Crane and Mrs. Simpson crawled out from beneath the bed that had served as a hurricane-cellar, they found little left of the house but its framework and a mass of débris. Crane, however, was almost drunk with excitement and the exaltation of the storm, as though he had recognized in its unleashed violence and destruction a counterpart of his own rages, which towered in him from time to time like a sudden insanity. In spite of the devastation about them he was seized with a mood of crazy joy, and digging out his victrola from the wreckage together with one of the unbroken discs, he turned on a popular jazz tune of the day; then balancing a sodden pillow on his head and proffering another to Mrs. Simpson—who, nothing daunted, followed his lead—he whirled her off in a one-step. But later they investigated the death and desolation in the town and finally returned to the bungalow somewhat sobered, to salvage what they could of their belongings.

We shoveled and sweated; watched the ogre sun
Blister the mountain, stripped now, bare of palm,
Everything—and lick the grass, as black as patent
Leather, which the rimed white wind had glazed.
Everything gone—or strewn in riddled grace—
Long tropic roots high in the air, like lace.
And somebody's mule steamed, swaying right by the pump,
Good God! as though his sinking carcass there
Were death predestined! You held your nose already
Along the roads, begging for buzzards, vultures. . . .

The mule stumbled, staggered. I somehow couldn't budge
To lift a stick for pity of his stupor.

After several days spent in helping Mrs. Simpson to settle
in a habitable place and another day or two talking to the
sailors and marines in the town, who had been sent down
by the government to aid in the reconstruction work, Crane
was ready to leave the island. The "little land that is still
ours in the world" had almost been torn from under him;
but it had served its purpose in part. Towards the end of
October Mrs. Simpson lent him enough money to pay his
passage north, and with the manuscript of *The Bridge* in
his luggage he set sail for New York.

~ IX ~

"Dawn's broken arc! the noon's more furbished room!
Yet seldom was there faith in the heart's right kindness.
There were tickets and alarm clocks. There were counters
and schedules. . . ."

From the time he returned to New York in the fall of 1926 to his departure for Europe in 1928, Crane's life followed an increasingly erratic and painful course. Only one month out of the twenty-four brought a revival of the tremendous creative drive he had experienced on the Isle of Pines; the rest were consumed in despair and doubt and anxiety. Driven on the one hand by the obligation to earn his own living, and on the other, by the desperate desire to finish *The Bridge*, he vacillated between subsidized retirement in the country and respectable employment in the city. When he received from Kahn the five hundred dollars that had failed to reach him in the Caribbean and went to live in Patterson, his conscience tormented him with his choice. During the idle winter months it accused him of irresponsibility, tortured him with guilt: Worst of all, it held up a constant mirror to the future which showed closing in on him the blind fog of his insoluble dilemma. Had he been able to make progress with *The Bridge*, these terrors would have vanished. But this failing, his life began to disintegrate under the pressure of the old irreconcilables. Unable to endure the reproaches of his conscience, he eventually abandoned his original choice and returned to the city, only to be harried by the specter of *The Bridge* still unfinished, his reason for being still unjustified. His irresolution grew upon him, his shuttling back and forth between New York and Patterson became more frequent, more frenzied. In his drunken rages he stormed about shouting that he was "caught like a rat in a trap," a cry that from sheer repetition came to be almost a burlesque of his extreme distress, a signal to his friends that Crane was "off" again. And in his anguish he turned more and more for relief to the blind alleys of alcoholic and sexual debauchery, wilfully seeking escape in the most brutal degradations.

Inextricably involved in this impasse was his concern for his mother's welfare. With apprehension and despair he had noted the first signs of marital unhappiness in the letters she had sent him during the past summer, marking the rising note of hysteria which he knew from former experience meant a siege of nervous disorders. He had no sooner established himself at Patterson in November than he received a letter from Mr. Curtis saying that he was suing for a divorce. His mother instituted a counter-suit and the following spring she was awarded the decision with permission to resume her former name.

In the meantime, as Hart had anticipated, the legal proceedings proved too much of a strain for her. Her letters reported a constant state of poor health; she was again without a home of her own; and the care of her mother, whose advanced age made her quite helpless, added substantially to her difficulties. In many ways the situation recalled to

Hart the painful period in 1917 when he and his mother were living in New York after her divorce from his father. But now he felt, for the first time, a growing resentment of the bond that had the power to disturb him so profoundly.

"I don't want you to think," he wrote her, "that you haven't my sympathy these days. You don't know how horribly upset I am—and have been for many months. I could hardly withhold my sympathies from you—no matter how much I might disagree with you on the question of your judgment etc. which brought about the present state of affairs. Affection is something that overrules reason always and I suffer with you much more than you think. . . . For the present we will have to be separated. I can't even get enough money together to get to Cleveland at present. And what would I do when I got there! It takes weeks to get work, you know that. If I can get anything in N. Y. I'll send you something from that. I'm trying as best I can to get a connection."

Like other difficulties he was unable to cope with, his mother's distress became a kind of indictment accusing him of moral weaknesses and reminding him of his own precarious status as a dependent on the generosity of others. He wanted desperately to be of some help, and did manage, once, to send a small sum of money home; but he clearly recognized his helplessness. "In the long ponderings—sometimes very painful, that I've gone through lately," he wrote his grandmother bitterly, "I don't see how I am, or can be, much good to anyone." His resentment was also rooted in more selfish reasons, however.

"I don't want to do anything to hurt *anyone*'s feelings," he wrote the Rychtariks in November, "but I think that unless I isolate myself somewhat (and pretty soon) from the avalanche of bitterness and wailing that has flooded me ever since I was seven years old, there won't be enough left of me to breathe, not to mention writing."

He recognized, in short, that because of his peculiar susceptibility to any suffering on his mother's part—a condition acquired perhaps during the nights he had stood beside her bed as a child—he could not sympathize too deeply with her without being himself victimized by emotional disorders. Accordingly, he was driven in self-defense to asserting his own problems against hers, matching her grievances and sufferings with those of his own.

"Insomnia seems now to have settled on me permanently," he wrote her in December, "and when I do 'sleep' my mind is plagued by an endless reel of pictures, startling and unhappy—like some endless cinematograph. I am making as much effort as possible to free my imagination and work the little time that is now left me on my Bridge poem. So much is expected of me via that poem that if I fail on it I shall become a laughing stock and my career closed.

"I take it that you would not wish this to happen. Yet it may be too late already for me to complete the conception. My mind is about as clear as dirty dishwater—and such a state of things is scarcely conducive to successful creative endeavor. If it were like adding up a column of figures—or more usual labors—it would be different. . . . Well, I'm trying my best—both to feel the proper sentiments to your situation and keep on with my task. *The Bridge* is an important task—and nobody else can ever do it."

Whatever the reason, whether anxiety for his mother or more esoteric psychological factors, he was unable to resume writing. Certainly his outward circumstances were favorable enough. There were none of the social distractions and disturbances of the previous winter, for both the Browns and the Tates were living in the city; and he was alone except for Mrs. Turner, who daily forsook her "Aunt's part" of the house to do his cooking and housekeeping. Furthermore, it might have been expected that the publication of *White Buildings* in December would stimulate a renascence of creative excitement; but he received its appearance with comparative apathy. He was robbed of his major triumph in its publication in that his family, for whom he had hoped it would stand as a vindication of his life, were too overwhelmed by their own personal troubles to appreciate its full importance. His mother and grandmother were the only ones in Cleveland to write him their congratulations, and their letters describing the reading of the book at the Garretsville Federated Women's Clubs made him roar with laughter. But his father, whom he had wished to impress more than all the others, was silent. Hart sent him several letters enclosing clippings of laudatory reviews without receiving any reply. Finally he was seized by the fear that his father's old contempt for him had returned, and wrote to his mother in a rage of resentment.

"For a long time he has seemed to me as thorough a specimen of abnormality as I have ever heard of. . . . He probably likes to build up the picture that he is creeping around in utter disgrace on account of the public 'disgrace' his son has made of himself. Well, the thirty thousand people that read the *New Republic* probably wouldn't give him much sympathy—regardless of their estimate of my particular value."

Even when he heard that Mr. Crane's second wife had just died after a tragic illness, he remained convinced that his father's silence expressed only ridicule; and it was not until he saw him in April, during a visit with his mother in Cleveland, that he was reassured of his good will.

Although the actual publication of the book did little to counteract his depression of mind, his spirits began to rise with the appearance of reviews and notices in the press. This is not to say that *White Buildings* galvanized the literary world and brought him Byronic fame. On the contrary, it did not even win in most instances the distinction of a column to itself, but was mentioned in passing together with other volumes of current poetry. Whenever it was singled out for particular criticism, more often than not the critic ridiculed its obscurity, quarrelled with Tate's analysis of the poetry in the Foreword, or attacked the "cult" of Crane admirers who advanced his work as "the most distinguished poetry of the age." In the Literary Supplement of the *New York Herald Tribune* Genevieve Taggard maintained that Crane was unable to write an actual poem, and scoffed at "his mannered obscurity, his slightly faked sonority." In *The Dial* Conrad Aiken accused him of "what one might call high class intellectual fake"; and the critic of *The Saturday Review of Literature* sarcastically confessed that he could scarcely understand the Foreword, not to mention the poetry itself. Other reviewers, like Mark Van Doren in *The Nation*, with more sensibility and less prejudice, recognized the distinction and power of the work while confessing at the same time to an imperfect understanding of its meaning. Indeed, the only critics who praised the book with forthright conviction were Waldo Frank with his article in *The New Republic*, Yvor Winters in Harriet Monroe's *Poetry*, and Allen Tate, whose Introduction to the volume was an acute critical essay. Without hesitation, almost without qualification, these men ranked Crane among the greatest living poets, as one of the few important American poets of all time, and compared his work freely with that of Whitman, Marlowe, Rimbaud, and Melville.

In the act of praising him, however, they unwittingly did him a subtle, but nonetheless serious, disservice. Doubtless hoping to anticipate the stones of the philistines, they not only admitted the difficulty of Crane's poetry, they even belabored it with attention in an effort to explain and justify it until, indeed, it almost seemed that Genevieve Taggard might have been right when she unpleasantly remarked that what Crane needed most was to be rescued from his admirers. Frank was eager to interpret the obscurity in terms of Crane's mysticism, and incorporated in his review a diagram which he described in the language of Kantian metaphysics; while Tate with scrupulous care defined Crane's method of composition as "oblique" and gave an exegesis of it which, however brilliant, had the unfortunate effect of exaggerating its difficulty and distracting the reader's attention from the poetry itself. But more importantly, their painstaking analyses of the obscurity of the verse led them to focus upon its weaknesses—the strain of its vision and its disintegration into isolated sensations—which in turn indicated, by implication at least, similar faults in Crane himself. From this point there remained but one step to take before arriving at a criticism of the poetry in terms of the poet's personal life, using his moral vices to explain his artistic failures. This was a mistake that Tate was in no danger of making since even in the Foreword to *White Buildings* he had decried the tendency of modern criticism to confuse the values of art with those of "moral and social aspirations." Nor was Frank any more likely to slip into this error. But Winters, whose conception of poetry was deeply rooted in ethical dogmas, was decidedly susceptible to such entanglements, and undertook to lecture Crane privately on the shortcomings not only of his poetry but also of his character—a dangerous task, since knowing him only by correspondence, he was completely ignorant of the details of his personal life.

Despite his intense admiration for Crane's poetry, which had led him a few months earlier to open the correspondence between them, Winters came to the conclusion that the flaw in his work was due to its almost exclusively metaphysical bias, which, he stated with evangelical dogmatism, was simply an effort to escape the full responsibilities of life. His own alternative, which he urged upon Crane as the ideal that would bring his poetry to its highest pitch of perfection, was the conception of the poet as "the complete man," respectably employed, holding a normal position in society, actively cognizant of moral obligations, and freely participating in the various departments of living. This was an ideal he shared in common with the critic, Edmund Wilson, who had just written an article for *The New Republic*, attacking several contemporary poets, including Crane, for their unintelligibility and evasion of social responsibilities. But however admirable an objective this was, Crane had long since recognized the impossibility of himself ever achieving it. He was only too keenly aware of the deficiencies of temperament and training that crippled his life; in fact, it was his hypersensitive consciousness of them that made him so painfully susceptible to fantasies of persecution and betrayal. Winters's letter with its evangelical fervor and lack of imagination struck heavily at the very heart of his tragic dilemma; even its unfortunate reference to the homosexual artist, Leonardo da Vinci, as a type of the "incomplete man," seemed contrived by fate to add insult to injury. The violence of Crane's reply bore sufficient witness to the effect of the criticism.

In answer to Winters's attack on the metaphysical character of his work he had little to say. If he were a metaphysical poet, he wrote, he was content to remain one, despite the critics who, when faced with such poetry, "immediately close their eyes or stare with utter complacency at the page —assuming that black is black no more and that the poet means anything but what he says." The criticism of Leonardo's sexual nature as a serious limitation on his work, however, aroused him to angry protest, all the more savage for fear it might possibly be true. "One doesn't have to turn to homosexuals," he wrote, "to find instances of missing sensibilities. Of course I'm sick of all this talk about b . . . s and c . . . s in criticism. It's obvious that b . . . s are needed, and that Leonardo had 'em—at least the records of the Florentine prisons, I'm told, say so." But he vented the full flood of his indignation on the assumption that the poet in order to become a "complete man," and consequently a greater artist, needed only to make a modicum of effort to be immediately rewarded with that distinction. All the bitter experience of a lonely childhood, a distorted adolescence, and a maturity harried by unemployment and the fear of insecurity, isolated by an indifferent society to the precarious periphery of life without any compensation but his own spirit: all the experience of his twenty-eight years rebelled against such facile precepts.

"You need a good drubbing," he wrote Winters, "for all your recent easy talk about the 'complete man,' the poet and his ethical place in society, etc. . . . Wilson's article was just half-baked enough to make one warm around the collar. It is so damned easy for such as he, born into easy means, graduated from a fashionable university into a critical chair overlooking Washington Square, etc. to sit tight and hatch little squibs of advice to poets not to be so 'professional' as he claims they are, as though all the names he had just mentioned had been as suavely nourished as he—as though 4 out of 5 of them hadn't been damned well forced the major part of their lives to grub at *any* kind of work they could manage by hook or crook and the fear of hell to secure! Yes, why not step into the State Dpt. and join the diplomatic corps for a change! indeed, or some other courtly occupation which would bring you into wide and active contact with world affairs! As a matter of fact I'm all too ready to concede that there are several other careers more engaging to follow than that of poetry. But the circumstances of one's birth, the conduct of one's parents, the current economic structure of society and a thousand other local factors have as much or more to say about successions to such occupations, the naïve volitions of the poet to the contrary. I agree with you, of course, that the poet should in as large a measure as possible adjust himself to society. But the question always will remain as to how far the conscience is justified in compromising with the age's demands."

The question of the poet's relation to society was a subject that Crane could rarely discuss without rage and bitterness. In fact, one of the obsessive ideas which, like that of being caught in a trap, haunted his mind increasingly was that there was no longer any place in the world for a poet. Moreover, Winters's letter had arrived at a very unfortunate time; for Crane was depressed by the realization that in spite of subsidies, the publication of a book, and the reputation of being one of the greatest living poets, his position was still as anomalous and insecure as ever. It was already May, and having spent the money received from Kahn in November, he was faced with the prospect of another harrowing period of job-hunting and a summer of mechanical office routine in the city. At the last minute, however, he was saved from that particular purgatory by the generosity of his father, who for the first time offered to provide him with an allowance, amounting to fifty dollars a month, which he calculated would enable Hart to pay his expenses in the country. Possibly because of a dawning recognition of his son's achievement, but more probably because of his loneliness after his wife's death and his discouragement in the gradual decline of his business, a more affectionate relationship grew up between Mr. Crane and Hart during the latter's visit to Cleveland in April. Mr. Crane, indeed, seems to have wanted to establish some kind of home with his son, for several times during the summer he suggested in his letters to Hart that he join him in the management of a country inn which he proposed to buy outside of Cleveland. But it was an invitation that Hart had the good sense to refuse; he would have chosen the torments of office work, in fact, rather than risk a repetition of the mental anguish he had suffered in his earlier relations with his father.

Once assured of a small income, he made plans to spend the summer at Patterson in the meager hope that he might still be able to finish *The Bridge* before autumn. The long period of inactivity was already beginning to result in the usual symptoms; and Mrs. Turner in her "Aunt's part" of the house was more and more frequently alarmed by the violent tumults from Crane's end of the building. The hurling of his typewriter through the window, which was rarely open at the time, became one of his favorite gestures, symbolizing, perhaps, the sentiment he confided in a letter to Underwood that he was almost tired of being a poet. He was also making many trips to the city in search of sailors and the blind escape he achieved through sexual gratification. There was no longer any question of romantic attachment in these relationships. The confusion of his mystical exaltations with his "love affairs" was a phenomenon of an earlier and less experienced day. When the affair with the sea-going friend of the "Voyages" had collapsed in the inevitable sordid dénouement, Crane seems to have finally recognized the impossibility of establishing a satisfactory homosexual love relationship; and thenceforth, almost as though in revenge for having been thwarted of the fulfilment of love, he became more brutal and insatiable in his lusts. In addition to keeping a small address book full of names, he subscribed to a navy bulletin which reported the movements of the fleet; and whenever one of the battleships or cruisers dropped anchor in the Hudson River and established communication with the city, Crane would rush to the telephone, address book in hand. When none of the sailors he knew were in port, however, he was not above paying for his pleasures in the dark pungent streets and seamen's dives along the Brooklyn and Hoboken waterfronts.

In the more quiet periods that intervened between these efforts to achieve release and compensation, though he was unable to add substantially to *The Bridge*, he spent much time in revising the work he had done on the Isle of Pines. As the various sections gradually took on the perfection of their final form, he began dispatching them to magazines for publication, and received a more generous reception than he had ever encountered before. Although he wondered in a letter to Tate "how much longer our market will be in the grip of two such hysterical virgins as the *Dial* and *Poetry*," still both Miss Moore and Miss Monroe accepted several of his poems. Where the former favored unconditional excision or rejection, the latter, less autocratic and more conservative, asked for revision and prose paraphrases for editorial enlightenment. Indeed, Crane had been able to sell "At Melville's Tomb," the first poem he contributed to *Poetry*, only by dint of a month's correspondence with Miss Monroe and an exhaustive analysis of the poem's meaning, which was published along with the poem.* Despite her continued skepticism, Miss Monroe also printed "Cutty Sark" and "Carib Isle" during this period. Miss Moore, for her part, while incomprehensibly rejecting "The River" later in the summer, accepted both the "Proem" and "The Dance." T. S. Eliot's London *Criterion* printed "The Tunnel," and *The Calendar* the "Three Songs" from *The Bridge*; the Paris *Transition* published "Harbor Dawn" and "Van Winkle," two short pieces which had been added to *The Bridge* during the winter; and the "Ave Maria" was solicited by Paul

---

* *See Appendix.*

Rosenfeld for the first *American Caravan,* an anthology of contemporary writing.

During the winter and the following summer Crane was also revising and polishing the short pieces he had written on the Isle of Pines. He made substantial changes in "The Air Plant," "O Carib Isle," and "Royal Palm." From time to time, as his imagination returned to the experiences of the past summer, he composed other lyrics to be included in the collection "Key West": "The Mermen," "Island Quarry," "And Bees of Paradise," and perhaps most striking of this group, "The Hurricane"—a powerful recreation of the violent, god-intoxicated whirlwind that had practically swept him out of his Caribbean exile. This poem, so strangely unlike Crane's usual style, has been cited by almost all his critics as being heavily indebted to the poetry of Gerard Manley Hopkins. The truth of the matter is that in August 1927, when Crane completed the first draft of the poem, which he originally called "The Hour," he had never read a line of Hopkins's verse and probably had not even heard of him. The Jesuit poet was almost unknown in America at that time; his poems had been out of print for several years and were not reprinted till 1930. Crane himself first heard of him through Yvor Winters; and it was not until 1928 during his stay in California, when he borrowed Winters's first edition of the poems, that he had an opportunity to read him. He immediately wrote excited announcements of his "discovery" to many of his friends; he begged Isidor Schneider, who was about to leave for England, to ransack the London bookshops for a stray copy of Hopkins; and from the volume he had borrowed from Winters he made, or had made, careful transcripts of the poems he liked best. Doubtless this voluble enthusiasm, coupled with the fact that "The Hurricane" was not published till 1931, gave rise to the impression that Crane had been considerably influenced by Hopkins. But since "The

Hurricane" is the only poem of Crane's in which the style and quality may possibly be considered Hopkinsesque, and since it was written before he had read the English poet, this conclusion would seem to be completely mistaken.

It was not until June and the coming of summer to Patterson that Crane's muse granted him the full measure of inspiration necessary to launch himself into "The River," one of the major sections of *The Bridge*. During the preceding months he had struggled with the problem of how to maneuver the movement of the poem so that its progress from the close of the "Ave Maria" would include the various historical periods of America. With a sure instinct he had discarded the straightforward and plodding chronological approach to his material, and with a leap that included the whole time span of the work, opened the second part with the poem "Harbor Dawn," in which the poet's consciousness wavers between sleep and waking, as though between past and present, weaving the sounds of twentieth-century Manhattan with the dim awareness of his lover at his side. The following piece, "Van Winkle," served to begin the movement backward into the past again by accompanying the poet on his morning walk to the subway, the while his mind mingles recollections of his own childhood with the "childhood of the continental conquest" and its legendary figures—Cortes, Pizarro, Captain Smith, and Priscilla Alden. By taking Rip Van Winkle as an indigenous genius of memory, Crane made him the "pathfinder of the journey into the past," a kind of Virgil to his poet's Dante. It remained for "The River" to bridge the gap backwards from the modern city to the Indian world of "The Dance," including in its span the content of the pioneer period—a difficult task, but one which Crane finally mastered with extraordinary ingenuity and craftsmanship. And in the act of solving the problems of "The River" he wrote some of his greatest poetry, direct in expression and universal in its breadth of emotional power.

The structure of this section is made essentially simple by the motif of the journey, which at the same time gives it a steady and progressive movement throughout. The preceding poem completely prepares one for the excursion into the past, indicating both the imagery and direction of what is to come. The last stanza binds together both the subway and the transcontinental highway:

> Macadam, gun-grey as the tunny's belt,
> Leaps from Far Rockaway to Golden Gate. . . .
> Keep hold of that nickel for car-change, Rip,—
> Have you got your *"Times"*—?
> And hurry along, Van Winkle—it's getting late!

With the stage thus set, "The River" opens with an extravagant burst of speed—the westbound Twentieth-Century Limited—which Crane intended as an "intentional burlesque on the cultural confusion of the present," written in a ragged jazz rhythm.

> Stick your patent name on a signboard
> brother—all over—going west—young man
> Tintex—Japalac—Certain-teed Overalls ads
> and lands sakes! under the new playbill ripped
> in the guaranteed corner—see Bert Williams what?

When the rush of the train is past, the reader is left some place in the Middle West with three hoboes "still hungry on the tracks." The rhythm then settles into a "steady pedestrian gait, like that of wanderers plodding along," and the movement of the poem progresses by means of the tramps, who, like the subway and the express, are "psychological vehicles." "They are the leftovers of the pioneers," Crane wrote in the synopsis he sent Kahn, ". . . abstractly their wanderings carry the reader through certain experiences roughly parallel to that of the traders, adventurers, Boone and others." Easily, skillfully, and often with sheer inspiration Crane made the hoboes serve his purpose, investing them with both pathos and a powerful elemental dignity.

> John, Jake or Charley, hopping the slow freight
> —Memphis to Tallahassee—riding the rods,
> Blind fists of nothing, humpty-dumpty clods.
>
> Yet they touch something like a key perhaps.
> From pole to pole across the hills, the states
> —They know a body under the wide rain;
> Youngsters with eyes like fjords, old reprobates
> With racetrack jargon,—dotting immensity
> They lurk across her, knowing her yonder breast
> Snow-silvered, sumac-stained or smoky blue—
> Is past the valley-sleepers, south or west.
> —As I have trod the rumorous midnights, too, . . .

Identifying himself with each new motif and movement, Crane led the poem backwards "into interior after interior, all of it funneled by the Mississippi." The River is first introduced casually and with a moving simplicity by means of popular songs sung by the tramps.

> Southward, near Cairo passing, you can see
> The Ohio merging,—borne down Tennessee;
> And if it's summer and the sun's in dusk
> Maybe the breeze will lift the River's musk
> —As though the waters breathed that you might know
> *Memphis Johnny, Steamboat Bill, Missouri Joe.*
> Oh, lean from the window, if the train slows down,
> As though you touched hands with some ancient clown,
> —A little while gaze absently below
> And hum *Deep River* with them while they go.

And then, because "you, too, feed the River timelessly," all
movements and subjects—the train, the tramps, pioneers, past,
present and future time—all gather up and flow with fine
inevitability into the Mississippi, the central artery of the
country's physical body and historical spirit, the Indian's
"Father of Waters," now become a symbol of the endless
current of humanity and fate. From the slow pedestrian
pentameters of the preceding stanzas the rhythm enlarges
and lifts in measured, majestic quatrains.

> Down, down—born pioneers in time's despite,
> Grimed tributaries to an ancient flow—
> They win no frontier by their wayward plight,
> But drift in stillness, as from Jordan's brow.
>
> You will not hear it as the sea; even stone
> Is not more hushed by gravity. . . . But slow,
> As loth to take more tribute—sliding prone
> Like one whose eyes were buried long ago
>
> The River, spreading, flows—and spends your dream.
> What are you, lost within this tideless spell?
> You are your father's father, and the stream—
> A liquid theme that floating niggers swell.
>
> Damp tonnage and alluvial march of days—
> Nights turbid, vascular with silted shale
> And roots surrendered down of moraine clays:
> The Mississippi drinks the farthest dale.

The eloquence and power are sustained with a rising crescendo to reach a magnificent conclusion as the River drains
into the Gulf.

> And flows within itself, heaps itself free.
> All fades but one thin skyline 'round. . . . Ahead
> No embrace opens but the stinging sea;
> The River lifts itself from its long bed,

Poised wholly on its dream, a mustard glow
Tortured with history, its one will—flow!
—The Passion spreads in wide tongues, choked and slow,
Meeting the Gulf, hosannas silently below.

With the completion of this section in July *The Bridge*
was again at a standstill. According to a synopsis of the entire work that Crane sent to Kahn a month or two later,
there remained four major parts still to be written as well as
the "Indiana" poem which was to round out the second
part.* Actually only one of these, "Cape Hatteras," which
was conceived as an ode to Whitman, was included in the
final draft. The other three, "The Cyder Cask," "The Calgary Express," a version of the John Brown legend through
the medium of a Negro pullman porter, and "1927 Whistles,"
a New Year's Eve fantasy, were never finished, if, indeed,
they were ever really begun. In the end the only other section besides "Cape Hatteras" to be added to the poem was
"Quaker Hill," a lament for the vulgar suburbanite invasion
of the Connecticut hills, the land that his forbears had once
cultivated in chaste hardihood. It was indicative of the loose
and flexible structure of *The Bridge* that Crane could discard
three major sections of the poem, as he had conceived it,
without finding it necessary to replace them by other parts.
Contrary to the opinions of many critics, this structure was
intentional, for Crane imagined each poem as a separate excursion into the historical and cultural past of America, always in terms of the present, and always having as a common
denominator the spirit of the poet-protagonist. In the letter
to Kahn which accompanied the synopsis of the work Crane
described his own conception of the interrelationships between the parts of the poem and the whole.

* *See Appendix.*

"Each section of the entire poem," he wrote, "has presented its own unique problem of form, not alone in relation to the materials embodied within its separate confines, but also in relation to the other parts, *in series*, of the major design of the entire poem. Each is a separate canvas, as it were, yet none yields its entire significance when seen apart from the others. One might take the tableaux of the Sistine Chapel as an analogy."

Obviously the capacity for expansion in a poem of such character was practically infinite, and it is not unlikely that this was one of the reasons why Crane each year both expected and failed to finish the work.

A more basic reason for this continual delay lay in the temper of his spirit which was becoming more constantly susceptible to despair. Despite his clear recognition that "The River" was one of his greatest achievements and the high praise it received from his friends, he relapsed into a state of despondent apathy as soon as it was finished.

"It's no use to tell you how futile I feel most of the time," he wrote Underwood a few weeks later, "no matter what I do or conceive of doing, even. Part of the disease of modern consciousness, I suppose. There is no standard of values in the modern world—it's mostly slop, priggishness, and sentimentality. One had much better be a wild man in Borneo and at least have a clear and unabashed love for the sight of blood."

Such sentiments were a far cry indeed from the spirit in which he had written Munson four years earlier, when he felt himself a potential Pindar of the machine age. Then the conception of *The Bridge* was radiant to his imagination with the pristine shine of its genesis and fired his faith in humanity with a mystical fervor. Even two years later, when he wrote his "General Aims and Theories," his convictions still stood firm; he felt himself as a "potential factor" in the realization in America of "certain as yet undefined spiritual quantities, perhaps a new hierarchy of faith not to be developed so completely elsewhere." But in the period between 1925 and 1927 his spirit began to flag. The vigor and idealism of his earlier days was sapped from without by the incessant demands of a society persistently indifferent to what he had conceived to be its national destiny, and consumed from within by the cancerous growth of his own moral conflicts. He himself had written that without faith in his materials he could not create, and the fact that "The River" was his last major achievement would seem to corroborate the statement. Henceforth his progress on *The Bridge* was painfully slow. At times he deliberately sought distractions, fleeing from the hypocrisy of completing a work in which he no longer believed, only to return to it eventually, driven by the fear of ridicule and conclusive failure. It was a failure he could not face, for almost from the day he had written his first poem he had placed in his writing his only hope of attaining security and recognition. Much more than is easily understood, it was a question of life and death for him that he finish *The Bridge*. Accordingly, his poetry had become an activity of the will rather than of the spirit. But even his will at times threatened to founder in the dark flood of despair or the void of bitter isolation.

"I envy the buck-and-wing dancers and the Al Jolsons of the world sometimes," he wrote Tate. "They don't have to encounter all these milksops . . . and they do *please*. They're able to do some 'good' to somebody. And when they laugh, people don't think they're crying. Out here one reads the paper—one sees evidence mounting all the time that there is no place left for *our* kind of minds or emotions. Unless we can pursue our futilities with some sort of constant pleasure, there is little use in going on—and we must apprehend some element in our mock ceremonies or even our follies aren't amusing."

As the first premonition of autumn crisped the night air of the Connecticut hills, he began to worry about the oncoming winter. Although it would have been possible for him to exist in the country on the fifty dollars a month allowance, this solution was prohibited by the mere thought of long months of inactivity in a snow-bound exile that promised to be but a frozen and deathly counterpart of his spiritual solitude. The only other possibility open to him was the all-too-familiar one of an office job in New York; and half-heartedly he began to make frequent trips to the city, resuming the old nightmare rounds of advertising and publishing houses, bookshops and steamship lines. But he found that his two years of retirement served only to disqualify him still further in the world of business. By the end of August his patience was exhausted and he wrote to Kahn, soliciting his aid and advice, despite the fact that he had already received the two thousand dollars originally guaranteed him by the banker. That he again made application to his benefactor witnessed the extremity of his discouragement, for however much he yearned aloud for the times of Maecenas and the munificent patronage of letters, he was too thoroughly schooled in the precepts of bourgeois ethics to accept such help without considering himself an object of charity. When his first letter was not answered at once, he wrote a second, outlining at great length his achievements thus far on *The Bridge* and suggesting specifically that Kahn advance him another thousand dollars on the same basis of insurance security that had covered the first subsidy. The letter was marked by a note of defiant self-vindication, increasingly characteristic of his attitude towards his life and work.

"There is no monetary standard of evaluation for works of art, I know," he wrote, "but I cannot help feeling that a great poem may well be worth at least the expenditure necessary for merely the scenery and costumes of many a flashy and ephemeral play, or for a motor car. *The Aeneid* was not written in two years—nor in four, and in more than one sense I feel justified in comparing the historic and cultural scope of *The Bridge* to this great work. It is at least a symphony with an epic theme, and a work of considerable profundity and inspiration."

Although this won him a gratifying interview with Kahn and a check for another five hundred dollars, he could still not muster sufficient courage and peace of mind to resume work on his poem. He had no sooner received the money than he went to Cleveland to help his mother and grandmother entrain for Hollywood, California, whither they had decided to remove for reasons of health and economy. Upon his return to New York in October he tried to settle down in his old "home" at 110 Columbia Heights and wrote Kahn, strangely enough, that he was in "pursuit of employment." A few days later, however, he suddenly decided to book passage on a ship bound for the island of Martinique, apparently in the hope of achieving another period of rich creative activity such as he had experienced on the Isle of Pines. He informed his father of his plans and received in reply a check for two months' allowance to swell his funds; he sent to the Browns in Patterson for his clothes; and he seems actually to have reserved a cabin for the voyage. But at the last minute he changed his mind, offering the somewhat dubious explanation that "family worries too complicated to explain made it seem useless to attempt—at least for the present—any sort of creative work, far or near." As an alternative he took a position in a small bookshop on 57th Street, hoping to save the Kahn money until a later date. Within two weeks, however, he heard of a more attractive opportunity through the interest of Eleanor Fitzgerald, who introduced him to a wealthy stock broker by the name of Herbert Wise. Mr. Wise, who had been ordered to California for his health, was eager to take with him as a kind of secretary and companion, a young man of intellectual accomplishments; and after one or two interviews with Crane offered him the position. Possibly Crane was persuaded to accept by a serious concern for the fate of his mother and grandmother and the wish to be near them; but it is more likely that he was moved to take the step by a desperate desire to escape from the responsibilities of creative effort. In any case, towards the middle of November, after writing his mother a joyful warning of his imminent arrival in California, he left for the West with Mr. Wise and his entourage of servants and chattels. One of his farewell gestures to New York was an impassioned speech for freedom of action delivered to a crowded court-room in a Brooklyn police station where he had spent the early hours of the morning as the price of a cocktail celebration with E. E. Cummings and his wife.

The California episode was the most unfortunate failure conceivable. Within a few weeks after their arrival at the estate Mr. Wise had rented in Altadena, Crane's childish delight in the novelty of living in a plush and padded luxury was succeeded by a sense of suffocation. Similarly, his momentary pleasure in the brilliant cinematic youth and gaiety of Hollywood turned almost overnight into a revulsion towards "this Pollyanna greasepaint pinkpoodle paradise with its everlasting stereotyped sunlight and its millions of mechanical accessories and sylphlike robots of the age of celluloid." Indeed, the quintessence of all the national vices and manias seemed to have been distilled in the neighborhood of Los Angeles. Added to the crazy formlessness of life, the vulgarity, and the rush for money, which had oppressed

him in New York, there was a cheap dissoluteness peculiar to
the parasitic life of the place. He could scarcely have chosen
a society better qualified to destroy whatever last remnants
of faith he might have had in the American spirit.

Needless to say, there was no question of working on *The
Bridge*, or on any other poem for that matter. His intellectual
life during the five months in California was confined to the
reading of two or three books and a few days of gratifying
talk with Yvor Winters, who spent some time in Los Angeles
over the Christmas holidays. "God knows," Crane wrote to
Frank, "some kind of substantial synthesis of opinion is
needed before I can feel confident in writing about anything
but my shoe-strings. . . . These Godless days! I wonder if
you suffer as much as I do. At least you have the education
and training to hold the scalpel." His activities for the most
part reflected the hysteria of his environment; as was always
the case when he could not write, he became the victim of
his circumstances. Since his duties in the Wise household
proved negligible, he was free to follow his own inclinations,
which were, as usual, towards sex and alcohol, commodities
more than available in the neighborhood of Los Angeles. In
both vices his indulgences reached new extremes. Night after
night he spent in the poolrooms and bars of San Pedro, which
were crowded with sailors from the fleet anchored in the
harbor, risking danger and violence in his search for escape
and gratification. One night, in fact, he and his friend Emil
Opffer, who had just arrived in port on a ship from New
York, were severely beaten and robbed in one of the dark
waterfront streets by a group of sailors who had been enjoying drinks with them in one of the bars.

It was probably the thought that his mother would sooner
or later hear rumors of these debauches which finally
brought Crane to realize the desire, so long postponed, to tell
her of his abnormality. An opportunity for such a confession

offered itself one evening during a week-end visit she made him in Altadena. With what must have been an heroic effort to conceal his painful emotions, Crane told his mother in a matter-of-fact way, calculated to diminish the shock of the announcement, that he was homosexual. He explained the aberration in its simplest terms, and went on to mention certain experiences of his adolescence which had conditioned him towards it; he described the years he had suffered from the sense of his difference from other men and the corrosive consciousness of guilt; he told also of his vain efforts to cure himself by attempting normal relationships; and he concluded by insisting vigorously—too vigorously to be convincing—that he was no longer ashamed of it, that in his reading on the subject he had learned to recognize it as a common phenomenon of all societies and all races. Needless to say, it was not by any means true that he had come to accept his status with complete equanimity, and doubtless his mother realized this. In any case, she understood her son well enough to know that any expression of horror or remonstrance on her part might well destroy the relationship which had bound them together so intimately since his childhood. Without committing herself either to approval or disapproval, she gave Hart to understand that she concurred with him in his attitude towards the subject, and promised faithfully to read the books on it that he recommended to her. The only false move she seems to have made lay in her sudden decision to spend the night at a hotel in town rather than with Hart, as she had originally planned. Very probably she wanted to be alone after experiencing such a profound shock, but her action was liable to other, less pleasant interpretations, especially to a mind so distorted as that of her son. Indeed, she was to discover during the following months that she was no more exempt than the least of his friends from his suspicions and fears. For the time being, however, the incident passed without any apparent ill effect on Hart.

Their relationship seemed to be strengthened, if anything, as though Hart, having shared his guilt with his mother, was able to accept her into even greater intimacy than before. When he resigned his position with the Wise establishment towards the end of February, having endured the cere-monials of luxury as long as possible, he relinquished his de-sire to return to New York in favor of joining his mother and grandmother in Hollywood. His anxiety over their financial difficulties was increased by concern for the com-fort of his grandmother, who, almost completely bedridden with age and illness, was expected to die at any moment. His extraordinary devotion to her had been one of the few pure emotions in his life, suffering from neither distortion nor reversals, and he knew that he could not return to New York without being constantly preoccupied with her fate.

"The experience of the last two years," he wrote Frank, "has taught me the futility of any retreat from what I, after all, must regard as my immediate responsibilities. The fur-ther I might go from the actual 'scene' of operations the more obsessed I tend to become with the inert idea. So I am re-maining here with the hope of securing some 'literary' con-nection with the movies which will bring me enough to be of some substantial help."

But this resolve, however unselfish, only prepared a fur-ther disaster. Since his own funds were limited to the few hundred dollars he had saved from Kahn's last gift, he could do little more than contribute to the support of the house-hold by paying his room and board. His efforts to establish a steady income from a job were futile. He had neither ex-perience in scenario work nor training in the legitimate theater to recommend him. Even the arrival in Hollywood of his perennial patron, Otto Kahn, and the forthcoming introduction to Jesse Lasky, the producer, proved useless. In the meantime life was becoming more than difficult in the small bungalow. Mrs. Crane, exhausted by months of daily attendance upon her mother, was in a precarious state of health herself; while Hart, suffering from his failure to relieve their distress and, moreover, brooding on the apparent impossibility of completing *The Bridge*, was becoming increasingly irritable. To be constantly reminded of his inability to meet the exigencies not only of living but of writing as well was a form of spiritual torture he could not endure. As the weeks dragged by, aggravating the nervous tension with frequent misunderstandings, he became convinced that his gesture of assistance had been an ill-advised piece of quixotism, and his original sympathy for his mother's condition began to turn into a bitter resentment. The crisis came towards the end of May when in the midst of a quarrel Hart seized upon his mother's suggestion that he leave the house as a legitimate excuse to escape. An investigation of his finances revealed that he had just enough money left to buy a ticket to New York via New Orleans by rail and water. A week or two later, when his clandestine preparations were completed, he fled in the middle of the night, leaving a brief note pinned to his pillow to say that he had "gone East."

Although his flight does Crane little credit, objectively considered, it would seem to have been an inevitable step towards the final estrangement from his mother, which a tragic fate had predetermined. When this last stage was reached a few months later and their misunderstandings broke forth again with climactic violence, Crane's conscience was still tormenting him with recollections of his behavior in California. In a long letter written at this time to his aunt, Mrs. Deming, in explanation of his ignominious flight, he confessed that he had outraged himself by deceiving as he had never done before.

"I was desperate, and desperately firm," he continued. "I could not take the chance of being frank, for it involved the hazard of other wild demonstrations, perhaps even worse than the last. Grace was walking about again two days before the date on my ticket. I had never acted before, and in the process I discovered that she was doing a good deal of it herself, timing her recovery by gradual degrees, quite confident, in fact, also—that she had completely subdued me to a kind of idiotic jelly of sympathetic responses. Well, I carried it through—packing by infinitesimal degrees and labyrinthine subterfuges (it sounds like a comedy, but I was ill and nearly dead for sleep) until on the appointed hour the taxi drove up with darkened lights—and I was on my way—'home'—the only one I ever hope to have—this supposedly cruel city, but certainly better for me than either of my parents."

These reactions, however, were not immediately apparent, and during the months between his return to New York and their final quarrel his relations with his mother, though somewhat restrained, continued with the appearance of friendliness.

Whatever other effects later became evident, it is certain that this incident impressed upon Crane with painful clarity the utter rootlessness of his life and so contributed to the hysteria that was fast disintegrating his spirit. For despite all criticisms and reproaches his mother and grandmother had represented a solid nucleus of emotional security, a kind of spiritual sanctuary where he could be sure of finding genuine devotion and encouragement, even if not complete understanding. They had provided the means and substance of the only home he had known; and they had championed the precious and lonely cause of his poetry from its earliest period. Now, his grandmother on her deathbed, a gulf of inexorable estrangement widening between himself and his mother, and lacking even the anchor of creative work, he felt more footloose and lost in the world than ever. His state of mind was reflected in the attempt he made, shortly after returning to Patterson in June, once more to buy a home in the country, an effort which this time failed to carry beyond his father's refusal to supply the necessary funds. Unlike his friends who had all married at an early age, Crane was unable to achieve the moral and spiritual support of a marital relationship. He was also deprived of another resource which granted most of them a modicum of self-confidence in his lack of a university training which would have qualified him to hold permanent editorial and teaching positions. During the two months he spent in Patterson the far-reaching import of these conditions was forcefully borne in upon him by the necessity of borrowing constantly from his more fortunate friends and from his father, who doled him out small amounts of money with generous, well-meaning criticisms. It was scarcely surprising that he often felt that "the past would evidently like to destroy me."

In August he plunged once again into the competitive rush and mêlée of the city in search of work, burdened with the hopeless knowledge that whatever position he might secure would be but another flimsy makeshift. "There's nothing left to struggle for except 'respectability,' " he complained to Underwood. "Occasionally some sailor gives me a jolt—but I guess I'm getting old." For several depressing weeks he lived at the apartment of the Cowleys, who were absent for the summer, spending the suffocating days in vain efforts to locate employment. Finally, in desperate need of money, he wrote to his father:

"My shoes are giving out as well as the several small loans that friends have given me. . . . I agree with you completely in what you say about learning a trade; in fact, I have wanted to learn some regular trade like typesetting, linotyping, etc. for a long time back. . . . I'm going to do my best during the next few days to find a job as a plumber's or mechanic's helper."

In reply his father wired him money and a message to come home immediately. But Hart, recalling the late disaster in California, used the money to pay his debts, and at the same time managed to secure a temporary job in a book-shop. By the beginning of October he once more found work with an advertising firm, though his services were needed only for a few weeks, and was able to move back into his old "home" at 110 Columbia Heights. When this brief respite came to an end, another period of anxiety followed, and it was not until late in November that he again obtained employment, this time in the filing department of a broker-age house in Wall Street, where his friend Walker Evans, the photographer, was also drudging for a meager living. It was a kind of nightmare existence, a breathless scramble for footholds over the sheer gulf of dereliction.

"Moving around, grabbing onto this and that, stupid land-ladies—never enough sense of security to relax and have a fresh thought," he wrote to the Rychtariks, "that's about all the years bring besides new and worse manifestations of fam-ily hysteria. It's a great big bore! I feel like saying what the Englishman did: 'Too many buttons to unbutton. I'm through!'"

Meanwhile, towering over the senseless tangle of his life, spanning the river and the sunken subway journeys of his daily traffic with the city, stood the Bridge, erstwhile symbol of a new spiritual order, become at last a dramatic stage for drunken homecomings, midnight assignations and arrests, and violent threats of suicide.

The only possible escape from the maze of this delirium opened up in September, when the death of his grandmother made available to him a five-thousand-dollar bequest. Frantic with the desire to flee as far as possible from the torments of the past years, he seized upon the prospect of this inheritance and began making plans to sail for Europe, impatiently awaiting the time when the estate would be settled. Meanwhile, he was not without concern for his mother. Despite the strained relations between them, he immediately sent her telegrams, flowers, and letters of genuine sympathy. Furthermore, knowing that she herself would receive almost nothing from the estate, he wrote his father to persuade him to make some provision for her welfare—a suggestion the latter firmly declined. But beyond this he would not go. With a desperation akin to fear, he was determined not to become involved again in the intimate details of her life.

When he received no reply to his letters, however, his mind began to revolve through the usual phantasmagoria of suspicions. He brooded over the quarrel in Hollywood, interpreting her words and gestures in new lights; recalled the evening in Altadena when she had left him to spend the night at a hotel; anticipated a host of imminent calamities. When, towards the middle of October, after a silence of more than a month, he received a startling wire from her saying that she was seriously ill and wished him to come to her at once, he was too distraught to believe it and replied that he could not make the journey for lack of money, which was, in fact, only too true. A few days later a letter arrived from a friend in Hollywood which implied that his mother was in good health and added to his fear that he was being victimized. Hearing nothing further from his mother, he wrote to the Guardian Trust Company, which was administering the estate, to get more reliable news and to inquire about his inheritance. When he heard in reply that his mother had wired them she was too ill to write or even to sign the papers which would release the money, he was completely convinced that he was being ensnared by a plot against his freedom.

At this time, early in November, the relationship hung in the balance. Though Hart's mind was inflamed by fear and resentment, he had as yet no desire to sever connections with his mother nor to wound her in any way. His primary concern was to protect himself from the spiritual disintegration that he felt to be threatening him, and to achieve a sufficient peace of mind to complete *The Bridge*.

"I feel very sorry for her," he wrote to his aunt in explanation, "for certainly she is miserably unhappy, but on the other hand I think that commiseration only renders her more helpless. She is profoundly attached to me, really loves me, I know. But there are mixtures of elements in this attachment that are neither good for her nor for me. Psychoanalysis reveals many things that it would be well for Grace to know. But I think that she is at present too prejudiced to give ear to any counsel. I'm really alarmed. But what can I do? I now live in that constant state of wondering 'what next?'. I shall not be surprised at almost anything.

"Nevertheless, I am now making a strong effort to discipline myself against the obsession with this and other wasteful family problems that have robbed me of my vitality during the last twenty years—unmanned me time and again and threatened to make me one of those emotional derelicts who are nothing but tremulous jellyfish might-have-beens. I may already be in that latter class, although I have done already too much solid writing to believe that to be true. I can't continue, however, to harbor this insatiable demon of morbidity without committing myself to destruction.

"One's conscience ripens somewhat by the age of thirty. I must respect my emotions or I can't feel the necessary solidity to create anything worthwhile. It is a spiritual crisis. Really serious. Perhaps you understand what I mean. If I am to continue in my sympathies for Grace she must not abuse the confidence that I would like to place in her sincerity. I won't be dragged into hell—and live there forever for anybody's joke—not even my mother's. That is, not unless the hold is already too strong on my unconscious emotional nature, for hope of escape,—which remains to be proved. If she continues with her present methods she may drive me to drastic methods of isolation."

Had either Hart or his mother written the other directly at this time, the tragic conclusion to their misunderstandings might still have been avoided; but both of them, full of mistrust, maintained a stubborn silence, relying upon the treacherous means of indirect communication and devious maneuvers. Towards the end of November Hart, completely unnerved by the protracted delay and the nightmare of suspicion, telephoned the Guardian Trust in Cleveland to demand that a five-hundred-dollar advance on his inheritance be sent him at once and that the balance be paid within a week. In reply he learned that his mother was withholding her signature from the papers the bank had sent her in the hope of persuading him by indirect pressure to join her in Hollywood. Enraged that she had enlisted the bank to lecture him on his filial responsibilities and terrified lest his opportunity to escape from the country be wrested from him at the last moment, he dispatched a violent telegram asking her to sign the papers immediately, in default of which he was prepared to bring legal action against her. It was an ugly threat for a son to make to his mother; indeed, it would have been incomprehensible had not Crane been almost crazed with the fury of his emotions. His mother's return message equalled the rage of his own. She replied indignantly that she had already signed the papers, and, matching threat for threat, added that she was prepared to urge his father to use his influence with the bank against paying him his inheritance on the grounds of his drinking habits. This bitter exchange of hostilities brought their unhappy relationship to an end. The only further step Hart took in the matter grew out of the fear that his mother might also report to his father his sexual aberrations, and hoping to protect himself somewhat, he wrote his aunt asking her to show his father the long letter he had written her analyzing his relations with his mother. He ended the letter with a violent declaration which bears terrible witness to the distortion of his spirit.

"Grace will probably never hear from me again," he concluded. "Nervous strain or simple hysterics could never explain the underhanded and insatiable vanity that has inspired her to attempt to crush her nearest of kin. And all for a bucketful of cash! I think I can say that my part in this long melodrama is almost over. I shall try to remain as unconcerned about the rest of it as possible."

It is practically impossible to disentangle from the hysterical, almost pathological, stuff of this rupture any clear pattern of cause and effect. The question of the inheritance, needless to say, was no more than the fortuitous incident which precipitated the full flood of poison secreted by years of anguish in the subconscious reservoirs of Crane's spirit. Later, when the money had been long since spent and he was again penniless, he steadfastly refused to answer his mother's letters and begged his friends and relatives to keep his whereabouts secret from her. There was more than a suggestion of the paranoiac in his attitude thenceforth. His primary emotion towards her seems to have been one of fear, amounting at times to a consuming terror, expressed in terms of hatred and vituperation. In his drunken rages he spread incredible stories among his friends concerning her character and morals. Once during a visit with his father in Cleveland when he heard of his mother's sudden arrival in the city, his state of mind was transformed in a moment from pleasant equilibrium to abject apprehension; he went out immediately in search of liquor and returned in such a miserable condition that Mr. Crane yielded to his pleas and put him aboard a New-York-bound train with the promise not to reveal his address.

That a profound devotion could be inverted to such fear and revulsion is one of the more obscure, though by no means uncommon, mysteries of human affection. Since Crane was well informed of the relation of the Oedipus complex to neurotic personalities and in particular to that of the homosexual, it is very likely that in the distorted retrospect over his "long-scattered score of broken intervals" he saw his mother as the sole cause of his crippled life, and made of her a symbol, a palpable fetish, of all his fears and grievances. That he actually tended to interpret their relationship symbolically may be gathered from the only other message he ever sent her, a cryptic postcard from Paris, scrawled with an obviously drunken hand, which wildly mentioned a flight into the Orient and bore the strangely prophetic signature, "Atlantis," and the hieroglyph of a five-pointed star. He might well sign himself by the name of the sunken island. Severed at last from the mainland of his past life, he achieved no escape when he boarded the ship for England shortly before Christmas; the inscrutable flood that was finally to engulf him rose only the more steadily around the isolated confusion and insecurity of his life.

X

"Now while thy petals spend the suns about us, hold—
(O Thou whose radiance doth inherit me)
Atlantis,—hold thy floating singer late!"

Lɪᴋᴇ the California sojourn,
the seven months Crane spent abroad between December
1928 and July 1929 were only another effort to sidestep the
task of completing *The Bridge*. With fully three-fourths of
the poem already published and the critics awaiting the appearance of the finished work, which had been announced as
the great national epic, Crane had felt the succession of un-
productive months as a clear indictment of failure. It was undoubtedly this sense of literary guilt as much as the painful
episodes of his personal life that made him so desperately
eager to quit the country. He planned, it is true, to vindicate
his flight by going to Mallorca, where in the insular peace of
the Mediterranean he could write the remaining sections of
the poem. But his plans were never accomplished. Between
him and the island lay London and Paris, the Scylla and
Charybdis of so many American exiles voyaging in search of
their Muse.

Since the dangers of London were the more subtle and unsympathetic to Crane's temperament, he weathered his brief stay of two weeks there without suffering any misadventure. Upon his arrival he put up at a hotel and set out at once to call on his old friend Laura Riding, whom he had not seen since she left America in 1925. A few days later, when he fell ill with a slight attack of grippe, Miss Riding invited him to stay for a while at her flat in Hammersmith. Close by in a houseboat moored on the Thames lived her friends, Robert Graves and his family, with whom they had Christmas dinner. In the following days, besides meeting other friends of hers, he spent some time with Paul Robeson and his wife, old friends from New York, who were staying in London for the production of "Show Boat" in which the great baritone was starred. He called on Edgell Rickword, who had given his poetry such a generous reception in his magazine *The Calendar*. He also took long walks through all parts of the city, and before long he found his way to Whitechapel and Limehouse, the Bowery and Sand Street of London, in the hope of meeting with exciting adventures. His disappointment was somewhat amusing, for he discovered that "most of the young toughs drank only lemonade—and after I had had several swigs of Scotch they all seemed to be afraid of me!" Finding little to interest him in that part of town, he was content to chat with old charwomen in Bedford Street over a glass of wine, and spend long hours in the National Gallery, where he always returned to stand before the magnificent canvas of El Greco, the "Agony in the Garden," which he had conceived as related to his "Proem" to *The Bridge*.

But despite these innocent pleasures, his behavior often showed evident signs of desperation. Miss Riding was deeply distressed by the tortured confusion of his moods, which alternated unreasonably between great affection and incoherent attack. At times he acted as though she had done him a personal injury, and again as though she were the only person in the world who understood him. When drunk, he spent money recklessly and then accused his companions of having cheated him. Evidently the obsessions of the last weeks in New York still swarmed in his mind. One night at the theater, having sat halfway through the performance, he suddenly became convinced that he had been cheated at the box office and refused to be quieted until the matter had been settled. Later the same evening, he sighted a couple of American sailors in the audience. After that nothing could hold him; for a few minutes he squirmed about in his seat and finally, having borrowed several pounds, deserted Miss Riding and her party in search of more exciting pleasures. It was his farewell gesture to London. The next day he crossed the Channel towards the French capital.

Tormented as he was by mental and spiritual disorders, it was almost inevitable that Crane should succumb to the whirlpool that was Paris. The American occupation of the city had reached its height, and the days and nights reeled around on the drunken carrousel of continual delirium and sensation-seeking. The artistic circles, which had preserved a comparative integrity during the days of Dada, were now inextricably entangled with the crazy fringes of social dereliction and hysteria. Surrealist art was ultra-fashionable, the final polish of sophistication; and its indiscriminate intercourse with parasites and camp-followers had infected it with their vices and betrayed it into extremities of affectation and self-consciousness. All sense of values disintegrated; the Subconscious, hypostatized as the Absolute, gave license in writing to pathology and charlatanry alike; conversation shifted promiscuously from discussions of literature, to the gossip of perverts and the fantastic dreams of drug addicts. Confusion, hallucinations, disintegration became ends in themselves. In the spring of 1929 *Transition* under the editorship of Eugene Jolas and with the collaboration of Harry Crosby and others printed an almost senseless manifesto in pseudo-philosophical jargon advocating the artist's right to ignore the laws of grammar and syntax in favor of using words and constructions of his own invention. It was a document signed by many of the well-known writers of the day, among them Crane, drunkenly following where the Romans led, though in a later and more sober moment he confessed his shame. But the sober moments were very rare during the months in Paris, and for the most part Crane abandoned himself to the dizzy current around him. As in Hollywood, so in Paris he became the victim of his circumstances; but where, in the former instance, his integrity had been protected from any serious corruption by the recognition of his superiority to his environment, it was now stripped of this last defense by his constant sense of inferiority. In Paris the most flimsy pretenses had the power to impose upon him: the sophistication, the deliberate, self-conscious depravities, the literary affectations—all vices and buffooneries commanded his tolerance and even his admiration, if only because they made him feel crude and inadequate by the simple fact of their foreignness. He was too deeply naïve to recognize his own discomfort as a token of his essential sincerity, and too provincial to remain unmoved by abject respect in the presence of great wealth or a noble title. He himself felt the potential threat to his spiritual health. "Paris really is a test for an American, I'm beginning to feel," he wrote to Frank. "And I'm so far from certain that I'm equal to it in my present mood that I'm quite uneasy." But the same letter announced his intention to remain indefinitely in Paris in preference to pushing on to Mallorca.

His change of plans seems to have been occasioned by his

meeting with Harry Crosby, "the heir of all the Morgan-Harjes millions," as Crane somewhat wildly described him in his letters, who with his wife, Caresse, conducted the Black Sun Press, a de luxe publishing establishment in the rue Cardinale. Deeply impressed by their first reading of *The Bridge* and eager to bring out a limited first edition of it, the Crosbys urged Crane to remain in Paris and finish the poem as soon as possible, offering him as an inducement the use of an old mill on the estate of the Comte de la Rochefoucauld at Ermenonville, which they had remodelled as a week-end retreat. Flattered as much by the wealth and position of the Crosbys as by their enthusiasm for his work, Crane accepted both propositions, and thenceforth spent almost as much of his time at the "Moulin" as at the house in town, which he shared with the painter Eugene MacCown. Although he had written Cowley that "I've an idea I shall soon wear off my novelty," as though he felt himself to be some kind of court jester, he discovered as the weeks passed that there was no limit to the Crosbys' hospitality. He was installed in one of the towers of the Mill where for a few days now and then he enjoyed the solitary pleasures of a warm hearth, solicitous service, walks in the snow-weighted forests of the park, and above all the endless supply of Crosby's whiskey, which by a happy coincidence proved to be the "Cutty Sark" brand. Although sometimes during these quiet interims he managed to do a little writing, more often he was overwhelmed by a feeling of desolation. He "dreamed of getting back to himself," and confessed in a letter to Frank that he "needed more strength than ever." But each week-end he drowned his pangs of conscience in a drunken whirl of excitement. Besides the French and American writers of the *Transition* group, all sorts of titles and reputations gravitated to the brilliant maelstrom that marked Crosby's progress towards his death.

"Mob for luncheon," Crosby noted in his diary during one of these week-ends, "poets and painters and pederasts and lesbians and Christ knows who and there was a great signing of names on the wall at the foot of the stairs and a firing off of the canon and bottle after bottle of red wine and Kay Boyle made fun of Hart Crane and he was angry and flung the American Caravan into the fire because it contained a story of Kay Boyle's (he forgot it had a poem of his in it) and there was a tempest of drinking and polo harra burra and an uproar and confusion so that it was difficult to do my work on the Bible."

Thus the months in Paris went by, and still Crane made no effort to tear himself away. On the contrary, in reaction to the crazy tempo of life about him, he committed new excesses of self-indulgence, and, almost constantly drunk, created violent scenes that at times were little more than buffooneries. At one party he tattooed his face with India ink and danced the "Gasotski"; another time he read Marlowe's *Tamburlaine* in a loud voice and proclaimed his own greatness as a poet. Again he would appear early in the morning, haggard and wild from a night in Montmartre, his sweater pinned all over with stars and anchors in token of his debauchery. More and more, whether in the city or at the Mill, he brandished his homosexuality in public, boasting defiantly of the numbers of his conquests, while his companions spurred him on with laughter, quips, and jibes. Although Eugene Jolas and the Crosbys introduced him to such French poets as Soupault and Aragon, and Frank had supplied him with letters to Gide and Larbaud, he showed no taste for literary interests. Doubtless the doctrines of the Surrealists and the manifestoes of *Transition* seemed to him but another current of the Parisian vertigo. Aside from his discussions with the Crosbys concerning their plans for the publication of *The Bridge*, his activities had no relation to the world of literature.

Finally with the arrival of early spring he left for the South; but even there he was unable to achieve equilibrium, if, indeed, he wished to. Excepting a short visit with Roy Campbell, the South African poet who was living at Martigues, and a week or two in the little fishing village of Collioure near the Spanish border, he spent his time in Marseille. The Cannebière became his Montparnasse, the Vieux-Port his Montmartre, and his dissipations continued unabated. Towards the end of June Crosby recorded in his diary: ". . . then back to the house to find Hart Crane back from Marseille where he had slept with his thirty sailors and he began again to drink Cutty Sark (the last bottle in the house)."

Crane's European sojourn was almost at an end, however. The episode that punctuated it with appropriate final violence occurred during the first week of July. One evening, having left a group of friends at La Closerie des Lilas, he strolled down the Boulevard Raspail until he arrived in front of the Café Select, where he stopped to have a few drinks. When he came to pay his bill, he discovered that he had only fifty centimes in his pocket, a deficiency that the waiter reported at once to the proprietress, a formidable woman known as Madame Select, who was notorious for her vindictiveness towards Americans. This Tartar immediately threatened to call the police, refusing at the same time to accept the offer of other Americans in the café to pay the bill. As might have been expected, Crane flew into a rage, and when one of the waiters tried to oust him from the terrace, knocked the fellow down with a blow. Pandemonium broke loose. Other waiters joined the fracas only to meet with a like fate; a gendarme appeared and, receiving the same treatment, summoned a horde of his confrères with a blast of his whistle; finally after several minutes, during which three or four of the *flics* suffered minor mutilations, Crane was subdued by a club and dragged away with traditional brutality, feet foremost, his head bumping along the curbing. Before being thrown in a cell at La Santé, he received a further bludgeoning with a rubber hose in the French equivalent of a third degree. Unfortunately, none of his friends had witnessed the incident, and since he was held *incommunicado*, several days passed before word leaked into the offices of the *Herald Tribune* via the French press that some unknown American was in jail. Thereupon Whit Burnett, who was then a reporter for the newspaper, Crosby, MacCown, and other friends rallied to his aid, hiring lawyers, pleading with judges, citing Byron and Shelley to the Chief Prefect of Police, in an effort to free him. A trial was inevitable, however, and it was not until a week after Crane's imprisonment that his case was brought before the court.

"Hart was magnificent," Crosby wrote in his diary. "When the Judge announced that it had taken ten gendarmes to hold him (the dirty bastards, they dragged him three blocks by the feet) all the court burst into laughter. After ten minutes of questioning he was fined 800 francs and 8 days in prison should he ever be arrested again. A letter from the Nouvelle Revue Française had a good deal to do with his liberation. They wouldn't let him out right away so I went with Marks to Le Doyen to eat and to drink sherry cobblers in the sun. . . . Apparently Hart had been sent back to the Sante so Burnett and I drove over there (we saw a truck run over a cat) and here we had to wait and to wait from six until long after eight (we spent the time drinking beer and playing checkers and talking to the gendarmes). At last the prisoners began to come out, Hart the last one, unshaved hungry wild. So we stood and drank in the Bar de la Bonne Sante right opposite the prison gate and then drove to the Herald office where Burnett got out to write up the story for the newspaper, Hart and I going on to Chicago Inn for cornbread and poached eggs on toast (Ginetta and Olivares were there and Ortiz) and Hart said that the dirty skunks in the Sante wouldn't give him any paper to write poems on. The bastards."

In the soberness of the day of his release Crane discovered he did not even have enough money left to buy a return passage to America; but Crosby with unfailing generosity bought his ticket and a few days later saw him aboard ship, having won from him the promise to complete *The Bridge* before October.

It was impossible, indeed, to postpone finishing *The Bridge* any longer, and upon his arrival in New York towards the end of July Crane took a room at 130 Columbia Heights with the desperate determination to make good his word to Crosby. Fortunately, he had left almost half of his inheritance in the safe-keeping of a bank before his flight to Europe, so that now he was free at least from the necessity of earning his livelihood. But despite his financial security the task of completing his poem was one of almost insurmountable difficulty. For two years he had written nothing except random phrases and fragments—an intermission that he could ill afford in view of his peculiar temperament. The loss of faith in his material, which he had felt even before his California sojourn, had been disastrously abetted in the meantime by a loss of confidence in his own powers, and this in turn was aggravated by a constant sense of guilt. Immediately upon his return to New York, in fact, he avoided his old friends for fear of being reproached with his wasteful months abroad; and it was not until he met Slater Brown on the street one day that he again felt certain of their loyalty to him. But even this reassurance could not restore his self-confidence. While he was completing *The Bridge*, his friends received telephone calls from him at all hours of the night and were forced to listen to a torrent of denunciations and complaints, pleas for assistance, violent declamations of his latest passage of verse; and the next day other calls followed, penitent and sober, asking forgiveness. On one occasion he telephoned Brown early in the morning to say he was dying and begged him to come to him at once, though when Brown arrived, he discovered that Crane was simply more drunk than usual. At other times his condition was actually serious. At least once during the fall, when a bad attack of delirium tremens left him quite helpless, one of his most devoted friends, a young woman whom he affectionately called "Twidget," stayed with him for several days, nursing him back to health and reassembling the wreckage of his rooms. It was only the unquestioning affection of one or two such people that had the power to calm him during these periods. Most of his friends, however fond he was of them, usually irritated him to further violence, by what he suspected must be their unvoiced criticisms and reproaches—the echoes of his own guilty conscience.

In spite of all difficulties, however, whether drunk or sober, he continued to work on *The Bridge* in a desperate effort to keep pace with the printer who had already started to set the poem in type at the Black Sun Press in Paris. In October he was able to dispatch to the Crosbys the final version of "Cape Hatteras," and a month later he sent off "Quaker Hill" and "Indiana," which he completed in a rage of disappointment.

Released at last from the long struggle of finishing *The Bridge*, Crane still found no escape from the familiar nightmares of anxiety and fear. None knew better than he that these last three sections fell far short of the rest of the poem, and no one doubted his achievement more than himself. Where he had once been terrified lest he should never complete his major work, he was now haunted by the suspicion that he had lost the power to write anything. He knew well enough that he had lost his faith and that the temper of his spirit had become almost diametrically opposed to his original vision. It was more than fortunate—perhaps it was even prophetic—that "Atlantis," the final apocalyptic paean, had been written first; for it is doubtful whether he could now have recaptured the intense mystical conviction of his early years.

He found it difficult enough to write "Cape Hatteras," which he had conceived as an ode to Whitman, a reaffirmation of his faith in the American spirit. In the effort to whip himself up to the buoyant breath of optimism that the subject demanded he fell into bathos and committed aesthetic sins that never ceased to plague his conscience. Besides apostrophizing Whitman, he incorporated into the poem panegyrics on the aeroplane and modern machinery and even attempted to deal obliquely with the philosophical problem of time and space. Having no means to integrate these unrelated subjects, he handled them in alternation and tried to conceal the essential confusion of the poem by resorting to technical fireworks. Sensational metaphors crowded one upon another in a kind of hysterical haste that made any musical cadence or basic rhythm impossible. The sprawling pentameter lines, rhymed in couplets or irregularly or not at all, had neither form nor progression. And often the coupling of unfortunate onomatopoeia and strained imagery produced an effect almost of parody. Probably all great poets at their worst have unconsciously burlesqued their own style, but few have done it more obviously than Crane in such lines as:—

Power's script,—wound, bobbin-bound, refined—
Is stropped to the slap of belts on booming spools, spurred
Into the bulging bouillon, harnessed jelly of the stars . . .

or, with a rhetoric even more flashy and empty:—

> As bright as frogs' eyes, giggling in the girth
> Of steely gizzards—axle-bound, confined
> In coiled precision, bunched in mutual glee
> The bearings glint,—O murmurless and shined
> In oilrinsed circles of blind ecstasy!

And nothing but the incredible strain of forced creation can explain the lapse of humor and taste that allowed him to apostrophize Whitman in one breath as "Panis Angelicus" and in the next as "Thou, Vedic Caesar, to the greensward knelt!". Only in a few lines of natural description and several others on Whitman, where his expression was not taxed by having to simulate a sincerity he did not feel, was there any poetry worthy of his best effort. His true state of mind found a more faithful reflection in the resigned disillusionment of "Quaker Hill." Still tormented by an almost pathological obsession with the quarrel over his inheritance, he wrote into one passage of this section a testimony of what he imagined was his mother's guilt.

> Shoulder the curse of sundered parentage,
> Wait for the postman driving from Birch Hill
> With birthright by blackmail, the arrant page
> That unfolds a new destiny to fill. . . .

> So, must we from the hawk's far stemming view,
> Must we descend as worm's eye to construe
> Our love of all we touch, and take it to the Gate
> As humbly as a guest who knows himself too late,
> His news already told? Yes, while the heart is wrung,
> Arise—yes, take this sheaf of dust upon your tongue!

Actually *The Bridge* could not have been finished at a less fortunate time. His creative impulse exhausted and yet in no condition to endure the irritations of unemployment, he was

probably more incapable than ever before of finding work
and submitting to the discipline of daily business routine.
Furthermore, jobs were no longer so easy to get. The country was facing economic disaster; the great depression, which
had an effect on literature comparable to that of the War,
was about to break over the world, ushering in new literary
generations with manifestoes of new social-economic faith.
Against such odds it was hardly surprising that Crane failed
to regain his balance. Throughout the winter the pace of disintegration continued unchecked. Weeks of violence and
debauchery in the city were followed by respites at Patterson, where he still kept his rooms at Addie Turner's house;
but even these invariably ended in similar outbreaks. Nothing was safe from his destructive rages, and his behavior
often seemed nothing short of insane. Sometimes, Peter
Blume, the painter, who was also renting rooms from Mrs.
Turner, had to stop him by force. Once, when Crane was
plunging about the house stark naked, smashing everything
he could lay hands on, Blume had to throw him to the floor
and sit on him till he calmed down—Crane shouting incoherently all the while that they might get *him* down, but
The Bridge was on its way to Paris. For a short time in December, however, he was somewhat sobered by the tragic
death of his friend, Harry Crosby, who with his wife was
paying a visit to New York. Only a few days after Crane
had entertained in their honor, on the very evening he had
been invited to join them for dinner and the theater, Crosby
was found dead, a bullet hole in his head punctuating his
search for the extreme sensation.

Despite the tragedy, Mrs. Crosby courageously returned
to Paris to see *The Bridge* through the press, and by February the copies of the limited first edition arrived in New
York, though it was not until April with the publication of
the Liveright edition that the reviews began to appear. Dur-

ing the intervening months Crane began to worry about his financial condition, which was growing steadily more precarious. In January he moved from 130 Columbia Heights to cheaper lodgings down the street at number 190, where he rented a furnished basement apartment. At the same time he applied to his publisher for a three-hundred-dollar advance, and began to cast about for employment—an almost hopeless task in a city stricken by the first shocks of economic disaster. The only opportunity came from his father, who offered him a job selling cheap prints of the popular paintings that he had bought for decorating the covers of his candy boxes. Needless to say, such door-to-door canvassing was not the kind of work for which Hart was qualified, and after a few half-hearted gestures of salesmanship the prints were stacked away in the closets of friends. When April arrived he was still unemployed, and fearful of being left again without any capital, he wrote in desperation to Kahn, asking his help in locating work. In reply the banker sent him a check for a hundred dollars and tried unsuccessfully to find him a position. Despite the publication of *The Bridge*, which Crane had hoped would win him some kind of editorial employment, May brought no better success and in June he fled to Patterson, thinking at least to save what little money was left.

The reviews of *The Bridge*, which began finally to appear in the press, far from improving his material situation, did not even serve to dissipate the sense of failure that haunted him. The critics, it is true, were forced by the sheer weight of Crane's reputation in literary circles to review the poem with more particular attention than they had accorded *White Buildings*, and in most instances their praise exceeded their censure. But even the most enthusiastic with one or two exceptions gave voice to qualifications and doubts which sounded in Crane's ears like echoes of his own fearful conscience. Since most of them had been familiar with the greatest sections of the poem for several years, the faults of the unpublished material were all the more obvious and drew attention to the defects of the work as a whole, which came almost as an anti-climax. Furthermore, Crane, ironically enough, had scattered the seeds of suspicion far and wide among the critics by his behavior; in his drunken violence he had repeatedly betrayed his own dissatisfaction with *The Bridge*, and his manner of life was such common gossip in the literary circles of New York that even those who did not know him personally sensed a fatal weakness in the discrepancy between the splendid intentions of the poem and the desperate tragedy of his personal dilemma. Yvor Winters, reviewing the book for *Poetry*, suspected with what seemed to Crane a cruel innuendo that he was "temperamentally unable to understand a very wide range of experience." Indeed, Winters's review as a whole, written with a relentless ethical bias, was such a surprising and vicious attack in view of his earlier and excessive enthusiasm for *The Bridge* that Crane was completely crushed upon reading it and burst into tears. The indignant letter he wrote to Winters in reply elicited only a brief and chilly note that brought their correspondence to an end and confirmed Crane's belief that he had been "betrayed" because of his personal habits.

Actually, Winters's review, when stripped of its unjust invective and prejudice, reduced to the same criticisms that were made by Cowley in *The New Republic* and Tate in *Hound & Horn*, as well as by others. These objections focused on the poem's failure to realize its intentions, the break-up of the epical subject into lyrical impulses, the unresolved vacillation between philosophical optimism and pessimism, and the occasional lapses of poetic style into an uncontrolled rhetoric. But despite these reservations many of the critics recognized *The Bridge* as a successful, if not a great, work, and a few accorded it unqualified praise. Granville Hicks, who reviewed the book for *The Nation* and the *New York World,* wrote that it was "as important a poem as has been written in our time . . . a greatness beyond the reach of the reviewer's superlatives"; and Vincent McHugh in the *New York Evening Post* claimed that Crane had caught the "major qualities of the American spirit and tradition" and had "honorably advanced the tradition of Walt Whitman." On the other hand one or two critics remained imperturbably hostile and obtuse. Percy Hutchinson in the *New York Times* came to the incredible conclusion that *The Bridge* was a form of "cubism in poetry . . . in the main spurious"; while William Rose Benét, who had written silly burlesques of the poems in *White Buildings,* expressed the view in *The Saturday Review of Literature* that it was "a great deal of sound and fury in reality signifying very little."

Crane was beyond the reach of such popular reviewers, however. It was the criticism of men like Tate, Cowley, and Winters which held his respect and attention; and in their objections he was willing to admit much that was true. Indeed, he seems in many ways to have had a clearer, more impersonal understanding of the faults of *The Bridge* than they. In a letter to Tate, written after reading the latter's review in *Hound & Horn,* he defended himself in some points, confessed his guilt in others, and brought a few acute counter-charges against his critics in which there was much truth.

"The fact that you posit *The Bridge,* at the end of a tradition of romanticism," he wrote, "may prove to have been an accurate prophecy, but I don't yet feel that such a statement can be taken as a foregone conclusion. A great deal of romanticism may persist—of the sort to deserve serious consideration, I mean.

"But granting your accuracy—I shall be humbly grateful if

The Bridge can fulfill simply the metaphorical inferences of its title. . . . You will admit our age (at least our predicament) to be one of transition. If *The Bridge*, embodying as many anomalies as you find in it, yet contains as much authentic poetry here and there as even Winters grants,—then perhaps it can serve as at least the function of a link connecting certain chains of the past to certain chains and tendencies of the future. . . . This gives it no more interest than as a point of chronological reference, but 'nothing ventured, nothing gained'—and I can't help thinking that my mistakes may warn others who may later be tempted to an interest in similar subject matter. . . . Taggard, like Winters, isn't looking for poetry any more. Like Munson, they are both in pursuit of some cure-all. Poetry as poetry (and I don't mean merely decorative verse) isn't worth a second reading any more. Therefore away with Kubla Khan, out with Marlowe, and to hell with Keats! It's a pity I think. So many true things have a way of coming out all the better without the strain to sum up the universe in one impressive pellet. I admit that I don't answer the requirements. My vision of poetry *is* too personal to 'answer the call.' And if I ever write any more verse it will probably be at least as personal as the idiom of *White Buildings*, whether anyone cares to look at it or not.

"The personal note is doubtless responsible for what you term as sentimentality in my attitude toward Whitman. It's true that my rhapsodic address to him in *The Bridge* exceeds any exact evaluation of the man. I realized that in the midst of composition. But since you and I hold such divergent prejudices regarding the materials and events W responded to, and especially as you, like so many others, never seem to have read his *Democratic Vistas* and other of his statements sharply decrying materialism, industrialism, etc. of which you name him the guilty and hysterical spokesman, there isn't much use in my tabulating the qualified yet persistent reasons I have for my admiration of him, and my allegiance to the positive universal tendencies implicit in nearly all his best work. You've heard me roar at too many of his lines to doubt that I can spot his worst, I'm sure."

The tone of resignation in this letter, the acceptance of limitations, so different from his exalted enthusiasms and equally intense despairs, was token of a new state of mind for Crane. It was equivalent to a reasonable admission of partial defeat, and for a person of his temperament, one must suspect, even of total defeat. Though he never admitted as much, implications of such a conclusion were constantly heard in his talk and his letters bore frequent innuendoes to the same effect. In falling short of the extreme goal he had set himself, in failing to achieve the complete and radiant vision of the mysticism he so vividly felt and so sadly misunderstood and abused, he seems to have done his spirit an irreparable injury from which it never recovered. It was not without especial significance that during the aimless and violent months of the summer and fall of 1930 he discovered Dante for the first time and was suffused, briefly and reflectively, by the light of a spiritual faith which had persistently evaded his own most strenuous reach. He read one translation after another, and in his headlong enthusiasm pored over the Italian despite his complete ignorance of the language. He exclaimed over and over to his friends that he felt and saw exactly as Dante had and about the same things, and elaborated in astonished delight upon the similarities between them. The affinity that he felt for the great religious poet may best be described by quoting the passage from the thirty-third canto of the *Paradiso*, which Crane carefully copied in one of his notebooks together with Wicksteed's translation:

"O grace abounding, wherein I presumed to fix my look on the eternal light so long that I consumed my sight thereon! Within its depths I saw ingathered, bound by love in one volume, the scattered leaves of all the universe; substance and accidents and their relations, as though together fused, after such fashion that what I tell of is one simple flame. The universal form of this complex I think that I beheld, because more largely, as I say this, I feel that I rejoice."

It was a vision that Crane too had seen, imperfectly and inconstantly, it is true, but nonetheless poignantly. His own version of it comes in the last stanza but one of *The Bridge*:

> Unspeakable Thou Bridge to Thee, O Love.
> Thy pardon for this history, whitest Flower,
> O Answerer of all,—Anemone,—
> Now while thy petals spend the suns about us, hold—
> (O Thou whose radiance doth inherit me)
> Atlantis,—hold thy floating singer late!

But he had seen this vision most clearly several years earlier, and now not even his discovery of Dante had the power to restore in him a strong and living conviction of its reality. For the rest, his life in Patterson continued in irritable idleness and bouts of drinking. His rages became more maniacal in their fury and defiance, often turning against those of whom he was most fond and even more frequently exposing him to all sorts of dangers, as though a profound instinct in him were courting the uttermost peril of self-destruction. In one instance, he deliberately infuriated a group of farmers with whom he had been drinking by boasting obscenely of his homosexual practices in the presence of women, and was saved from the threat of an immediate beating only by the intervention of the barkeeper's wife. Mrs. Turner, his wrinkled old landlady, grew more and more terrified of his behavior; often when he left the house in a drunken condition, she locked the doors against his return, only to have both doors and windows smashed. More than once these outbursts were caused by a drunken inspection of a series of photographs of his mother, which he kept in his room and in which he professed to see a gradual progression of moral decay. Finally, after an afternoon and evening of unprecedented violence and destruction, when Blume, Cowley, and Brown were called in to pacify him, Mrs. Turner firmly demanded that he leave her house once and for all. Crane without saying a word moved his belongings down the road to the home of his friend Eleanor Fitzgerald, and there, though somewhat abated, his outrages continued.

Towards the middle of July, together with Lorna Dietz, one of the few friends whose affection he seems to have trusted, he left for New Hampshire for a fortnight's visit with E. E. Cummings and his wife at their country home. His attitude towards many of his friends during this time is well illustrated by an incident that occurred during his stay there. Having tormented himself with suspicions of Cummings's real feeling for him, and aroused himself to a pitch of unbearable anxiety and fear, he arose one night after the household was asleep, and waking Miss Dietz, persistently demanded to know whether Cummings was merely tolerating him or whether he was genuinely fond of him, until his host from the room below called up his reassurance and told him to go to bed. He was most suspicious of those friends who were writers, possibly because he realized that their regard for him was inextricably involved with their estimation of his creative activity, which was now at a complete standstill; and it was from them that he felt increasingly estranged. As the country plunged deeper into the slough of economic depression, most of them abandoned the cause of "pure" literature for a growing interest in political and social ideas; and tacitly relinquishing their first books of verse, their one or two novels to the limbo of "early works," dipped their pens afresh in the brilliant ink of the new thought. Somewhere, perhaps, Ernest Boyd indulged in a sibylline smile, recalling his prophecy of the aesthetes who would become journalists; for of all of them only Cummings and Crane shied clear of the new factionalism. Too honest, too stubborn, or possibly merely unable to make a compromise, Crane clung to his old way of life and his original conception of poetry, willing to stand or fall by the impulses that had governed his life. Whenever he was asked what his friends were doing, he stormed about shouting that they were only "cutting paper dollies."

Upon his return to Miss Fitzgerald's home at Gaylordsville, the township adjoining Patterson, financial worries again began to harass him. In August he made application for a Guggenheim fellowship; but having no assurance of winning the coveted award, and since, in any case, the judges' decision would not be rendered until the following spring, he was still faced by the difficult problem of supporting himself through the winter. Since his own small capital was too nearly exhausted to draw upon further, he started once more to borrow small amounts from his friends. In September he wrote to Kahn, forthrightly asking for a subsidy of twenty-five dollars a week, which would support him in the country until he could find employment. But his patron was travelling in Europe, and the plea was in vain. With the arrival of October, however, he received the Helen Haire Levinson prize of two hundred dollars, one of the annual awards of Harriet Monroe's *Poetry*, in recognition of his achievement in *The Bridge;* and thus flimsily reënforced, he returned to live in the city in the hope of finding work. For a time he made Eleanor Fitzgerald's apartment at 45 Grove Street his headquarters, but eventually he moved back to the neighborhood of Columbia Heights, this time to the Hotel St. George, where he rented a cheap room by the week. That he avoided taking a room in one of his old boarding houses was very likely owing to the fear of blackmail that had haunted him ever since the preceding spring, when a group of sailors had robbed him one night after he had lapsed into unconsciousness, not only stripping his room of clothes and valuables, but also carrying off with them the incriminating evidence contained in his address book.

Despite such experiences he plunged into the old round of debauchery, heedless of expense, health, and personal safety. Columbia Heights and the adjacent streets which slanted steeply down to the notorious waterfront under the Bridge were well known to the police for crimes and immoral practiçes of all sorts, and from time to time were rigorously and brutally patrolled. More than once during this time Crane was arrested for solicitation and drunkenness; and one night he was set upon by two plainclothesmen, who found him wandering in the streets, and severely beaten— a drastic method devised by the police as more effective than a night in jail. It was possibly this humiliating experience that drove him to use cabs in his midnight prowlings. In any case, as his money dwindled his extravagance increased. Night after night, unable to sleep, he set out in a taxi to make the rounds of his favorite haunts along Sand Street, collecting sailors and carousing—finally, as a rule, to end up drunk and penniless at the house of a friend begging for a loan to pay his accumulated fare. By November he was so exhausted by dissipation, anxiety, and insomnia that he proved completely incapable of qualifying for the opportunity which was finally available to him.

Through Archibald MacLeish, the poet, and Russell Davenport, both of whom were employed by the industrial magazine *Fortune*, he met the magazine's managing editor, Parker Lloyd Smith, who, knowing Crane's enthusiasm for bridges, offered him the assignment of writing an article on the George Washington Bridge, then in the process of construction. Immediately fired with excitement by the subject,

Crane spent a week or two collecting material. Despite the handicap of regular "hangovers," he turned up for several days at the scene of operations; interviewed engineers; was shot up high over the Hudson River in skeletal elevators; was whisked about by tug-boats; and was even offered the privilege of crossing the bridge on a "cat-walk"—an invitation he wisely declined. The spinning of the gigantic cables, in particular, fascinated him; and much of the little writing he actually did consisted in eloquent descriptions of this process. But his writing was either too poetic or too heavily burdened with advertising slogans to be acceptable; nor was he able to organize the material for consecutive presentation. Even the help of his friends, whom he phoned for advice at all hours of the night, and of MacLeish, in particular, who outlined the article for him, was unavailing, and in the end he confessed that the task was beyond him. A similar fate overtook his second assignment, an interview with J. Walter Teagle, the President of the Standard Oil Company of New Jersey. Having talked with him at great length and collected a bewildering amount of information, he was utterly helpless, despite his tremendous admiration for the man, to produce an article which would satisfy the requirements of the magazine, and finally proffered as an excuse the absurd story that all the material had been stolen from his mailbox.

Although there is undoubtedly some truth in the explanation for this fiasco that Crane wrote to a friend—namely, "the degree of paralysis that worry can impose on the functioning of one's natural faculties"—his drinking was more probably the cause of it. It is only surprising that he did not show even more serious symptoms of alcoholism. His appearance, however, remained practically unchanged. His hair, which had become completely grey, served but to emphasize the youthfulness of his face; and his heavy features, though somewhat coarsened by dissipation, still expressed the same magnetic charm and vitality. Wherever he appeared, in fact, whether at the Davenports, where he often turned up during the course of an evening, or at the homes of other friends, he still held the center of the stage, his conversation flowing as always in a stream of brilliant epithet and remarkable intuition and his body emphasizing his periods and inflections with irrepressible animation. But underneath this appearance of characteristic vigor he was actually nearing the limit of physical endurance. The amount of energy consumed by incessant drinking was doubled by what seems to have been almost chronic insomnia, which drove him to seek drunken unconsciousness as his only means of rest. His failure to complete the *Fortune* articles, adding the weight of shame and disappointment to the already intolerable burden of physical exhaustion, brought him to a sudden decision; and early in December he left New York for his father's inn outside of Cleveland, reeling as usual on the crest of a night of hilarious drinking.

XI

"*Hasten, while they are true,—sleep, death, desire,*
Close round one instant in one floating flower."

ALTHOUGH Crane had not planned to spend the winter in Chagrin Falls, Ohio, the months wore on without his making any move to leave. From time to time he wrote friends in New York that he might "dive back into the metropolis willy nilly, since there are several ways of dying," or again that he had "moments of regarding breadlines as less humiliating than parental duck and plum pudding." But however much he chafed under the pangs of pride and conscience, he was always restrained from leaving his snug refuge by the recollection of the city parks crowded with unemployed, the able-bodied workers and professional men selling apples and shoe-strings along the avenues. Moreover, he was not entirely unhappy despite his restlessness and sense of isolation. Owing to the sensible tact and kindliness of his step-mother, the third Mrs. Crane, a woman not a great deal older than himself, of whom he was very fond, his relations with his father were greatly improved. For the first time the two were able to meet on comparatively equal grounds, if not with understanding of one another, at least with a mutual respect which fostered the natural affection between them, so long distorted by circumstances. If in later months Hart ranted against his father for having made him perform menial tasks about the inn, it was owing more to a reversion to character than to any genuine resentment. Actually, he welcomed whatever chores were available, turning his hand to carpentry, painting, repairing; joking with the help, hobnobbing with the cooks in the kitchen, and amusing the whole household with his uproarious and fantastic stories. He even accepted restrictions of his personal habits with a good grace, humorously recognizing his father's objections to his smoking and chewing tobacco simultaneously, and confining his drinking to rare visits to friends in Cleveland.

It was little short of amazing that, having drunk to such habitual excess in New York, he was able to maintain almost complete abstinence for three months without evidently suffering any strain or reaction. This would seem to confirm the interpretation that his use of alcohol, together with its correlative defiance and violent egotism, was part of a complex mechanism of self-defense. In New York, in Paris, and presently in Mexico—in short, wherever he felt exposed to the abysmal insecurity and suspicions of the world—he needed the license of intoxication to override his fears and assert himself against the encroachments of doubt. But in the inn at Chagrin Falls where he was surrounded by simple people who, knowing little of his life in New York and caring less, still accorded him full measure of spontaneous affection for his human qualities, there was no necessity for such devices. Occasionally, it is true, when he was unable to find tasks to busy himself about, a profound spiritual *malaise* beset him; and brooding over the aimlessness of his life in a world where he seemed to have no place, he longed once more for the violent drunkenness which would blind him to the perspectives of despair.

"These are bewildering times for everyone, I suppose," he wrote to Frank in February. "I can't muster much of anything to say to anyone. I seem to have lost the faculty to even feel tension. A bad sign, I'm sure. When they all get it decided, Capitalism or Communism, then I'll probably be able to resume a few intensities; meanwhile there seems to be no sap in anything. I'd love to fight for—almost anything, but there seems to be no longer any real resistance. Maybe I'm only a disappointed romantic, after all. Or perhaps I've made too many affable compromises. I hope to discover the fault, whatever it is, before long. . . . Present day America seems a long way off from the destiny I fancied when I wrote that poem [The Bridge]. In some ways Spengler must have been right.

"On the water wagon two months now. . . . If abstinence is clarifying to the vision, as they claim, then give me back the blindness of my will. It needs a fresh baptism."

This was his prevailing mood throughout the winter. For the first time in years he was able to look at the world about him and, more importantly, at his own life in the clear light of protracted soberness and quiet; and what he saw appalled him. Excepting the goal of completing The Bridge, there had been no direction in his life for six years, no interior growth or clarification of personality, which presently would have put forth its pattern of purpose into the future, to burgeon with new meaning and seasonable fruits. There had been only a constant and violent furrowing of the spirit, a ravaging of its resources by wasteful impulses without subsequent renewal, until it was spent beyond the hope of possible germination. It was hardly surprising, then, that he should long once more for the blindness of his will, for if his spirit was exhausted, that will by which he had sworn as a boy to make his fate still remained, headstrong and intoxicated by the sense of its autonomous power of life and death.

When in March he received one of the Guggenheim fellowships and returned to New York, he immediately plunged back into the maelstrom of drunken violence. Apparently so reckless was he of the future, so avid of the sheer sensation of intense living again, that during the two weeks before his departure he spent almost the entire amount of the first quarterly payment of his stipend in carousing. Meanwhile, he had not even made any well-formulated plans of what he was going to do. Since the fellowship required residence abroad, he had stipulated in his application a desire to go to France; but for a project he had only the vague hope that he would again be possessed by some great theme. It was not until a few days before leaving, when on the advice of friends he suddenly decided to go to Mexico, that he began to speak of writing a long poetic drama of the Conquest, an inspiration originally conceived while on the Isle of Pines and thereafter almost forgotten. But however much his imagination might be inflamed from time to time by the brilliant barbaric pageantry of the Cortes-Montezuma history, he was not to achieve its recreation. His creative impulse was too scattered, too riddled by fears, to restore him to equilibrium. From the moment he set staggering foot aboard ship early in April, after a night of farewell rounds, until he took abrupt and final leave of the same ship a year later, the story of his life is also, almost exclusively, the story of his death.

The voyage south was an early indication of what the tempo of the following months would be. As the ship swung into the Gulf Stream and plowed deeper into the Caribbean, his drinking increased. By the time Havana was reached, his funds were exhausted and he was depending for his expenses upon Dr. Hans Zinsser, the well-known bacteriologist, who together with an assistant was also en route to Mexico City, where an epidemic of typhoid fever had broken out. Crane, with the dogged, almost animal-like affection characteristic of him, attached himself to the doctor during the trip, following him about the ship, plying him with questions concerning his work, and discussing poetry for hours on end. Dr. Zinsser, for his part, quickly recognizing his constant drinking and violent tempers as symptoms of a disordered spirit, developed a fatherly concern for Crane. Shocked on the one hand by his harsh, deliberate obscenity in talking of sexual matters and on the other hand deeply affected by the pathos and appeal of his occasional illuminations of child-like spirit, the doctor seemed, nonetheless, to understand Crane's dilemma with considerable insight. The prose poem "Havana Rose," in which Crane recorded his "humble, fond remembrances of the great bacteriologist," concludes with the sensible and sympathetic advice that Dr. Zinsser gave him one night when the ship was lying over in Havana:

"And during the wait over dinner at La Diana, the Doctor had said—who was American also—'You cannot heed the negative, so might go on to undeserved doom . . . must therefore loose yourself within a pattern's mastery that you can conceive, that you can yield to—by which also you win and gain mastery and happiness which is your own from birth.'"

Had he known Crane more intimately, he would have realized—and possibly he did suspect—that Crane had already yielded to a pattern far different from the one he recommended. It was wise counsel, however; and to show his gratitude for the affection which prompted it, Crane immediately borrowed several dollars from the doctor with which to order a few rounds of brandy. With the remaining money he bought himself a bottle of rum that he carried back to his cabin with him. Later in the evening, having consumed its contents and taken to prowling the decks in search of his friend, he surprised the doctor absorbed in the act of dropping overboard a parcel wrapped in newspapers. Leaning over the side, he saw the packet burst asunder as it struck the water, and dimly distinguished two white rats struggling frantically against the current. Knowing that the rats were two of four typhus-infected specimens that the doctor had smuggled aboard ship for experimental purposes in Mexico, Crane was seized by the drunken fantasy that his friend was diabolically poisoning the harbor of Havana, and began to shout frenzied warnings of the danger at the top of his voice. Dr. Zinsser's efforts to explain that the rats were almost dead and were being carried out to sea by an ebb tide were unavailing. Completely swept away by his hallucinations, Crane had identified the animals with those he had seen in the Paris jail, and overwhelmed by the feeling of persecution which so often accompanied his drunken states, associated the poisoning of the harbor with the brutal treatment he had received at the hands of the French police. There was no question of silencing him. Fortunately for Dr. Zinsser, however, the ship's officers who came running up to investigate the disturbance were convinced—without, indeed, being far from wrong—that Crane was suffering from delirium tremens; and for the rest of the night he was locked in his cabin, where his violence spent itself in vituperation.

Upon his arrival in Mexico City Crane installed himself in a cheap hotel with money borrowed from the doctor until he could replenish his funds by urgent wires to his father and numerous friends in the States. In the meantime he showed no signs of reorganizing his life to meet the demands of his new environment and to prepare himself for writing. His only adjustment seems to have been the substitution of *tequila*, the cheap, powerful native drink, for the less dangerous liquor of his own country, with a consequent increase in the pace of his dissipation. Certainly, Mexico offered no reassurance to a person in need of spiritual and mental stability; and it can not be doubted that Crane, with his acute sensitivity to the most trivial influences, was further unhinged by the pervasive qualities of its profoundly mysterious and hostile strangeness. At first sight, it is true, he fell in love with the country: the dramatic and dizzy ascent from Vera Cruz winding through humid jungles that breathed a heavy perfume of gardenias and exotic lilies through the train, coiling along the edge of breathless panoramas to the high floor of the plateau, where bristling fields of maguey stretched away in the clear rarefied air to the stark volcanic mountains that rose from the flat plain in massive misshapen forms to even greater heights—the remote, inscrutable, apparently lifeless roof of the world. But there was something unfriendly, something sinister in all this beauty. Behind the dark inflexible masks of the Indians one sensed an active resentment, an almost animal-like suspicion and hatred, as ancient and enduring as the centuries of oppression which had engendered it, likely at any moment to erupt into fatal violence. In a country where human life was cheap, casual and diminutive, the smell of death was constantly in the air. In the expressionless eyes, gleaming at night between the rim of sombrero and serape, in the lightning-like scuttle of a scorpion, even in the flame-colored flowers lighting a leafless tree in the grey rubble of mountain rock, there was always a signal of sudden death. And the pleasures of the people, whom Crane both loved and feared, were fierce momentary joys snatched like gratuities from a life neither joyful nor generous; and their songs had in them a wild tone of forsakenness. There was much in the spirit of

Mexico that carried a potential threat for Crane. Its silent antagonism served only to sharpen and drive home his sense of estrangement and isolation; its violent contrasts and intensities encouraged him in his own dramatic excesses, offering both irritation and example; and in the life of the people, as well as in the gigantic, ruthless nature that dominated them, he constantly sensed the ageless futility of human effort. Something of his reaction to the country may be seen in one of the poems found among his papers, significantly called "Purgatorio."

My country, O my land, my friends—
Am I apart—here from you in a land
Where all your gas lights—faces—sputum gleam
Like something left, forsaken—here am I—
And are these stars—the high plateau—the scents
Of Eden—and the dangerous tree—are these
The landscape of confession—and if confession
So absolution? Wake pines—but pines wake here.
I dream the too-keen cider—the too-soft snow.
Where are the bayonets that the scorpion may not grow?
Here quakes of earth make houses fall—
And all my countrymen I see rush toward one stall;
Exile is thus purgatory—not such as Dante built,

But rather like a blanket than a quilt,
And I have no decision—is it green or brown
That I prefer to country or to town?

Town or country, Mexico or the States—it mattered little in the end where he went; for the torments he longed to escape were spiritual. Although he had originally planned to settle down in some quiet mountain village, he accepted instead the invitation of Katherine Anne Porter, another Guggenheim Fellow, whom he had known in New York, to make his temporary quarters at her home in Mixcoac, a sleepy native suburb of Mexico City. Before many days had passed, however, she had reason to regret her hospitality; for Crane, caught in the quickening constrictions of his fate, which with every burst of maddened resistance entangled him the more securely, was fast becoming an insupportable companion. The moral fiber, which had sustained him in past crises, had long since rotted away by dissipation, and there was no longer any restraint to check the painful exhibition he made of his suffering. Regardless of pride, sensibility, and propriety, he threw himself with abandon upon friend and stranger alike, as though he could thus rid himself of his intolerable burden. And yet he never asked for help, for he knew full well that the only salvation lay in himself, who was helpless. Those of his friends who, like Miss Porter, tried to be of some assistance, discovered that commiseration only encouraged him in self-pity and that advice, however delicately or kindly proffered, was liable to bring down on their heads furious accusations of "betrayal." These drunken scenes were all the more painful to his friends in that during his sober moments he seemed so quietly reasonable, so full of his old humor, so tender and solicitous in his attentions, that their hopes for his ultimate recovery were constantly renewed. During the mornings, when he often spent pleasant hours helping Miss Porter tend her garden, he was still capable of taking a pure delight in the beauty of the flowers: the rich intense purple of the bougain-villea hanging with luxurious weight from the white sunlit wall, the curious intricate symbolism of the passion-flower, the delicate bell-like columbines, the forms and colors of all the exotic plants and blooms. And in the afternoons, dressed in his usual white sailor pants, Basque jersey, and kerchief, he was frequently seen in the great markets of the city, plung-ing excitedly from one stall to another, buying pottery and glass, serapes, huaraches, flowers, and toys, followed all the while by a little white dog and a patient *mozo*, who carried a canvas bag full of silver pesos—for there was no paper currency in Mexico at that time.

But if he sometimes refrained from drinking during the day, it was rarely that midnight found him sober. With the coming of night, as though the darkness in blotting out the life about him drove him back into the whirling interior cage of his dilemma, he began to drink heavily, wandering from one *cantina* to another in a blind, wilful effort to escape his conscience, till he became possessed by an almost insane rage of resentment and frustration. When Miss Porter, no longer able to endure the situation, persuaded him to find a home of his own, he rented the adjoining building, which, unfortunately for her, was vacant—a spacious house with its own garden and a small staff of servants. But there was no cessation of his midnight brawling, and the new arrangement proved of little protection. It was not so much this violence, however, nor even the shocking sordidness of his sexual life, that appalled his neighbor, as it was the terrible spectacle of a great talent, an essentially noble spirit, caught in the grip of a slow, inexorable disintegration. In some random recollections of this period, written in later years, Miss Porter left an eloquent record of Crane's spiritual disorder and anguish.

"The evening before this episode at the gate," she wrote, "I had stopped before his own iron gate and called out to him that his garden already looked like something not made with hands. He came out and we talked for a few minutes. I did not go in because I was on my way somewhere else. It was just after dark and he had been reading Blake by the light of a single candle. He was drinking somewhat, too, alone in the house. He repeated a few of the vast lines, and added almost in the same voice: 'You can't see them from here, but I have hundreds of little plants that I got at the market this morning.' Holding to the grill he suddenly began to cry and said, 'You don't know what my life has been.

This is the only place I ever felt was my own. This is the only place I ever loved.'

"The next evening, or rather some time after midnight, he arrived at our gate in a taxicab, and began the habitual dreary brawl with the driver, shouting that he had been cheated, robbed; calling for us to come and pay his fare, as he had been robbed in a café. At times he accused the driver of robbing him. This time he stood there jingling heavy silver coins in his pocket, and as he shouted, he took out half a dozen, looked at them, and returned them to his pocket. I gave the driver the usual fare and sent him away. (Hart always insisted that he could never remember anything of these events, but he never once failed to come or send the next day to return the money I had paid the drivers.) Hart then demanded to come in, but I was tired to death, at the end of my patience, and I told him plainly he must go home. It was then that he broke into the monotonous obsessed dull obscenity which was the only language he knew after reaching a certain point of drunkenness, but this time he cursed things and elements as well as human beings. His voice at these times was intolerable; a steady harsh inhuman bellow which stunned the ears and shocked the nerves and caused the heart to contract. In this voice and with words so foul there is no question of repeating them, he cursed separately and by name the moon, and its light: the heliotrope, the heaven-tree, the sweet-by-night, the star jessamine, and their perfumes. He cursed the air we breathed together, the pool of water with its two small ducks huddled at the edge, and the vines on the wall and the house. But those were not the things he hated. He did not even hate us, for we were nothing to him. He hated and feared himself.

"Sober, he tried to analyze his predicament, he would talk slowly in an ordinary voice, saying he knew he was destroying himself as poet, he did not know why, and he asked himself why, constantly. He said once that the life he lived was blunting his sensibilities, that he was no longer capable of feeling anything except under the most violent and brutal shocks: 'and I can't even then deceive myself that I really feel anything,' he said. He talked about Baudelaire and Marlowe, and Whitman and Melville and Blake—all the consoling examples he could call to mind of artists who had lived excessively in one way or another. Later, drunk, he would weep and shout, shaking his fist, 'I am Baudelaire, I am Whitman, I am Christopher Marlowe, I am Christ' but never once did I hear him say he was Hart Crane. . . . He talked of suicide almost every day. Whenever he read of a suicide in the newspapers, he approved and praised the act. He spoke of Ralph Barton's suicide as 'noble.' He described the suicide of Harry Crosby as 'imaginative; the act of a poet.' Once while he was still stopping at my house he ran out of his room—it was night, and the moon seems to have been shining, again—rushed up to the roof which was only one story high, and shouted that he was going to throw himself off. It happened rather suddenly after such a long silence in his part of the house that I thought he might be asleep. I called out to him, 'Oh don't. It's not high enough and you'll only hurt yourself.' He began to laugh immediately, a curiously fresh sober humor in the laughter, and came down by way of an apricot tree with branches spreading over the roof. He sat and talked a little while, went in and began to play the piano loudly and incoherently—it was very old and out of tune— and after about an hour of this he left the house, and did not return. He had got into difficulties in town and spent the night in jail. . . ."

His mind was so disordered by fantasies of persecution, betrayal, and guilt, that when early in July he received a telegram announcing the sudden death of his father, he suspected for a moment that it was a ruse on the part of the Guggenheim Foundation to entice him back to New York for disciplinary measures. Once convinced of the authenticity of the message, however, he immediately left Mexico by plane and arrived at Chagrin Falls in time for the funeral.

It must have been a strange bewildering moment: his father, for so long his most bitter enemy, now dead; his mother, he knew not where; and his only "home" in a remote and alien country, which threatened constantly to engulf him. But he found genuine consolation and a happiness, however forlorn, in the thought of the affection he had shared with his father during the last few years. That Mr. Crane, for his part, had become completely reconciled to his son was attested by the will he left, which specified that after a period of four years his substantial estate should be divided equally between Hart and his wife, and that Hart, in the meantime, should receive an annuity of two thousand dollars. It was a generous and just bequest, and not a little ironic after the years of financial anxiety his son had endured; but its potential benefits were wasted, for Crane had passed beyond the point where economic security could retrieve his peace of mind and health of spirit. During the following weeks, however, while he stayed on at Chagrin Falls in a kindly effort to be of service to his step-mother, his behavior gave no hint of his actual state of mind. Not until he returned to New York did he abandon himself once more to his fate, resuming his dissipations as though they had never been interrupted. As upon his return from Europe with *The Bridge* still unfinished, so now, empty-handed, with nothing to show, or even to say, of his new project, he was ashamed to meet his old friends. Fearful of their questions and reproaches, he confined himself for the most part to his room at the Hotel Albert, where he was waiting for his boat to sail, drinking heavily in the hope of obliterating the consciousness of his loneliness and doubt. His faith in himself was so far destroyed that he was able in all honesty to ask Slater Brown—who was again the first of his friends to find him wandering the streets—whether or not he believed that his poetry would live. Three days before his departure, Walker Evans, finding him in the dining room of his hotel, haggard, unkempt, and scarcely able to feed himself, was so shocked by his apparent helplessness that he undertook to care for him during the interim, buying his ticket, seeing to his luggage, and finally installing him in his cabin aboard ship.

Throughout the fall, as the circle of his acquaintances in Mexico widened, the opportunities for distraction and dissipation multiplied, offering an abundant supply of excuses to put off the day of reckoning. Shortly after his return to Mixcoac, he set out with a young American archaeologist, who later came to live with him, for a walking trip to Tepoztlan, a primitive Aztec village not far from Mexico City, where he participated with wild gusto in the barbaric ceremonies for a native god and was accorded the distinction of beating the ancient wooden drum atop the cathedral, "while a whole bevy of rockets showered into such a vocal sunrise." Under such bizarre conditions—"sitting there on the top of that church, with the lightning playing on one horizon, a new moon sinking on the opposite and with millions of stars overhead and between and with that strange old music beating in one's blood"—it was possible to achieve momentary relief, even to strike a spark of transcendent fire once more from the worn fiber of his sensibilities. Instinctively he sought out such conditions, contriving almost never to be alone, never to be without occasion for intense sensation or violent amusement. When he was not making expeditions into the hinterland or attending the local fiestas about the city, he was most often to be found in Taxco, where he visited William Spratling, a resident artist known as the "unofficial mayor" of the town, and later, Peggy Baird, whom he had known intimately for many years in New York as the wife of Malcolm Cowley. A charming native village terraced steeply into the precipitous mountains of Guerrero, Taxco was practically untouched by tourists in those days, and yet inhabited by a sufficient number of American and Mexican artists, and an occasional writer, to provide a lively spot for distractions. There he could hold forth in Doña Berta's bar on the Plaza, inflaming himself with tequila and talk of his great project without fear of criticism, and in the evening, perhaps, sit on the porch of a friend, high over the town, looking out into the scented darkness that was richly disturbed from time to time by the weird resonant voices of the village minstrels.

It was during one of these visits to Taxco that Crane met the well-known Mexican painter, David Siqueiros, and sat to him for his portrait. That the painting represented him with lowered lids was owing to the fact that Siqueiros, despite repeated efforts, could not paint his eyes, so startling were they, so desperately expressive of the fate that was poised within him, ripe for fulfilment. Not long after this, when the painter fell sick with malaria and had no decent refuge, Crane invited him and his wife to make use of his house in Mixcoac, at the same time extending the invitation to include political asylum for several of his friends and compatriots—Communists, who were seeking a hiding place. Although the resulting turmoil often drove him to Tepoztlan in search of rest and quiet, he preferred it to solitude and the uncomfortable company of his books and blank paper; and when Siqueiros upon his recovery took his leave, Crane urged the others to remain. Throughout the fall and winter his house was never empty of guests, his conscience never without excuses.

Needless to say, his devices were almost completely successful. As the term of his fellowship drew towards its close, he had practically nothing to show for his year's sojourn in Mexico: a few short poems, which he had not thought worthy of publication, and several pages of criticism—reviews he had agreed to write for *Poetry* and had been unable to finish; but of the dramatic epic of the Conquest, not a line. He discussed it at great length with his friends, particularly with Lesley Simpson, a professor of history from the University of California, who, remarking that his information was largely derived from Prescott's work, supplied him with an exhaustive bibliography of the subject. But such gestures of concrete assistance only angered Crane by their implied criticism. He preferred to play with his conception in the intoxicated freedom of his imagination, careful always to keep it at several removes from the conditions of actual creation. Excepting his conversation and letters the only evidence that he ever contemplated such a work was a typewritten sheet, printed as a title page for the poem, which he sent as token of his industry to a friend in New York who had reproached him with his idleness and wasteful living in Mexico. Harassed by the fear that he had completely lost the power to create, the thought of his friends of earlier days, for whom he was still the leading poet of his generation, was a constant torment to him. Unable to send them substantial proof of creative activity, he wrote them deliberately cheerful and serene letters in the hope of counterbalancing the rumors of his escapades that he knew were reaching them from Mexico. On several occasions he confessed to Lesley Simpson and others that he feared their reaction to every word he wrote. He wanted to introduce elements of satire and burlesque into his poetry, but was afraid they would consider it a kind of apostasy, a deviation from his proper idiom. The more he anticipated and brooded over their criticisms, their unvoiced imaginary strictures, the more surely were his faculties frozen in a strange kind of spiritual paralysis.

In January, however, such prohibitions notwithstanding, he was possessed once more, for the last time, by the demonic spirit of "divine madness," and with his old creative fury began the first verses of "The Broken Tower." In a letter written to the *New English Weekly* after Crane's death, to refute Gorham Munson's statement that the poem had been composed several years earlier, Lesley Simpson left a record of its immediate genesis.

"I was with Hart Crane in Taxco, Mexico the morning of January 27, this year," he wrote, "when he first conceived the idea of 'The Broken Tower.' The night before, being troubled with insomnia, he had risen before daybreak and walked down to the village square. It so happened that one of the innumerable Indian fiestas was to be celebrated that day, and Hart met the old Indian bell-ringer who was on his way down to the Church. He and Hart were old friends, and he brought Hart up into the tower with him to help ring the bells. As Hart was swinging the clapper of the great bell, half drunk with its mighty music, the swift tropical dawn broke over the mountains. The sublimity of the scene and the thunder of the bells woke in Hart one of those gusts of joy of which only he was capable. He came striding up the hill afterwards in a sort of frenzy, refused his breakfast, and paced up and down the porch impatiently waiting for me to finish my coffee. Then he seized my arm and bore me off to the plaza where we sat in the shadow of the Church, Hart the while pouring out a magnificent cascade of words. It was a Hart Crane I had never known and an experience I shall never forget."

Although this incident furnished Crane with an appropriate and powerful symbolism, as well as an immediate stimulus, the actual content of the poem—its mysterious portent of spiritual pregnancy, its almost mystical quality of an Annunciation—was engendered by more human factors. Certainly in the preceding months there had been nothing to arouse in Crane the hope of salvation. During the early part of January, however, while visiting in Taxco, the long-standing friendship between him and Peggy Baird suddenly developed into a more intimate and complete relationship in which he apparently saw the possibility of a rebirth, both physical and spiritual, and an integration of the scattered decaying impulses of his life. Drawn together by their loneliness and sense of desolation in a strange and hostile country, they were able to offer one another much comfort and reassurance. During the first weeks of their relationship, and especially after Miss Baird moved into Mixcoac to live with him, Crane showed a considerable change in his behavior. His friends noted a kind of domestic happiness about him, a refreshing temperance of mood that suggested he had partially recovered his equilibrium, and a boyish delight in his new status. For the moment he was flushed with a sensation of renascent confidence and power for which he felt a humble, almost abased, gratitude. Shortly before their common residence was inaugurated, he wrote Miss Baird that he could scarcely understand her love for him.

"I don't deserve it," he confessed. "I'm just a careening idiot with a talent for humor at times, and for insult and desecration at others. But I can, and must say that your love is very precious to me. For one thing it gives me an assurance that I thought long buried. You can give me many things besides—if time proves me fit to receive them: the independence of my mind and soul again, and perhaps a real wholeness to my body."

But time proved otherwise. During the two months that he labored over "The Broken Tower," cutting, revising, and rearranging it, his newly achieved confidence gradually deserted him, undermined on the one hand by difficulties in composition, for which he now had so little patience, and on the other by a sudden accumulation of problems in his daily living, which he found himself helpless to solve. His servant,

Daniel, one of his boon drinking companions, going his master one better, became completely insubordinate, arriving at the house at all hours of the day and night, obstreperously drunk, and often in a threatening mood. Unwilling to discharge him for fear of retaliation, as well as because of his own friendship with Daniel's two brothers, local policemen, who often came to play marbles in his patio and sing to him of nights, Crane retained the man despite the constant chaos he caused. At the same time, in the process of having his passport renewed, he became entangled with a shyster lawyer, lost his papers, and was driven almost frantic with anxiety. As usual, such irritations led to heavy drinking and violent quarrels, which in turn quickly reduced him to his previous state of haggard uncertainty. Despite the encouragement and praise of Miss Baird and a few other friends, by the time he finished the poem towards the end of March, the self-confidence of his brief recreation had utterly vanished. He was so abysmally unsure of his achievement that when a week or so later he sent the poem to Cowley, he implored his "honest appraisal of this verse, prose, or nonsense—whatever it may seem." At the same time he dispatched a copy of it to Morton Dauwen Zabel, the associate editor of *Poetry*, who had been begging him to submit some poetry for publication. That both of these men, quite unaware of the tragic significance of the poem, did not reply until it was too late, added heavily to the weight of despair that overwhelmed Crane during his last weeks in Mexico.*

There can be no doubt that the belief that he had failed in "The Broken Tower"—his first really finished poem in two years—sealed his conviction that his creative powers were exhausted, once and for all. Coming as it did at the end of March, all this served as a bitterly decisive punctuation to his fruitless term as a Guggenheim Fellow; and he read in the evidence a plain sentence of doom. In his imagination he

* *From evidence available only after the publication of the original edition, it is clear that Crane, though he wrote Mr. Zabel from Mexico that he was sending him a copy of a new poem, did not*

turned over the pages of the months to come, and they were blank—empty of hope, or purpose, or meaning. Deprived of his only function in life, the single source of spiritual nourishment and satisfaction run dry, it mattered little, he well knew, where he went or what he did. Should he remain in Mexico on his own money? There was small likelihood that the magnificent mirage of the epic tragedy would suddenly materialize out of nothing. Should he go home, then—and where was "home"? Certainly not New York. The very thought of meeting his old friends shrivelled his conscience with apprehension and shame; and even should he be able to face out their reproaches, he no longer shared with them any vital community of purpose. Almost all of them—Cowley, Brown, Burke, Schneider, Josephson, even Frank—had shifted the emphasis of their interests, and renovated the system of values to which they had subscribed in the "twenties." Should he go to Chagrin Falls, then? He knew he would find a permanent welcome there and genuine affection, but the sterile monotony of such a life was a desolate prospect. There was no question of making a home of his own. The relationship in which he had recently seen so much hope of a new life had been caught up in the plunge back into disintegration; with his return to his old habits every impulse towards moral recreation was cut short. Where should he go, then? The dark reply, which more than one of his friends in Mexico heard him make, was that he had no place to go, and that no place to go was easy enough to find.

Gripped in this vertigo of despair, his drinking became increasingly heavy, his behavior more and more violent and eccentric, and his feeling of persecution completely obsessive. In his constant round of *cantinas* he would seize upon the most casual acquaintances and overwhelm them with fantastic stories, building up sagas of "betrayal" out of im-

in fact do so, and that Mr. Zabel, contrary to Crane's assertions at the time, never had the opportunity of passing judgment on "The Broken Tower."

aginary slights, pouring out torrential curses on Mexico, which had seduced him with a Judas kiss, reviling the Guggenheims, their Foundation, and their officers. In Mixcoac he quarrelled furiously with Miss Baird, often disturbing the midnight quiet with such an uproar that his friends, the policemen, arrived to carry him off for a night in jail, where he amused himself by wrecking the meager furnishings and shouting obscenities through the grating. At other times he fled the house only to continue his outrages at some hotel in town. He seemed to be abroad at all hours of the day and night, showing up at the apartments of his friends with the inevitable cab driver clamoring at his heels for payment. On one occasion, early in the morning he appeared at the home of Caroline Durieux, a painter whom he had met in Taxco, with his right palm slashed across by a razor drawn against him in a brawl in some "dive" of the city. And yet, there were moments, sometimes even in the midst of his outbursts, when he would make some pun or Rabelaisian remark, that would send him off in gales of apparently genuine merriment, to the utter mystification of his companions. To many of them he seemed poised on the brink of insanity, and certain changes of expression—the accusing glare of his eyes, the intense strain evident in the lines of his face—caused them serious anxiety on this score. To others, who knew him less well and had seen too much Hollywood influence in the behavior of Americans in Mexico, it seemed that he was indulging in an excessive orgy of melodrama.

This latter point of view gained considerable credence after the events of the day two weeks before his final departure, when the perilous tension of his suffering snapped and precipitated an almost fatal climax. On that day Crane had invited Louise Howard, and Mary Doherty, one of his closest friends in Mexico, to spend the day with him and Miss Baird at Mixcoac. Upon their arrival they were told by Miss Baird that Crane was in a dangerous mood, and the three of them retired to the back part of the house in order to leave him free to his own devices. Before long Crane himself appeared, haggard and untidy, carrying under his arm the Siqueiros portrait which had hung on the wall of his own room. Setting the painting up for their inspection, he burst into a stream of criticism and abuse, pointing out with voluble wrath that the pigments, which were applied on burlap according to Siqueiros's habitual technique, were cracking and peeling, and reviling the artist and all his ilk for a painter of doormats. Suddenly, when his fury had reached a towering height, he seized a razor and despite cries of protest from the women, slashed the portrait to tatters. Then, as though carried away by the implicit symbolism of the destruction, he rushed from the room, to return a moment later with the announcement that he had drunk a bottle of iodine and would be dead within three hours. A hasty investigation disclosed the empty vial, and the women, completely beside themselves with horror, dispatched the servant for a doctor and tried to prevail upon Crane to come to his senses. But there was no quieting him. Striding up and down the room, his disordered mind whirling around the worn grooves of his usual delusions, he raged through all the grievances and torments of his life, until finally, somewhat exhausted, he ordered Miss Baird out of the room and demanded that Miss Doherty take down the dictation of his will.

The servant, in the meantime, had returned with the doctor's report that the dose of iodine would not be fatal, especially in view of Crane's alcoholism. Their fears slightly allayed, the women tried to pacify him by following out his directions. But early in the afternoon, when Crane realized that the poison was not taking effect, he rushed into the bathroom and drained a bottle of mercurochrome. For the rest of the day he continued to dictate his will, discarding one version after another, cutting and revising and polishing as though he were composing a poem, ranting against the mistakes made in the typing, and interspersing his dictation with bitter abuse of those who had betrayed him. Significantly, the bulk of the money he was to inherit from his father's estate he left to a sailor; and despite his disordered state of mind the letter he wrote this friend the same afternoon was curiously sober and restrained. Although all the copies of the will were carefully destroyed the next day, this note, which was never sent, remained as a moving and prophetic testimony of what was to come.

"Won't be living at all any more if this ever reaches you," he wrote. "But hope you are all right. . . . I have very wilfully killed myself. I hope you will happily marry and realize some of the conversations we have had together, sometimes. Dear B—, I remember so many things, and I have loved you always, and this is my only end."

Towards evening, when Crane recognized that his desperate attempt to put an end to his suffering had failed, he became quite calm and finally submitted to the doctor's care, who administered antidotes and a heavy injection of morphine.

It might have been expected that the violence of this episode would relieve his anguish of spirit. But apparently nothing could subdue or exhaust his torments; and after a day or two of convalescence, his life continued at its customary tempo, now accelerating to shocking paroxysms, now diminishing to charming sobriety with such sudden shifts of mood that his friends scarcely knew what to expect next. In the meantime, he was still undecided as to what course of action to take, when towards the middle of April a telegram arrived from his step-mother, reporting that his father's estate was being sued for a large sum of money which, should the executors be required to pay it, would force her into bankruptcy, and that pending the outcome of the case his own allowance would have to be suspended. In the hope of being of some help to Mrs. Crane, and realizing that in any case he could not remain in Mexico without funds, he immediately began to make preparations to return to Chagrin Falls. It was decided that Miss Baird, who was also planning to leave Mexico, should book passage on the same steamer, the *S.S. Orizaba*, sailing from Vera Cruz on the twenty-fourth of April.

The last days were full of confusion and violence. In the midst of packing Crane quarrelled bitterly with his servant and accused him of stealing. In retribution several of Daniel's family branches, combining in common fury, stormed at Crane's gates with such blood-curdling threats that he called upon the Embassy for protection. Another time, suddenly convinced that Miss Baird had been kidnapped, he combed the city for hours in a frenzy of apprehension; aroused the Embassy in the middle of the night to demand that President Hoover be notified, that the Marines be summoned, that the Mexican government be impeached; and was finally thrown into jail once more for disturbing the peace. At such moments he appeared to be driven insane by rage, terror, hatred —by the abandoned fury of all destructive passions. His eyes, polished with a furious glare, started from his head, and his face was distorted by uncontrollable convulsions. Some of his friends, fearful of what might happen aboard ship, tried to persuade him to stay on in Mexico a few more days and return by train. On the day of his departure, however, they were somewhat reassured. Apparently happy and in complete possession of himself, he bade many of them goodbye at one of the popular restaurants in the city. Far from showing any anxiety over the reports of his financial condition, he seemed to welcome the prospect of having something to occupy his time and attention. He made engagements to meet some of his friends upon their return to the States; others he promised faithfully to write to; and when the train for Vera Cruz finally pulled out of the station, there were more than a few who felt that their fears had been unfounded.

During the passage from Vera Cruz to Havana his equable frame of mind persisted, and if he was drinking somewhat, there were, at least, no serious disturbances. When the ship docked in the harbor of Havana on the morning of the twenty-fifth to lie over for the day, Crane set out alone to make the round of his favorite bars and cafés. Possibly he took luncheon at La Diana, recalling with a pang the dinner table of the year before and the doctor's prophetic remark— "so might go on to undeserved doom." Doubtless he visited many of the haunts where he had caroused six years ago during his stay on the Isle of Pines, for some time that afternoon together with other casual messages he sent off a postcard to Aunt Sally Simpson to remind her of his love. And if memories of that rich period crowded his mind, what a wrench of anguished nostalgia and despair must have gripped him to remember that "tremendous rondure floating somewhere," which had transported him to the very height of creative power! Little wonder that he was drunk when he returned to the ship that evening, a bottle of rum under his arm with which to pass the night!

As the ship weighed anchor, he set out to look for Miss Baird, whom he discovered at last in her cabin, where she was being attended by a stewardess for a painful burn on her hand, caused by a packet of ignited matches. For some time Crane lingered beside her bed, offering clumsy ministrations and sympathies, until at length Miss Baird asked him to leave. Later, however, as his drinking continued, he returned time after time, now overwhelming her with endearments, now breaking out into harsh and bitter abuse, apparently without any provocation or aim beyond relieving the intolerable suffering again seething within him. He seemed not even to hear her pleas to be left alone. Exhausted at last by his persistent violence, she summoned the steward and demanded that Crane be locked in his cabin. Late that night when he eventually broke out and began to prowl the decks, it was almost inevitable that his steps should lead him, as though automatically retracing a well-known pattern, down to the sailors' quarters. What happened there was never ascertained, though Crane's own story the following morning that he had been beaten and robbed would have been a likely enough consequence.

Upon returning at last to the open, he found the decks deserted. Everything was dark except for the lights along the promenade, which cast brief burnished gleams on the black heaves of water that rose and fell with heavy regularity as the ship rolled forward on the long swells. Clearly there was no question of finding excitement now. The only sounds were the occasional grating of the steering gear and the constant sigh of the liner's progress, shearing the waves. From the warm waters of the Gulf Stream there was a soft odor of salt and sea-substance. Astern, the constellation of the Cross settled towards the southern horizon; to the north, somewhere out of sight, the lights of New York cast a metropolitan glare on the sky. Just as he was about to plunge overboard into the darkness, the night watch, who had seen him from the shadows of the foredeck, seized him from behind and escorted him back to his cabin.

The next morning, the 26th of April, 1932, the ship was sailing just out of sight of the Florida coast, ten miles off Jupiter Light. Crane, awakening rather late, threw on a light topcoat over his pyjamas and sought out Miss Baird to ask her to have breakfast with him in his stateroom. During the meal he told her of his experience in the seamen's quarters, without, however, mentioning the final episode on deck, and complained bitterly of the brutal treatment he had received. His companion, only too well aware of his condition the night before, did not sense any premonition of disaster in the profound despair which seemed to weigh upon him, and attributed it to his drinking. Later, leaving him to his own devices, she returned to her own cabin to have her injured hand dressed. Shortly before noon, however, still clothed in pyjamas and topcoat, Crane once more knocked on her door, and entering, said that he wanted to say good-bye. Too preoccupied with what she was doing at the moment to fully comprehend the significance of his remark, Miss Baird asked him to get dressed and meet her for luncheon in a half hour. Without replying, he went out, shutting the door behind him, and ascended directly to the promenade deck. The sea was mild, and the sun, striking against the gentle motion of its surface, polished the delicate blue with sudden ripples of fire. Heedless of the curious glances that followed his progress along the deck, Crane walked quickly to the stern of the ship, and scarcely pausing to slip his coat from his shoulders, vaulted over the rail into the boiling wake.

The alarm was general and immediate. There was a clangor of bells as the ship's engines ground into reverse; life preservers were thrown overboard; a lifeboat was lowered. Some claimed they saw an arm raised from the water and others that a life preserver turned over as though gripped by an unseen hand. But the officer in charge of the bridge maintained they had only seen the white disc lifted on a sudden wave. For more than an hour the steamer circled round and round in the quiet blue morning, crossing and recrossing its broad white wake, while the lifeboat crew, resting on their oars or rowing aimlessly, scanned the inscrutable water. At last, the search was abandoned, the boat recalled, and the ship headed resolutely northwards on its proper course.

⤞ XII ⤝

"And so it was I entered the broken world
To trace the visionary company of love, its voice
An instant in the wind (I know not whither hurled)
But not for long to hold each desperate choice."

I<small>N</small> KEEPING with the special
fate reserved for poets whose deaths are violent and dramatic, the news of his suicide won for Crane a larger audience
than he had ever commanded during his life. It was a
social commentary he would have bitterly appreciated that
his final gesture of self-destruction interested the public
more vitally than all his years of creation. For a day or two
the press of the nation displayed his photograph; ran news
items reviewing his life, ineptly quoting passages of his
verse, mentioning as motives his discouragement in money
matters and his despair over the state of poetry in the world;
and even printed one or two editorials by way of sentimental
homilies. To the literary world, however, the report of his
death came as a serious shock. For some time afterwards its
representative magazines carried poems to his memory, articles estimating his achievement, and inquiries into the causes

and significance of his suicide. As there had been much controversy over his poetry, so now there was much confusion regarding the reasons for his act. The periodicals of sociological bias tended to see him as the victim of a disordered society—a refugee from chaos; others of more eclectic character variously indicated his psychopathic dilemma and his exhaustion after composing a poem of such large scope as *The Bridge*. Even his friends, somewhat bewildered by the rumors of his wild life in Mexico, differed among themselves in their interpretations. More than one, recalling the vigorous joy he had taken in living and his apparently inexhaustible vitality, refused to consider his action as anything more than a drunken accident. Others, remembering rather the destructive rages, the insane fear and desperation, felt that it was an inevitable conclusion.

Clearly there is much truth in all these points of view. After tracing the course of his life and particularly the swift decline of the last years, beginning with the fall of 1927, there should be little need to insist upon the complex and organic character of his suicide. One may see it as an escape either from a society in which he had no function or from a psychic impasse which had no solution; one may see it morally as the violent issue of debauchery or, mystically, as the last desperate effort to achieve a transcendent unity through his favorite symbol, the sea; or finally, one may take a more general and inclusive view of it, such as the one so constantly stressed in these pages—namely, the lack of security, both spiritual and worldly, which, like an interior cavity hollowed by fear, distorted the surfaces and substrata of his life with fatal displacements.

But whatever interpretation is adopted, it can not be denied that any one motive, when carefully investigated, will lead back to his childhood. Like Poe, whose career offers so many striking parallels to his own, Crane was conditioned towards the disorder of his life and its abrupt ending by the circumstances of his childhood and adolescence. With less cause, perhaps, but with equal intensity, he suffered fears and humiliations during his boyhood that were very much like those Poe experienced in the Allan's household in Richmond. Both of them had a consuming desire for unquestioning devotion and admiration, which, being largely frustrated—partially because of the fear of ridicule in themselves—tormented them in later years with fantasies of persecution and drove them to insane outbursts of defiant egotism that amounted at times to delusions of grandeur. Significantly, it was only when this desire was realized—when Poe was safe in the cottage at Fordham with Virginia and "Muddie," when Crane found refuge with "Aunt Sally" on the Isle of Pines or at Chagrin Falls—that either of them could achieve any peace of mind. In the midst of literary circles they felt single, isolated, anomalous. Each of them, caught in the constricting mesh of a psychopathic dilemma, produced his writing under incredible strain, maintaining a precarious equilibrium only by various defenses and compensations, which, when they finally crumbled, gave way to the swift flood of dissolution. And seized with terror in this last fatal mill-race, each began to lose control of his creative power—Poe in "Eureka" and "Ulalume" and Crane in "Cape Hatteras." Hounded by financial difficulties, too disordered by drink and anxiety to secure steady employment, they were both outcasts from society.

The parallelism must not be carried too far, however, for beyond a certain point there is nothing in common between them. Where Poe, both in his life and in his works, was almost completely a creature of his pathological condition, Crane, essentially healthy in body and mind, was little more

than a victim of recurrent obsessions and constant dissipations which, since he recognized them honestly, and clearly
understood their causes, were in no danger of restricting
the scope of his work or seriously conditioning its spirit.
But it is not without significance that as early as 1926 Crane
recorded his haunting vision of Poe in the subway, and
asked:

> And why do I often meet your visage here,
> Your eyes like agate lanterns—on and on
> Below the toothpaste and the dandruff ads?
> —And did their riding eyes right through your side,
> And did their eyes like unwashed platters ride?
> And Death, aloft,—gigantically down
> Probing through you—toward me, O evermore!

In the end there is little doubt that the most immediate
factor in determining Crane's suicide was his conviction
that his creative powers were exhausted, or at least seriously
diminished. Whether or not this conviction had any basis
in actuality must remain unknown. Certainly "The Broken
Tower" would seem to prove that his fears were unfounded,
for it must rank among his better works. But even in this
poem, in the midst of the brief spiritual recreation that inspired it, he posed the fatal question that was tormenting
him, and his strange use of the past tense gave it the final
tolling quality of a "hail and farewell."

> My word I poured. But was it cognate, scored
> Of that tribunal monarch of the air
> Whose thigh embronzes earth, strikes crystal Word
> In wounds pledged once to hope—cleft to despair?

Stricken with doubt and humility, he could make no reply:—

The steep encroachments of my blood left me
No answer (could blood hold such a lofty tower
As flings the question true?) . . .

And finding no reassurance during the following weeks of nightmare, he became convinced that the answer was negative, and the conviction proved fatal. Thus, the decline of his creative powers must be explained rather by the ultimate triumph of his fear than by any absolute failure of his genius. The distinction is, perhaps, unimportant except as it serves to emphasize that his suicide was not the result of a single incident or crisis, but the simple issue of that complex growth which, stretching backwards through his life with web-like ramifications, had so riddled his spiritual substance that even his faith in his work was cut off from nourishment and destroyed. He was left only the will to make the final *coup de grâce*.

When, as a boy, he had determined to "make his fate," he had set his foot on the ladder to fame, the one tower equally invincible to the treacheries of human life and the siege of time. And poetry became both his ladder and his tower. By comparison his other supports—the affection and faith of family and friends—were ephemeral. But as they were gradually withdrawn from him—first by the separation from his mother, then by his father's death, and finally by estrangement from his friends—a rising tide of terror, swollen by multiple tributaries of doubt, surged at the base of his fortress, undermined it, and plunged him to his death. Even as the pattern of his life had often portended his fate, so also do certain passages of his poetry, almost as though in moments of clairvoyance he had clearly understood the nature of the end in store for him. The closing lines of the third "Voyage," written in 1924, might well have been composed as his epitaph:

And so, admitted through black swollen gates
That must arrest all distance otherwise,—
Past whirling pillars and lithe pediments,
Light wrestling there incessantly with light,
Star kissing star through wave on wave unto
Your body rocking!
                              and where death, if shed,
Presumes no carnage, but this single change,—
Upon the steep floor flung from dawn to dawn
The silken skilled transmemberment of song;

Permit me voyage, love, into your hands . . .

The confusion concerning the causes of his suicide was paralleled by the divergence of critical opinion as to the importance of his work. At the time of his death his name stood variously for "one of the great masters of the Romantic movement," for "the most distinguished poetry of the age," for "the cult of unintelligibility" and "the leader of the decorative school," for the defeat of poetry in the modern world; indeed, for so many things that it seemed in danger of becoming a fetish for the critics. The arbiters and purveyors of popular poetry, who had been mortally offended by their inability to understand Crane's verse, comfortably insisted that his name and works would be comparatively unknown in a few years. Among the most discerning critics and writers, however—not only in America, but in France and England as well—there was a small, powerful group who recognized that a great poet had died and voiced their opinion that his work, whatever its defects, entitled him to a place among the first poets of his country.

Certainly Crane's technical contributions to modern poetry alone justify such an estimate. Of these probably the most important was his rehabilitation of blank verse, a form which since the days of the Elizabethans had been robbed of much of its potential richness. Although Pound and Eliot had been largely responsible for reviving an interest in the poetry of the sixteenth and seventeenth centuries, they were themselves temperamentally incapable of doing more than adapting, imitating, and assimilating certain of its characteristics, with the result that much of their own poetry, however effective and admirable in its artistry, was marked by an archaic, retrospective quality. Even Eliot's most perfectly dramatic passages had about them something of the close, artificial, indoor atmosphere of the library and theater, which had been his chief means of intimacy with that literature. It remained for Crane, unschooled, unspoiled by scholastic nostalgia and self-consciousness, to use the medium in a completely modern way, easily and naturally combining in it rhetoric, conversation, and discursive thought, and sounding afresh the grand note so rarely heard in modern times. This is not to say that the Elizabethan influence is not distinctly traceable in his blank verse. On the contrary, the rhetoric of certain passages could have had no other source:—

> Series on series, infinite,—till eyes
> Starved wide on blackened tides, accrete—enclose
> This turning rondure whole, this crescent ring
> Sun-cusped and zoned with modulated fire
> Like pearls that whisper through the Doge's hands
> —Yet no delirium of jewels! O Fernando,
> Take of that eastern shore, this western sea,
> Yet yield thy God's, thy Virgin's charity!

Yet even here, the spirit that moves the lines is so spontaneous, the bombast so much a part of Crane's own breath, that one feels it as an affinity rather than an influence. The same passion for dramatic inflated metaphor is found in his love poems:

Knowing I cannot touch your hand and look
Too, into that godless cleft of sky
Where nothing turns but dead sands flashing.

"—And never to quite understand!" No,
In all the argosy of your bright hair I dreamed
Nothing so flagless as this piracy.

In the intense energy and excitement of such lines, in the torrential imagination, so often cosmic in its reaches, one may find more than ample confirmation of Crane's belief that he was possessed by a Marlovian demon. The same qualities in his personality earned him the Elizabethan nickname of "the roaring boy." But since his mastery of blank verse was an original achievement, and not an imitation or mannerism, it varied with his subject matter and mood, ranging from the exaltation of the "Ave Maria" to the homely pedestrian stanzas of "The River," and was always pre-eminently his own.

In the process of renovating blank verse Crane also re-vivified the poetic language of his time. And here again his lack of education was a distinct advantage to him. Although it often led him to commit such amusing mistakes as confusing "cask" and "casque," "wrapt" and "rapt," and apostrophizing Whitman as "Panis Angelicus" under the impression he was hailing him as Holy Pan, it also left his mind comparatively free of conventional meanings and associations. He was able to discover words, and use them, almost as things in themselves, prizing their colors, sounds, and shapes as more meaningful than their strict definitions. This passion for the sensuous qualities of language encouraged him in the use of rare exotic terms. Sometimes, even, he was not sure whether these were not the products of his imagination, as in the case of the word "findrinny"—originally used in the line, "The seal's findrinny gaze toward Paradise"—which neither he nor his

friends could unearth in any dictionary. Prodigal in his use of
brilliant colloquialisms, barbarisms, and metaphors, and convinced that the resources of poetic language were "not to be
limited by a scientific and arbitrary code of relationships
either in verbal inflections or concepts," he restored to poetry
a dramatic vigor and immediacy it had long been lacking.
With the exception of Hopkins and, to a lesser extent, Brown-
ing, no other modern poet writing in English has so thoroughly and successfully exploited the resources of his medium.

Another contribution he made to modern poetry—and one
peculiarly his own—was the incorporation into his verse of
the complex machinery and mechanical activities of industrial
civilization. With an urgent sense of the modern poet's need
for "gigantic assimilative capacities" he was the first, and
for some time the only, poet who could write naturally and
eloquently of aeroplanes, subways, skyscrapers, and at the
same time relate them organically to the spiritual life of
man. On the one hand he could write of the Bridge:

> Again the traffic lights that skim thy swift
> Unfractioned idiom, immaculate sigh of stars,
> Beading thy path—condense eternity:
> And we have seen night lifted in thine arms.

on the other, in a passage of pure description:

> Down Wall, from girder into street noon leaks,
> A rip-tooth of the sky's acetylene . . .

or, drawing from the subway a powerful imagery of intro-
spection as in the vision of Poe:

> Whose head is swinging from the swollen strap?
> Whose body smokes along the bitten rails,
> Bursts from a smoldering bundle far behind

> In back forks of the chasms of the brain,—
> Puffs from a riven stump far out behind
> In interborough fissures of the mind . . . ?

The figures of machinery became one of his most effective means of communication. Having come into a vivid contact with the industrial world during his most impressionable years, he knew it not only as a concrete, overpowering reality, but also as a factor of incalculable importance in the social and spiritual life of the country: at once a cause for despair and for hope. He needed no knowledge of economics or training in sociology to be aware of the tremendous potentialities of the machine which made for oppression and corruption, and which might equally make for freedom and enlightenment. From this consciousness, however inarticulate and ill-defined on the level of social and political thought, he drew an original and powerful symbolism that expressed more profoundly than any other contemporary poetry the dilemmas of his age. Thence came the concept of the Bridge, "symbol of our constructive future, our unique identity." Thence, too, came those naked and bitter visions of the City, "with scalding unguents spread and smoking darts"—the modern purgatory of the spirit:

> The City's fiery parcels all undone,
> Already snow submerges an iron year . . .

or again—

> The phonographs of hades in the brain
> Are tunnels that re-wind themselves, and love
> A burnt match skating in a urinal—

That these two attitudes—a buoyant idealism and an almost macabre pessimism—exist side by side in his work in irreconcilable opposition is a further token that he was completely a man of his time. His own maturity coincided with the coming of age of his country, which at the end of the World War discovered itself to be foremost among the world powers, and aroused by the recognition, plunged forward in a steadily increasing tempo of industrial expansion. As always during such periods, the national consciousness of America at that time was intense. The thrill of this widespread excitement was undoubtedly the spark which fired Crane and his contemporaries with the belief that the arts, participating in the general growth, would attain a truly great stature, expressive of the race that would become the fine eventual flower of this renaissance. It was a belief, however short-lived, significantly like that of Whitman, who had also grown up during a time of national expansion and optimism. But such epochs, as Whitman learned at the end of his life, are also characterized by a corrupt and powerful materialism, which far from nourishing the spiritual faculties of the people constantly threatens to destroy them. This dual aspect of a national resurgence was the background and, in part, the cause of Crane's divided spirit. Even before his early idealism had had time to strike healthy roots in secure soil, it was shadowed, surrounded, and shut in upon itself by the swarming growth of materialism: the indifference, the crass preoccupations and amusements, the hypocrisy, the misdirected and diseased vitality of a world that was "flying into trillions of tabloids." The public had already found its Pindars in the daily press, which supplied tragedies, comedies, and panegyrics to its own taste. For the rest, it was unconcerned.

But however darkly at times this overwhelming tide of materialism flooded him with despair, Crane could not entirely relinquish his idealism. His religious impulse was too constant in him, too positively active, to be stifled by pessimism or deflected into those retrospective channels that would have led him, like Eliot, to resignation and the acceptance of the dogmas of the Church. He was fitted neither by education nor by temperament to achieve such synthetic reconciliation and refuge. Irrevocably divorced from all the institutions of tradition and security, from family, marriage, and established religion—and in this he again symbolized the rootlessness of his age—he was at once possessed by the desire to discover an absolute faith and by an abhorrence of all rational discipline. In assimilating the life of his time with his enormous indiscriminate appetite for experience, he became too deeply entangled in its intellectual and spiritual confusions, as well as its vices, ever to be able to resolve this dilemma. Consequently his religious impulse was never definitively clarified. It appeared now as a form of pantheism, now as a Whitmanian vision of social utopia, "a pact, new bound, of living brotherhood," and again, more frequently, as a purely individual expression of subjective mysticism. Many of the critics of *The Bridge*, seizing upon this ambiguity and the dualism of spirit underlying it as the basic flaw of the work, the fault in the material that undermined the structure, characterized the poem as "a magnificent failure." Themselves poets, for the most part, deeply concerned for the spiritual predicament of the times and the future of poetry, they tended to lose sight of the greatness of the poetry in their disappointment that *The Bridge* was not what it never could have been: a panacea, a religious or philosophical epic that would have integrated the cross-purposes of the age. Some of them even assumed that this was Crane's intention in writing the poem, and that he committed suicide because he had made a prophecy for the future of America which by 1932 had proved false.

But to suppose that Crane's visionary idealism was messianic is completely to misunderstand the temper of the man and his work; and to complain that *The Bridge* is not philosophically consistent or sociologically sound is to support the misdirected, wish-thinking kind of criticism that condemns in a work the lack of what it had hoped to find. That Crane for a very short time believed in an imminent transfiguration of national life seems to be true, judging from his letters of the winter of 1922–23. But this belief was the immediate reflex of his first creative excitement over *The Bridge* coupled with his reading of Ouspensky's *Tertium Organum*, and was mystical rather than messianic. Furthermore, like many other poets carried away by enthusiasm, he often admitted to ambitions with which his admirers credited him and which actually he did not have. But he consistently and vigorously disclaimed any messianic intentions with a strong revulsion for everything that the term implied. Nor was he interested, at least as regards his work, in social panaceas. In the letter to Tate, quoted in Chapter X, he bitterly condemned the current tendency among poets and critics alike to abandon "poetry as poetry" in favor of searching for some "cure-all," which is precisely the attitude, however subtly disguised with aesthetic terms, of those who criticize *The Bridge* from a philosophical or sociological bias.

It should be clear from Crane's personality, from his letters, from all the evidence of his life that he was singly and purely an artist, a poet for poetry's sake. That he had a strong mystical impulse gave his work a greater scope and a spiritual intensity and vision that it might otherwise have lacked. But this does not justify the assumption that he wished to be a prophet. To confuse mysticism and clairvoyance is to ignore completely the intensely personal and subjective character of the former. And to say that Crane's symbol of the Bridge was false simply because its implications failed to materialize in the world or because its content did not conform in a one to one relation to "reality" or to any "real" system of values, is to read the poem on the one hand as a kind of clairvoyant journalism, or on the other, as a rational philosophical treatise. Had Crane been primarily concerned with the "real," if by that is meant the quotidian, world, he would undoubtedly have shared with his contemporaries the new interest in social and political questions, and joined with them in the leftist movements. Feeling as he did that there was no place for poetry in the world as he found it, he surely had reason to support any cause that promised to improve society. But whatever enthusiasm he showed in such matters was largely a question of sympathy with friends who were engaged in political activities. For the rest, the letter he wrote to Lorna Dietz just two weeks before his death proves that essentially he remained indifferent:

"Yes, the wholesale conversion of most of our friends around New York has made me feel quite guilty at times. Instead of donning the prevalent sack-cloth and ashes I've been sitting around cold evenings in the most comfortable and flamboyant serapes I could lay my hands on. I'm convinced of the logic of it all—perhaps also of the inevitability, but it runs so against my precious individualistic 'grain' (if I have any left) that I can't really feel very sterterous about it."

His religious impulse was too subjective, too mystical, to be transposed into the terms of a political or philosophical rationale, or indeed of any category except poetry. He resented the encroachments of rationalism on any part of the poet's province, and, like the natural Platonist he was, consistently maintained that poetry, to remain true to its own nature, must transcend the dictates of scientific logic, and function only according to laws of its own making. Similarly in his life, modelling his moral code after his aesthetics, he claimed for himself freedom from all discipline other than artistic. He felt that he could not identify himself with "all of life" if he were restricted by ethical dogmas, any more than poetry when subjected to rational principles could express the rich mysterious stuff of experience. This attitude was the source of the ambiguity that marked the religious impulse in his work. In a letter replying to the essay on his poetry in Gorham Munson's volume, *Destinations*, he defended what he called his "alternate 'gutter sniping' and 'angel kissing'" on the grounds that any arbitrary limitation of the poet's subject matter could be nothing more than "a meretricious substitute for psychological sincerity." * Thus his spiritual ambivalence is seen to be a reflection of life as he experienced it, and must be considered as inevitable in *The Bridge* as Dante's completely articulated religious dialectic was in *The Divine Comedy*, the work so frequently on the lips of Crane's critics. Had it been otherwise, *The Bridge* would not be what it preeminently is—a powerful, authentic expression of Crane's times, a record of the American spirit, both past and present, caught up and entangled in the spiritual dilemmas of the twentieth century, and a work that for the greatness of its poetry alone must take its place in the foremost ranks of American literature.

Crane's death is still too recent to allow of any predictions as to what part his work will play in the developments of poetry in the decades to come; when it will command the general recognition that it must some day receive; and in exactly what relation it will stand to other great works of our literature. More than a little time may have to pass before his poetry comes into its own, for his death coin-

* See *Appendix*.

cided with a great social and economic crisis, international in scope, which brought to an abrupt close the period that had been the background of *The Bridge*, and inaugurated an era characterized by social and political consciousness. Since that time the current of modern poetry and the predominant interests of criticism have been set in increasing momentum towards the "revolutionary" expressions of the leftist movement with which Crane had no affiliations and but slight sympathies. Practically all the younger poets, and many of Crane's contemporaries, were drawn into the movement, finding in its broad humanitarian idealism the faith that had been painfully lacking in the previous decade, and an objective system of thought and value by which they could integrate and direct their experience. It was the inevitable reaction against a vicious materialism. And yet, despite the difference in temper between them and Crane, there is scarcely one of the younger poets whose work does not betray the influence of Crane's poetry; and he has had more than a few direct imitators among them. Whether one selects a "proletarian" anthology or one of more catholic tastes, the evidence is equally remarkable. In their use of the metaphor of machinery, in their density of imagery, in their free adaptations of blank verse and conversational and dramatic idioms, it is Crane who is most often their master. Together with Whitman he shares the distinction of serving as a model for the younger poets.

And why should he not? In his character as a national poet he expressed major qualities of the American spirit which had not been heard in poetry since *Leaves of Grass*. In his own work he combined the best traditions of English verse with innovations and idioms without which poetry would become formalized, static, and lifeless. Rooted in the past, furnished towards the future, and standing at the heart of his age, his poetry promises to be a rich source of discovery and inspiration for poets to come. The least that may be said of it—which is the least that Crane himself could hope for—is that it will perform "the function of a link connecting certain chains of the past to certain chains and tendencies of the future." But with more than a little confidence one may also say that it constitutes an important and permanent contribution to English poetry.

APPENDIX

NOTE: The following material is included in the book primarily for students of Crane's poetry. The essay and the three letters form a relatively compact body of the poet's critical and aesthetic thought both in respect to his own work and to poetry in general. They are: I—an unpublished essay written during 1925 that clarifies his intentions in the poetry of *White Buildings;* II—a letter to Harriet Monroe, editor of *Poetry,* in reply to questions concerning "At Melville's Tomb"; III—a letter to Otto Kahn outlining the subject matter of *The Bridge;* IV—a letter to Gorham Munson in reply to the essay on Crane in his *Destinations.*

I

General Aims and Theories

WHEN I started writing Faustus & Helen it was my intention to embody in modern terms (words, symbols, metaphors) a contemporary approximation to an ancient human culture or mythology that seems to have been obscured rather than illumined with the frequency of poetic allusions made to it during the last century. The name of Helen, for instance, has become an all-too-easily employed crutch for evocation whenever a poet felt a stitch in his side. The real evocation of this (to me) very real and absolute conception of beauty seemed to consist in a reconstruction in these modern terms of the basic emotional attitude toward beauty that the Greeks had. And in so doing I found that I was really building a bridge between so-called classic experience and many divergent realities of our seething, confused cosmos of today, which has no formulated mythology yet for classic poetic reference or for religious exploitation.

So I found "Helen" sitting in a street car; the Dionysian revels of her court and her seduction were transferred to a Metropolitan roof garden with a jazz orchestra; and the *katharsis* of the fall of Troy I saw approximated in the recent World War. The importance of this scaffolding may easily be exaggerated, but it gave me a series of correspondences between two widely separated worlds on which to sound some major themes of human speculation—love, beauty, death, renascence. It was a kind of grafting process that I shall doubtless not be interested in repeating, but which is consistent with subsequent theories of mine on the relation of tradition to the contemporary creating imagination.

It is a terrific problem that faces the poet today—a world that is so in transition from a decayed culture toward a re-organization of human evaluations that there are few common terms, general denominators of speech that are solid enough or that ring with any vibration or spiritual conviction. The great mythologies of the past (including the Church) are deprived of enough façade to even launch good raillery against. Yet much of their traditions are operative still—in millions of chance combinations of related and un-related detail, psychological reference, figures of speech, precepts, etc. These are all a part of our common experience and the terms, at least partially, of that very experience when it defines or extends itself.

The deliberate program, then, of a "break" with the past or tradition seems to me to be a sentimental fallacy. . . . The poet has a right to draw on whatever practical resources he finds in books or otherwise about him. He must tax his sensibility and his touchstone of experience for the proper selections of these themes and details, however,—and that is where he either stands, or falls into useless archeology.

I put no particular value on the simple objective of "modernity." The element of the temporal location of an artist's creation is of very secondary importance; it can be left to the impressionist or historian just as well. It seems to me that a poet will accidentally define his time well enough simply by reacting honestly and to the full extent of his sensibilities to the states of passion, experience and rumination that fate forces on him, first hand. He must, of course, have a sufficiently universal basis of experience to make his imagination selective and valuable. His picture of the "period," then, will simply be a by-product of his curiosity and the relation of his experience to a postulated "eternity."

I am concerned with the future of America, but not because I think that America has any so-called par value as a state or as a group of people. . . . It is only because I feel persuaded that here are destined to be discovered certain as yet undefined spiritual quantities, perhaps a new hierarchy of faith not to be developed so completely elsewhere. And in this process I like to feel myself as a potential factor; certainly I must speak in its terms and what discoveries I may make are situated in its experience.

But to fool one's self that definitions are being reached by merely referring frequently to skyscrapers, radio antennae, steam whistles, or other surface phenomena of our time is merely to paint a photograph. I think that what is interesting and significant will emerge only under the conditions of our submission to, and examination and assimilation of the organic effects on us of these and other fundamental factors of our experience. It can certainly not be an organic expression otherwise. And the expression of such values may often be as well accomplished with the vocabulary and blank verse of the Elizabethans as with the calligraphic tricks and slang used so brilliantly at times by an impressionist like Cummings.

It may not be possible to say that there is, strictly speaking, any "absolute" experience. But it seems evident that certain aesthetic experience (and this may for a time engross the total faculties of the spectator) can be called absolute, inasmuch as it approximates a formally convincing statement of a conception or apprehension of life that gains our unquestioning assent, and under the conditions of which our imagination is unable to suggest a further detail consistent with the design of the aesthetic whole.

I have been called an "absolutist" in poetry, and if I am to welcome such a label it should be under the terms of the above definition. It is really only a *modus operandi*, however, and as such has been used organically before by at least a dozen poets such as Donne, Blake, Baudelaire, Rimbaud, etc. I may succeed in defining it better by contrasting it with the impressionistic method. The impressionist is interesting as far as he goes—but his goal has been reached when he has succeeded in projecting certain selected factual details into his reader's consciousness. He is really not interested in the *causes* (metaphysical) of his materials, their emotional derivations or their utmost spiritual consequences. A kind of retinal registration is enough, along with a certain psychological stimulation. And this is also true of your realist (of the Zola type), and to a certain extent of the classicist, like Horace, Ovid, Pope, etc.

Blake meant these differences when he wrote:

> We are led to believe in a lie
> When we see *with* not *through* the eye.

The impressionist creates only with the eye and for the readiest surface of the consciousness, at least relatively so. If the effect has been harmonious or even stimulating, he can stop there, relinquishing entirely to his audience the problematic synthesis of the details into terms of their own personal consciousness.

It is my hope to go *through* the combined materials of the poem, using our "real" world somewhat as a spring-board, and to give the poem *as a whole* an orbit or predetermined direction of its own. I would like to establish it as free from my own personality as from any chance evaluation on the reader's part. (This is, of course, an impossibility, but it is a characteristic worth mentioning.) Such a poem is at least a stab at a truth, and to such an extent may be differentiated from other kinds of poetry and called "absolute." Its evocation will not be toward decoration or amusement, but rather toward a state of consciousness, an "innocence" (Blake) or absolute beauty. In this condition there may be discoverable under new forms certain spiritual illuminations, shining with a morality essentialized from experience directly, and not from previous precepts or preconceptions. It is as though a poem gave the reader as he left it a single, new *word*, never before spoken and impossible to actually enunciate, but self-evident as an active principle in the reader's consciousness henceforward.

As to technical considerations: the motivation of the poem must be derived from the implicit emotional dynamics of the materials used, and the terms of expression employed are often selected less for their logical (literal) significance than for their associational meanings. Via this and their metaphorical inter-relationships, the entire construction of the poem is raised on the organic principle of a "logic of metaphor," which antedates our so-called pure logic, and which is the genetic basis of all speech, hence consciousness and thought-extension.

These dynamics often result, I'm told, in certain initial difficulties in understanding my poems. But on the other hand I find them at times the only means possible for expressing certain concepts in any forceful or direct way whatever. To cite two examples:—when, in Voyages (II), I speak of "adagios of islands," the reference is to the motion of a boat through islands clustered thickly, the rhythm of the motion, etc. And it seems a much more direct and creative statement than any more logical employment of words such as "coasting slowly through the islands," besides ushering in a whole world of music. Similarly in Faustus and Helen (III) the speed and tense altitude of an aeroplane are much better suggested by the idea of "nimble blue plateaus" —*implying* the aeroplane and its speed against a contrast of stationary elevated earth. Although the statement is pseudo in relation to formal logic—it *is* completely logical in relation to the truth of the imagination, and there is expressed a concept of speed and space that could not be handled so well in other terms.

In manipulating the more imponderable phenomena of psychic motives, pure emotional crystallizations, etc. I have had to rely even more on these dynamics of inferential mention, and I am doubtless still very unconscious of having committed myself to what seems nothing but obscurities to some minds. A poem like Possessions really cannot be technically explained. It must rely (even to a large extent with myself) on its organic impact on the imagination to successfully imply its meaning. This seems to me to present an exceptionally difficult problem, however, considering the real clarity and consistent logic of many of the other poems.

I know that I run the risk of much criticism by defending such theories as I have, but as it is part of a poet's business to risk not only criticism—but folly—in the conquest of consciousness I can only say that I attach no intrinsic value to what means I use beyond their practical service in giving form to the living stuff of the imagination.

New conditions of life germinate new forms of spiritual articulation. And while I feel that my work includes a more consistent extension of traditional literary elements than many contemporary poets are capable of appraising, I realize that I am utilizing the gifts of the past as instruments principally; and that the voice of the present, if it is to be known, must be caught at the risk of speaking in idioms and circumlocutions sometimes shocking to the scholar and historians of logic. Language has built towers and bridges, but itself is inevitably as fluid as always.

II

From Mr. Crane to the Editor [Harriet Monroe]

YOUR good nature and manifest interest in writing me about the obscurities apparent in my Melville poem certainly prompt a wish to clarify my intentions in that poem as much as possible. But I realize that my explanations will not be very convincing. For a paraphrase is generally a poor substitute for any organized conception that one has fancied he has put into the more essentialized form of the poem itself.

At any rate, and though I imagine us to have considerable differences of opinion regarding the relationship of poetic metaphor to ordinary logic (I judge this from the angle of approach you use toward portions of the poem), I hope my answers will not be taken as a defense of merely certain faulty lines. I am really much more interested in certain theories of metaphor and technique involved generally in poetics, than I am concerned in vindicating any particular perpetrations of my own.

My poem may well be elliptical and actually obscure in the ordering of its content, but in your criticism of this very possible deficiency you have stated your objections in terms that allow me, at least for the moment, the privilege of claiming your ideas and ideals as theoretically, at least, quite outside the issues of my own aspirations. To put it more plainly, as a poet I may very possibly be more interested in the so-called illogical impingements of the connotations of words on the consciousness (and their combinations and interplay in metaphor on this basis) than I am interested in the preservation of their logically rigid significations at the cost of limiting my subject matter and perceptions involved in the poem.

This may sound as though I merely fancied juggling words and images until I found something novel, or esoteric; but the process is much more predetermined and objectified than that. The nuances of feeling and observation in a poem may well call for certain liberties which you claim the poet has no right to take. I am simply making the claim that the poet does have that authority, and that to deny it is to limit the scope of the medium so considerably as to outlaw some of the richest genius of the past.

This argument over the dynamics of metaphor promises as active a future as has been evinced in the past. Partaking so extensively as it does of the issues involved in the propriety or non-propriety of certain attitudes toward subject matter, etc., it enters the critical distinctions usually made between "romantic," "classic" as an organic factor. It is a problem that would require many pages to state adequately—merely from my own limited standpoint on the issues. Even this limited statement may prove onerous reading, and I hope you will pardon me if my own interest in the matter carries me to the point of presumption.

Its paradox, of course, is that its apparent illogic operates so logically in conjunction with its context in the poem as to establish its claim to another logic, quite independent of the original definition of the word or phrase or image thus employed. It implies (this *inflection* of language) a previous or prepared receptivity to its stimulus on the part of the reader. The reader's sensibility simply responds by identifying this inflection of experience with some event in his own history or perceptions—or rejects it altogether. The logic of metaphor is so organically entrenched in pure sensibility that it can't be thoroughly traced or explained outside of historical sciences, like philology and anthropology. This "pseudo-statement," as I. A. Richards calls it in an admirable essay touching our contentions in last July's *Criterion*, demands completely other faculties of recognition than the pure rationalistic associations permit. Much fine poetry may be completely rationalistic in its use of symbols, but there is much great poetry of another order which will yield the reader very little when inspected under the limitation of such arbitrary concerns as are manifested in your judgment of the Melville poem, especially when you constitute such requirements of ordinary logical relationship between word and word as irreducible.

I don't wish to enter here defense of the particular symbols employed in my own poem, because, as I said, I may well have failed to supply the necessary emotional connectives to the content featured. But I would like to counter a question or so of yours with a similar question. Here the poem is less dubious in quality than my own, and as far as the abstract pertinacity of question and its immediate consequences are concerned the point I'm arguing about can be better demonstrated. Both quotations are familiar to you, I'm sure.

You ask me how a *portent* can possibly be wound in a *shell*. Without attempting to answer this for the moment, I ask you how Blake could possibly say that "a *sigh* is a *sword* of an Angel King." You ask me how *compass, quadrant and sextant* "*contrive*" tides. I ask you how Eliot can possibly believe that "Every street *lamp* that I pass *beats* like a fatalistic *drum!*" Both of my metaphors may fall down completely. I'm not defending their actual value in themselves; but your criticism of them in each case was leveled at an illogicality of relationship between symbols, which similar fault you must have either overlooked in case you have ever admired the

Blake and Eliot lines, or have there condoned them on account of some more ultimate convictions pressed on you by the impact of the poems in their entirety.

It all comes to the recognition that emotional dynamics are not to be confused with any absolute order of rationalized definitions; ergo, in poetry the *rationale* of metaphor belongs to another order of experience than science, and is not to be limited by a scientific and arbitrary code of relationships either in verbal inflections or concepts.

There are plenty of people who have never accumulated a sufficient series of reflections (and these of a rather special nature) to perceive the relation between a *drum* and a *street lamp*—*via* the *unmentioned* throbbing of the heart and nerves in a distraught man which *tacitly* creates the reason and "logic" of the Eliot metaphor. They will always have a perfect justification for ignoring those lines and to claim them obscure, excessive, etc., until by some experience of their own the words accumulate the necessary connotations to complete their connection. It is the same with the "patient etherized upon a table," isn't it? Surely that line must lack all eloquence to many people who, for instance, would delight in agreeing that the sky was like a dome of many-colored glass.

If one can't count on some such bases in the reader now and then, I don't see how the poet has any chance to ever get beyond the simplest conceptions of emotion and thought, of sensation and lyrical sequence. If the poet is to be held completely to the already evolved and exploited sequences of imagery and logic—what field of added consciousness and increased perceptions (the actual province of poetry, if not lullabyes) can be expected when one has to relatively return to the alphabet every breath or so? In the minds of people who have sensitively read, seen and experienced a great deal, isn't there a terminology something like short-hand as compared to usual description and dialectics, which the artist ought to be right in trusting as a reasonable connective agent toward fresh concepts, more inclusive evaluations? The question is more important to me than it perhaps ought to be; but as long as poetry is written, an audience, however small, is implied, and there remains the question of an active or an inactive imagination as its characteristic.

It is of course understood that a street-lamp simply can't beat with a sound like a drum; but it often happens that images, themselves totally dissociated, when joined in the circuit of a particular emotion located with specific relation to both of them, conduce to great vividness and accuracy of statement in defining that emotion.

Not to rant on forever, I'll beg your indulgence and come at once to the explanations you requested on the Melville poem.

> "The dice of drowned men's bones he saw bequeath
>   An embassy."

Dice bequeath an embassy, in the first place, by being ground (in this connection only, of course) in little cubes from the bones of drowned men by the action of the sea, and are finally thrown up on the sand, having "numbers" but no identification. These being the bones of dead men who never completed their voyage, it seems legitimate to refer to them as the only surviving evidence of certain messages undelivered, mute evidence of certain things, experiences that the dead mariners might have had to deliver. Dice as a symbol of chance and circumstance is also implied.

> "The calyx of death's bounty giving back," etc.

This calyx refers in a double ironic sense both to a cornucopia and the vortex made by a sinking vessel. As soon as the water has closed over a ship this whirlpool sends up broken spars, wreckage, etc., which can be alluded to as livid *hieroglyphs*, making a *scattered chapter* so far as any complete record of the recent ship and her crew is concerned. In fact, about as much definite knowledge might come from all this as anyone might gain from the roar of his own veins, which is easily heard (haven't you ever done it?) by holding a shell close to one's ear.

"Frosted eyes lift altars."

Refers simply to a conviction that a man, not knowing perhaps a definite god yet being endowed with a reverence for deity—such a man naturally postulates a deity somehow, and the altar of that deity by the very *action* of the eyes *lifted* in searching.

"Compass, quadrant and sextant contrive no farther tides."

Hasn't it often occurred that instruments originally invented for record and computation have inadvertently so extended the concepts of the entity they were invented to measure (concepts of space, etc.) in the mind and imagination that employed them, that they may metaphorically be said to have extended the original boundaries of the entity measured? This little bit of "relativity" ought not to be discredited in poetry now that scientists are proceeding to measure the universe on principles of pure *ratio*, quite as metaphorical, so far as previous standards of scientific methods extended, as some of the axioms in *Job*.

I may have completely failed to provide any clear interpretation of these symbols in their context. And you will no doubt feel that I have rather heatedly explained them for anyone who professes no claims for their particular value. I hope, at any rate, that I have clarified them enough to suppress any suspicion that their obscurity derives from a lack of definite intentions in the subject-matter of the poem. The execution is another matter, and you must be accorded a superior judgment to mine in that regard.

III

A Letter to Otto Kahn

Patterson, New York
September 12th 1927

DEAR MR. KAHN:

I am taking for granted your continued interest in the progress of *The Bridge,* in which I am still absorbed, and which has reached a stage where its general outline is clearly evident. The Dedication (recently published in *The Dial*) and Part I (now in *The American Caravan*) you have already seen, but as you may not have them presently at hand I am including them in a ms. of the whole, to date, which I am sending you under separate cover.

At the risk of complicating your appreciation of Part II (Powhatan's Daughter), I nevertheless feel impelled to mention a few of my deliberate intentions in this part of the poem, and to give some description of my general method of construction. Powhatan's daughter, or Pocahontas, is the mythological nature-symbol chosen to represent the physical body of the continent, or the soil. She here takes on much the same role as the traditional Hertha of ancient Teutonic mythology. The five sub-sections of Part II are mainly concerned with a gradual exploration of this 'body' whose first possessor was the Indian. It seemed altogether ineffective from the poetic standpoint to approach this material from the purely chronological historic angle—beginning with, say, the landing of *The Mayflower*, continuing with a résumé of the Revolution through the conquest of the West, etc. One can get that viewpoint in any history primer. What I am after is an assimilation of this experience, a more organic panorama, showing the continuous and living evidence of the past in the inmost vital substance of the present.

Consequently I jump from the monologue of Columbus in Ave Maria—right across the four intervening centuries—into the harbor of 20th-century Manhattan. And from that point in time and place I begin to work backward through the pioneer period, always in terms of the present—finally to the very core of the nature-world of the Indian. What I am really handling, you see, is the Myth of America. Thousands of strands have had to be searched for, sorted and interwoven. In a sense I have had to do a good deal of pioneering myself. It has taken a great deal of energy—which has not been so difficult to summon as the necessary patience to wait, simply wait much of the time—until my instincts assured me that I had assembled my materials in proper order for a final welding into their natural form. For each section of the entire poem has presented its own unique problem of form, not alone in relation to the materials embodied within its separate confines, but also in relation to the other parts, *in series*, of the major design of the entire poem. Each is a separate canvas, as it were, yet none yields its entire significance when seen apart from the others. One might take the tableaux of the Sistine Chapel as an analogy. It might be better to read the following notes *after* rather than *before* your reading of the ms. They are not necessary for an understanding of the poem, but I think they may prove interesting to you as a commentary on my architectural method.

1. The Harbor Dawn:

Here the movement of the verse is in considerable contrast to that of the Ave Maria, with its sea-swell crescendo and the climateric vision of Columbus. This legato, in which images blur as objects only half apprehended on the border of sleep and consciousness, makes an admirable transition between the intervening centuries.

The love-motif (in italics) carries along a symbolism of the life and ages of man (here the sowing of the seed) which is further developed in each of the subsequent sections of Powhatan's Daughter, though it is never particularly stressed. In 2 (Van Winkle) it is Childhood; in 3 it is Youth; in 4, Manhood; in 5 it is Age. This motif is interwoven and tends to be implicit in the imagery rather than anywhere stressed.

2. Van Winkle:

The protagonist has left the room with its harbor sounds, and is walking to the subway. The rhythm is quickened; it is a transition between sleep and the immanent tasks of the day. Space is filled with the music of a hand organ and fresh sunlight, and one has the impression of the whole continent—from Atlantic to Pacific—freshly arisen and moving. The walk to the subway arouses reminiscences of childhood, also the 'childhood' of the continental conquest, viz., the conquistadores, Priscilla, Capt. John Smith, etc. These parallelisms unite in the figure of Rip Van Winkle (indigenous "Muse of Memory") who finally becomes identified with the protagonist, as you will notice, and who really boards the subway with the reader. He becomes the 'guardian angel' of the journey into the past.

3. The River:

The subway is simply a figurative, psychological 'vehicle' for transporting the reader to the Middle West. He lands on the railroad tracks in the company of several tramps in the twilight. The extravagance of the first twenty-three lines of this section is an intentional burlesque on the cultural confusion of the present—a great conglomeration of noises analogous to the strident impression of a fast express rushing by. The rhythm is jazz.

Thenceforward the rhythm settles down to a steady pedes-

trian gait, like that of wanderers plodding along. My tramps
are psychological vehicles, also. Their wanderings, as you
will notice, carry the reader into interior after interior, all of
it funneled by the Mississippi. They are the left-overs of the
pioneers in at least this respect—that abstractly their wanderings carry the reader through certain experiences roughly
parallel to that of the traders, adventurers, Boone and others.
I think I have caught some of the essential spirit of the
Great Valley here, and in the process have approached the
primal world of the Indian, which emerges with a full orchestra in the succeeding dance.

4. The Dance:

Here one is on the pure mythical and smoky soil at last!
Not only do I describe the conflict between the two races
in this dance—I also become identified with the Indian and
his world before it is over, which is the only method possible
of ever really possessing the Indian and his world as a cultural factor. I think I really succeed in getting under the
skin of this glorious and dying animal, in terms of expression,
in symbols, which he, himself, would comprehend. Pocahontas (the continent) is the common basis of our meeting,
she survives the extinction of the Indian, who finally, after
being assumed into the elements of nature (as he understood
them) persists only as a kind of 'eye' in the sky, or as a star
that hangs between day and night—'the twilight's dim per-
petual throne.'

5. Indiana:

This monologue of a woman of the 50's is a farewell to her
son who is leaving their Indiana farm for the sea. By her
story of the encounter with the half-breed squaw woman
and her child, passed on the road back from the western
gold-fields, I hope to signalize the transference of the role of
Pocahontas to the pioneer white woman, or, from another
angle, the absorption of this Pocahontas symbolism by the
pioneer white woman. The significance of the anecdote is
perhaps clearer without further explanation. This section is
psychologically a summary of Powhatan's Daughter in its

entirety. The entire section is "framed" by the sea again. In the beginning, Columbus and the Harbor Dawn,—finally the departure of the first-born for a life before the mast.

The next section, Cutty Sark, is a phantasy on the period of the whalers and clipper ships. It also starts in the present and "progresses backwards." The form of the poem may seem erratic, but it is meant to present the hallucinations incident to rum-drinking in a South Street dive, as well as reminiscent lurchings of a boat in heavy seas, etc. So I allow myself something of the same freedom of punctuation which E. E. Cummings employs.

Cutty Sark is arranged on the plan of a fugue. Two voices —that of the world of Time, and that of the world of Eternity—are interwoven in the action. The Atlantis theme (Eternity, or the Absolute) is the transmuted voice of the nickle-in-the-slot piano, and this voice alternates with that of the derelict sailor and the description of the action. It is into this Absolute that the finale to the whole poem (Atlantis) projects at the close of the book.

The calligramme of ships, seen as a phantom regatta from Brooklyn Bridge on the way "home" is simply a lyrical apostrophe to a world of loveliness forever vanished.

Cape Hatteras, which follows, is unfinished. It will be a kind of ode to Whitman. I am working as much as possible on it now. It presents very formidable problems, as, indeed, all the sections have. I am really writing an epic of the modern consciousness, and indescribably complicated factors have to be resolved and blended. . . . I don't wish to tire you with too extended an analysis of my work, and so shall leave the other completed sections to explain themselves. In the ms., where the remaining incompleted sections occur, I am including a rough synopsis of their respective themes, however. The range of The Bridge has been called colossal by more than one critic who has seen the ms. And though I have found the subject to be vaster than I had at first realized, I am still highly confident of its final articulation into a continuous and eloquent span. Already there are evident signs

of recognition: the following magazines have taken various
sections:

Dedication: To Brooklyn Bridge	THE DIAL
Ave Maria	THE AMERICAN CARAVAN
The Harbor Dawn	TRANSITION (Paris)
Van Winkle	TRANSITION (Paris)
The River	THE VIRGINIA QUARTERLY
The Dance	THE DIAL
Cutty Sark	POETRY (Chicago)
Three Songs	THE CALENDAR (London)
The Tunnel	THE CRITERION (London)

(I have been especially gratified by the reception accorded
me by *The Criterion*, whose director, Mr. T. S. Eliot, is
representative of the most exacting literary standards of our
times.)

IV

A Letter to Gorham Munson

Patterson, New York
March 17 '26

DEAR GORHAM:

My rummy conversation last Monday offered, I fear, but a poor explanation of my several theoretical differences of opinion with you on the function of poetry, its particular province of activity, etc. Neither was I able to express to you my considerable appreciation of many accurate distinctions made in your essay which certainly prompt my gratitude as well as applause. It would be probably uninteresting, as well as a bit excessive, for me to enumerate and dwell on these felicitations, however gratifying to myself they may be. Your essay is roughly divided in two, the second half including our present disagreement, and inasmuch as I have never really attempted to fulfil the functions therein attributed to the poet, your theories on that subject can be discussed from a relatively impersonal angle so far as I am concerned. Furthermore, it is *one* aspect of a contemporary problem which has already enlisted the most detailed and intense speculation from a number of fields, science, philosophy, etc., as you, of course, know. I'm not saying that my few hasty notes which follow are conclusive evidence, but the logic of them (added to the organic convictions incident to the memorized *experience* of the creative "act," let us say) is not yet disproved for me by at least such arguments as you have placed in your essay.

Poetry, in so far as the metaphysics of absolute knowledge extends, is simply the concrete *evidence* of the *experience* of knowledge. It can give you a *ratio* of fact and experience, and in this sense it is both perception and *thing perceived* according as it approaches a significant articulation or not. This is its reality, its fact, *being*. When you attempt to ask more of poetry,—the fact of man's relationship to a hypothetical god, be he Osiris, Zeus or Indra, you will get as variant terms even from the abstract terminology of philosophy as you will from poetry; whereas poetry without attempting to logically enunciate such a problem or its solution may well give you the real connective experience, the very sign manifest on which rests the assumption of god.

I'm perfectly aware of my wholesale lack of knowledge. But as Allen said, what do you mean by knowledge. When you ask exact factual data, ethical morality, or moral classifications, etc. from poetry you not only limit its goal, you ask its subordination to science, philosophy. Is it not equally logical to expect Stravinsky to bring his strings into dissent with Sir Isaac Newton? They *are* in dissent with this scientist, as a matter of fact, for the group mind that Stravinsky appeals to has already been freed from the limitations of experience and consciousness that Newton worked with. Science (ergo all exact knowledge and its instruments of operation) is in perfect antithesis to poetry. (Painting, architecture, music, etc. as well.) It operates from an exactly opposite polarity, and it may equate with poetry, but when it does so it is in entirely another terminology. I hope you get this difference between *inimical* and *antithetical*. It is not my interest to discredit science, it has been as inspired as poetry,

—and if you could but recognize it, much more hypothetically motivated.

What you admire in Plato as "divine sanity" is the architecture of his logic. Plato doesn't live today because of the intrinsic "truth" of his statements, their only living truth today consists in the "fact" of their harmonious relationship to each other. This grace is, or partakes of, poetry. But Plato was primarily a philosopher, and you must admit that grace is a secondary motive in philosophical statement, at least until the hypothetical basis of an initial "truth" has been accepted —not in the name of beauty, form or experience, but in the name of rationality. No wonder Plato considered the banishment of poets,—their reorganizations of chaos naturally threatened the logic of his system founded on assumptions that demanded the very defense of poetic construction which he was able to give them.

The tragic quandary of the modern world derives from the paradoxes that an inadequate system of rationality forces on the living consciousness. I am not opposing any new synthesis of reasonable laws which might provide a consistent philosophical and moral program for our epoch. Neither, on the other hand, am I attempting in poetry to delineate any such system. If this "knowledge" as you call it, were so sufficiently organized as to dominate the limitations of my experience (consciousness) then I would probably find myself automatically writing under its "classic" power and under that circumstance might be incidentally as philosophically "contained" as you might wish me to be. That would mean "serenity" to you because the abstract basis of my work would have been familiarized to you before you read a word of the poetry. But my poetry, even then,—in so far as it was truly poetic,—would avoid the employment of abstract labels, formulations of experience in factual terms, etc.,—it would necessarily express its concepts in the more direct terms of physical experience. If not, it must by so much lose its impact and become simply categorical.

I think it must be due to some such misapprehension of my poetic purpose in writing that leads you to several rather contradictory judgments which in one sentence are laudatory and in other contexts which you give them, put me to blush for the sentimental attitude implied. For instance, after having granted me all the praise you do earlier in your essay for "storming heaven" as it were, how can you later refer to that same faculty of verbal symphony as to picture me as "waiting for an ecstasy" and then "slumping"—rather as a baker would refer to a loaf in his oven. Granted your admiration for the yeastiness of some of my effusions, you should (in simple justice to your reader and your argument) here also afford the physical evidence (actual quotation or logical proof) of the "slump," the unleavened failure. And I'm saying there are plenty of lines to quote. What I object to is in my suspicion that you have allowed too many extra-literary pictures of me to enter your essay, sometimes for better, sometimes for worse. The same is true of your reference to the "psychological gaming" (Verlaine) which puts the slur of superficiality and vulgarity on the very aspects of my work which you have been at pains to praise.—And all because you propose a goal for me which I have no idea or interest in following. Either you find my work poetic or not, but if you propose for it such ends as poetry organically escapes, it seems to me, as Allen said, that you as a critic are working in a confusion of categories. Certainly this charge of alternate "gutter sniping" and "angel kissing" is no longer anything more than a meretricious substitute for psychological sincerity in defining the range of an artist's subject matter and psychic explorations. Still less should it be brought forward unless there is enough physical evidence in the artist's work to warrant curiosity on the part of the reader.

Your difficulties are extra, I realize, in writing about me at all. They are bound to be thus extra because of the (so far as your reader goes) "impurities of our previous literary arguments, intimacies of statements, etc., sometimes only half crystallized theories," etc., etc. But your preoccupations on the one hand with a terminology which I have not attempted and your praise on the other hand of my actual (physical) representation of the incarnate *evidence* of the very knowledge, the very *wisdom* which you feel me to be only "conjecturally" sure of—makes me guilty of really wronging you, perhaps, but drives me to the platitude that "truth has no name." Her latest one, of course, is "relativity."

Index

347